THE HUMANIZATION OF MAN

THE HUMANIZATION OF MAN

JOHN JULIAN RYAN

NEWMAN PRESS
New York, N.Y. Paramus, N.J.

ACKNOWLEDGMENTS

Material by Richard Goodwin is reprinted from *The New Yorker,* © 1969 Richard Goodwin; reprinted by permission of The Sterling Lord Agency, Inc. The excerpt from *Caravans* by James A. Michener, copyright © 1963 by Marjay Productions, Inc., is reprinted by permission of Random House, Inc. Excerpts from *The Revolution of Hope* by Erich Fromm are reprinted by permission of Harper & Row, Publishers. Material from *The Song of the Sky* by Guy Murchie is reprinted by permission of Houghton Mifflin Co. The excerpt from *The Discovery of the Child* by Maria Montessori is reprinted by permission of Fides Publishers. The piece entitled "Legibility" is reprinted by permission of *Print* magazine.

Library of Congress
Catalog Card Number: 72-79124

Published by Newman Press
Editorial Office: 1865 Broadway, N.Y., N.Y. 10023
Business Office: 400 Sette Drive, Paramus, N.J. 07652

Printed and bound in the
United States of America

to my friend
Graham Carey

INTRODUCTORY NOTE

One of the major problems encountered in the writing of this book was that of naming it accurately and fairly. There was a two-fold risk here. The book could be over-titled, thereby attracting a huge audience, only to disappoint some of them. Or it could be under-titled, thereby failing to attract its legitimate, wide audience.

The problem was not easy to solve—if, indeed, it has been solved—since the book could have gone out, justly enough, under any one of a number of titles, such as: *A Manifesto for Dropouts; Neither Communism nor Capitalism; Beyond Philistia; Walden III, Consciousness IV; The Professional Society; The Legitimate Technology;* or *Science Is Not Enough.*

The present title was settled on because the work offers partly a promise, but mainly a hope: a philosophically grounded hope. It is that we can forge a truly humane culture from our present ghastly one through learning to understand and follow the basic principles of a method which has been tragically overlooked and neglected.

CONTENTS

PART IV: THE METHOD IN DETAIL

APPENDICES

PART I

THE NEED FOR HUMANIZATION

CHAPTER 1

OUR PRESENT CULTURE AND ITS ILLS

In any systematic attempt to humanize our society, it is obvious that we must begin by taking four diagnostic steps. We must observe the difference between what we are and what we might be. We must examine the philosophy that is largely responsible for bringing us to our present state, and then that which should guide us in achieving a better state. And, finally, we must identify the method which the implementation of this latter philosophy dictates.

First, then, let us take account of the ills of our culture as these have been pointed out by expert social commentators. They may be summarized, fairly enough, as follows. Through idleness, lack of training or lack of opportunity, many of our young people are becoming rioters, vandals or drug addicts. Our workers stand in continuous fear of technological unemployment. Often, they settle, with despair and smoldering resentment, for a zombie-like, assemblyline, automated drudgery, compensating for the deadly boredom of their working lives by evenings of sports fanaticism, television trance, tavern-bred drunkenness, sexual dissipation. Our executives find themselves in not much better case as organization men or status seekers. Economic rank aside, many of us, deprived of creative outlets and of normal delight in the amenities, have become sex-obsessed, pleasure-seeking neurotics or alcoholics. Our most envied class, the suburbanites, are substituting the togetherness of the cocktail party and the Little League for the communion of loyal marriage, neighborliness, and thoughtful parenthood. Our cities are deteriorating into dirty crisscrossed hodgepodges of tenements, "projects" and aluminum office warrens. Our very scenery is somehow being given a standardized look by our thruways. So, too, is the course of our lives. And many of us subsist on a diet of tranquilizers, haunted by a subconscious uneasiness about our apparently meaningless and monotonous way of life. We suffer from a deep malaise that makes us envy intensely, as our television programs suggest, the private detective, the rancher, the lawyer and the doctor.

Indeed, as worker, the ordinary man feels himself to be in a chill state of isolation. He feels alienated from God even viewed minimally as Providence. Certainly, he can hardly be said to appreciate him as the Creator under whom he may work meaningfully through having been charged with filling out that part of the world known as civilization. He feels no less alienated from his client, whom he is ordinarily trained to regard, not as a fellowman to be served humanly, but as a "prospect" to be "sold." He feels alienated from his fellow workers, hardly sharing with them a professional code of honor and solicitude, a love of perfection, an admiration for skilled work, a basic technical sympathy and understanding, so much as a common envy and a common set of hatreds and "gripes." He feels alienated from his employer, under whom he has the status, not of fellow master, journeyman or even apprentice, but of hireling. And he feels alienated from his very work, which, technically, is hardly his at all, since it is not determined by his own inventive choices or responsible decisions.

Instead of being impelled by an adventurous hope and by the satisfactions of joyful creativity, he is likely to be governed by a greedy and overriding fear. He is afraid of not attaining a high standard of living, of pleasure and of financial security. He is afraid of not attaining and maintaining status, and therefore of not acquiring all the gadgets that are necessary for these purposes. He is afraid of competition. He is afraid of being thought an oddball: of being considered an un-American eccentric—not a "regular guy." He is afraid of "rocking the boat" economically, politically, socially—especially when this is likely in any way to endanger his security. He is often afraid of even listening to the "far out," who are dangerous because they raise disturbing questions about conformity. He is afraid of almost anyone who gets labeled a planner, much preferring to drift with the main current, salvage the inevitable wreck, and start all over again under another "practical" hardheaded captain. He becomes so afraid of change that he automatically rejects anything that is radically different from the present order, and smugly blinds himself to the needs of the "other America" in our midst.

Because he feels that, after all, somehow the system works, he is fearful of modifying it, even when he suspects that he has made himself subject to the tyranny of a dehumanizing mass production and to the manipulation of the hidden persuaders. He is so afraid, in other words, that he will lose everything if he tries to advance from a system of leveled-down quantity production to one of quality production that he settles for the second-rate as simply in the nature of things. ("Surely, it's better for everyone to have something, isn't it?") And he is even willing, as Berger has pointed-ed out in *The Noise of Solemn Assemblies,* to suborn his very churches to assuring his philistine security and bourgeois way of life. Too often he turns to his spiritual leaders, not as prophetic critics or as guides to freedom, but as sanctioners of the very things that enslave him. He goes to his place of worship, not to ask for God's help in transforming the city of man into what it should be, but to gain the comfortable assurance that he is right in conforming to it as it is.

THE POSSIBILITIES

So much for the society in which we live. What, by contrast, would a truly humane one be like?

First of all, it would be one in which work would be what it should be: a proper exercise of skill. It would be one in which—through the *artistically* dictated use of tool, powered tool, machine and automation—its members would have a real chance of satisfying their natural desire for the normal, vigorous use of tal-

5

ents and abilities in generously meeting the needs of others—with work seeming only negligibly different from play. A humane society would be one in which men worked as the various kinds of artists they were meant to be. Artists in investigation would afford knowledge. Artists in education, using much of this knowledge, would foster the various kinds of skills required by civilized living and occupational proficiency. Artists in production would fashion objects which, like our antiques, were true works of art. Artists in exchange and distribution would see that these products found their way into the hands of those who needed them. Artists in governing would assure the peace and justice, as well as the communal services and aids, requisite for enabling men to live together safely, cooperatively and harmoniously. Artists in communication would enchant men with visions of reality and inspire them to noble living. Artists in priestly ministry would help them in their efforts to attain earthly and ultimate salvation.

In short, a truly humane society would be one in which the primal rights of every man as a full human being would be respected as sacred, not the least of these being his right to lead a meaningful creative life as a worker serving others skillfully, personally and honorably.

Beyond this, a truly humane society would also be one in which the members would be relatively happy because normally skillful in all their noneconomic activities as well. Thus, they would be trained to move easily and gracefully, without apparent effort. They would speak resonantly and clearly. They would sing freely, melodiously, spontaneously. They would dance unselfconsciously, without any forced bacchanalian gaiety. They would write a hand that was pleasantly calligraphic. The casual maps or diagrams they had to sketch, in explaining something to a friend, would please both mind and eye. They would design and choose clothing which, while comfortably functional, would be expressively personal. They would build homes and shops that both in structure and appearance would foster a warmly human way of life. They would serve nutritious meals which would also be symphonies of tastes. They would converse or compose letters pointedly, wittily or compassionately, as occasion demanded. In these and the many other activities of daily living, therefore, they would continuously experience the delights both of performing things well themselves, and of enjoying the similarly skillful performances of others.

IMPLICATIONS OF THE CONTRAST

However biased these two descriptions may be—however caustic the one or idyllic the other—they do serve, when put side by side, to suggest strikingly just how appalling is the gap between what we are and what we might be. And, by the same token, they further suggest that it would be sheer folly for us to try and bridge that gap without taking into account the two creeds that produce these conditions.

For, when we analyze the first set, we see that they spring largely from these beliefs:

—That life is made up of two kinds of activity: work and play.

—That, since "work is for horses," play is the more determining of the two.

—That life consists of the satisfactions of consuming, thrill-seeking and fun.

—That to be free to enjoy these, "to be able to do the things you always wanted to do," you need to achieve independence.

—That business life itself, however, offers you the compensations of ingeniously competing with others in making a profit through satisfying the public's wants that you have largely "created."

—That workers are "hands," who, being essentially slothful, need the incentives of the stick (docking or firing) and of the carrot (good working conditions, short hours, good pay, fringe benefits and semi-suburban, luxurious living).

—That the fine arts are to be encouraged, of course; partly because they make for well-rounded businessmen, partly because they are superior forms of entertainment.

—That if many persons, especially young men and women, reject and rebel against this creed as dehumanizing, they are to be considered unrealistic malcontents, ne'er-do-wells who want things without being willing to work for them.

—That to lead a meaningful life means, therefore, to become successfully independent, to give jobs to many workers, to serve on civic boards as a public-spirited citizen and to make large philanthropic contributions, not all of them tax-deductible.

On the other hand, the second, the "ideal" condition has for its creed the following basic beliefs:

—That life consists in every activity you perform—whether of work, of play or of mere conduct (walking, talking, etc.).

—That no activity is merely "for" any other; they are all meant to be good in themselves *and* for one another.

—That their immediate satisfactions are twofold: the pleasure of executing them artistically, and the delight of seeing them well-executed by others—the pleasure of the performer, the delight of the spectator.

—That in order to lead a happy life in a sound society, you need to maintain and fit into a system of professional *interdependence*.

—That, properly, your economic life will offer you joys of exercising your talents strenuously and of cooperating with others in answering the real needs of your fellowmen as persons.

—That a worker, being something more than a higher animal, is happiest when he is most creative—when he does "a really good, a truly beautiful" job.

—That the fine arts are to be cherished as the crafts for communicating a kind of vision and a wise disposition of mind and heart which are not to be gained from textbooks or lectures—or even from laboratories and seminars.

—That those men, whether young or old, who rebel against conditions which frustrate them in their attempts to lead creative and generous, profoundly professional lives are the normal people in a culture, not the abnormal.

—That to lead a meaningful life, therefore, is to lead one which, in all its constituent activities, is as continuously creative, delightful and generous as one's talents permit.

Now, if we are to move on from the condition that has been mainly determined by an adherence to the first of these creeds to one that will be mainly determined by an adherence to the second, and if we wish to do so without loss, then we must obviously consider carefully how best to acquire and follow the method which this advance naturally calls for, namely, the artistic method. Or, to put this in currently popular terms: if, instead of merely relying on a change of heart in the young to enable us to lapse from Consciousness II into Consciousness III, if we wish to progress from one to the other responsibly, safely and smoothly, we must, at the very least, equip ourselves with a sound philosophy of technique.

It is to this requirement, therefore, that we turn our attention next.

PART II

TOWARD
A GENUINE WORLD

CHAPTER 2

THE ARTISTIC METHOD

Before considering the basic principles of artistic method, we must alert ourselves against two unfortunate habits of mind that may well interfere with our focusing on this subject properly.

First of all, there is the habit of taking the terms "art" and "artistic" in a very narrow sense—as if they necessarily referred to the fine arts alone, or, worse still, to only the most superb examples of their products. Yet there is no good reason, either etymological or historical, for us to limit these terms in this way; it is simply a practice born of the snobbery of the High Renaissance. Until that period, from the time of Aristotle, the word "art" had the much broader sense of "skill." Traditionally, artistic method was simply that followed, not only by great painters, sculptors or musicians, but also by anyone who did what we call "an artistic job" in no matter what field or at what cultural level. It would apply, for instance, to everything from the making of a kayak or the pitching of a baseball game to the composing of a symphony. And it is in this broad sense that it is being used here.

The other main tendency against which we must be on the alert is that of regarding artistic method as shallow, and therefore of not much use, because it seems, at first sight, both simple and obvious. We could hardly make a worse error. For what is true, in this regard, of scientific method is no less true of artistic.

13

In his classic essay, "The Method of Scientific Investigation," Thomas Huxley pointed out that the method we follow in ordinary investigation—as in examining apples for their ripeness before we buy them—is essentially like that which a scientist follows in testing a hypothesis for its adequacy. We are all, he suggests, potentially scientific; to become actually so, we need hardly do more than refine our common-sense notions and methods of discovery. Then, although we may start with what seems little other than an elaboration of the obvious, the techniques and conclusions we end up with are likely to be revolutionary and remarkably fruitful. The terms, the postulates and the axioms of mathematics, for instance, may seem, at first sight, ridiculously self-evident, not to say simple and shallow; but the ultimate results of an exploration of their significances are hardly that.

Much the same can be said of artistic method. Its basic terms are also quite familiar and apparently shallow. But, once we have rid ourselves of the common misconceptions of them, and have discovered their deeper meanings, we shall find that these can lead us to vital and astonishingly fruitful insights.

We all know, of course, if only subconsciously, what the four factors are that determine every act of skillful making or performing. We all realize that if we choose the right *material,* cast it into the right *form,* using the right *instrument,* all in accordance with the right *purpose,* we are likely to turn out something that is a real work of art. Or, to state this negatively: to the extent to which we work with an inadequate material, form, or instrument, and an ill-visualized purpose, we shall turn out something defective, something essentially inartistic.

The necessity here, then, is not to be thrown off by the apparent obviousness of these realizations, but to explore the full significance of their terms; so that, in the light of them, we may find our way out of the world of the shoddy and into the world of the genuine.

Purpose

To begin, then, with the most important of the four factors of every act of making or performing, namely, purpose: what is it, we may ask, that we particularly need to keep in mind about it? How are we to avoid being gravely misled, as even great authorities frequently are, by superficial and fallacious notions of it? And, beyond that, what is technically the most fruitful view of it?

TRUE PURPOSE

The first necessity we face here is that of having to make a simple but vital distinction—one that is of crucial importance, not only for assuring sound technique and technology, but also for maintaining a sound civilization. We must learn to distinguish carefully between strictly technical purpose and what is ordinarily identified falsely with it, namely, personal motive.

For, technically, the purpose of a maker or a performer is to produce something that does well what it is meant to do—that answers the need properly which it is meant to answer; it is *not* primarily to make money and to assure the comfort, status and power that money can purchase.

Nothing could be more harmful to a culture—nothing, indeed, could more certainly degrade it into a commercialized, philistine one—than the failure to make and maintain properly this vital distinction. For, once money, and therefore profit, becomes the primary objective of making or performing, the members of a culture become so obsessed by it that gradually, fatally, they begin to lose almost all sense of humane values. A product or a service becomes something to be turned out with just enough quality to make it acceptable, but at as little cost and as high a sales price as possible; this, through the use of mechanical efficiency and a niggardly cost accounting. It becomes interesting to the distributor as affording him a high percentage of rake-off, even if it is designed to pander to wants created by advertising. And it becomes prized by its user on the basis of whether it enables him to make money or to enjoy what money can buy.

15

As a result, every kind of product or performance becomes less and less appreciated for what, from a technical point of view, it really is. No longer is it the source of joy it is meant to be for everyone, producer, distributor and client alike. The producer does not experience the delight of exercising fully his skill on it, of contemplating its intrinsic rightness or of rejoicing in his client's gratitude for its satisfactoriness. Nor does the distributor take delight in similarly appreciating its essential goodness or in exercising his skill in efficiently and generously getting it into the hands of those who need it and receiving their thanks in return. And, finally, the client himself does not appreciate its excellence as a work of skill or its helpfulness in aiding him to live in a truly humane way. For all of them, moreover, the amenities of life—a beautiful script, a graceful walk, a resonant voice, good manners, and all the rest—these become readily dispensable (for where is the money in *them*); with the result that both the joy of performing them well and that of appreciating them when well-performed is lost almost irrevocably.

All this does not mean, of course, that a maker or a performer has no need *secondarily* of money, status and power as these may rightly be understood. He obviously needs to be given a fee for his work, if only that he may go on doing it and perfecting himself in it. He also needs the status that will enable him to gain the clientele and the respect due him. And he needs the power to determine, along with his fellow masters, the normal conditions for the fair and effective prosecution of his work. But these motives are not, from a purely technical point of view, his main purpose; this is to provide the particular kind of service that he has the talent and training for providing: the surgeon, health; the judge, justice; the architect, shelter; and so on.

The main point here is well brought out by the old story about three men breaking up rocks. When the first was asked what he was doing, he replied, "Making little ones out of big ones;" the second, "Making a living;" and the third, "Building a cathedral." Each of these men was, of course, doing all three; but it is the answer of the third that obviously suggests the basic meaning of purpose in technique.

DYNAMISM OF PURPOSE

The next thing that has to be realized about purpose is that it is to be thought of, not statically, but dynamically: it is the *role* played by a thing in answering a system of needs—the sequence of actions it goes through as it meets these one by one. Technically, for instance, the purpose of a beer stein is not to be thought of simply as the holding of beer. A stein is to be visualized as something that can readily be filled in such a way as to satisfy a drinker's need for a certain amount of beer, with a reasonable head of foam; that can be grasped by the whole fist easily and steadily; raised easily, but with enough weight to rhyme with the body of the beer and its slightly bitter taste; lifted gracefully aloft in a toast; tilted safely and emptied in the right volume for an easy swallow by an ordinarily large mouth; brought down firmly, yet stably, in the expression of strong satisfaction.

THE UNIQUENESS OF PURPOSE

Furthermore, a purpose is normally thought of as a particular purpose. A thing is made to fill, ordinarily, not a general system of needs like those just described, but a particular form of these as dictated by a particular person or group of persons.

This fact is likely to be ignored or overlooked because we have become so used to average products that we seem to have forgotten that these are by no means the only kind desirable or possible. Many of us would be inclined to ask, for instance, why have a particular stein for a given tavern, or for a social group frequenting it regularly for meetings and discussions? After all, any good stein would be good enough, would it not?

The answer is, no; and the only reason it might seem good enough is that we have become used to two assumptions, neither of them, from a technical point of view, legitimate: one, that what is desirable must be dismissed as undesirable as soon as it appears difficult or expensive under present conditions; and, two, it is foolish to assume that we can better present conditions, or that we can do better under them.

This doctrine of technological despair is fallacious, however, on both counts.

For, if it is desirable that the architecture, inner as well as outer, of every tavern be different from that of every other, both because of the individual owner's concept of it and his awareness of the tone and atmosphere of the social and economic life into which it is to fit, then there would seem to be good reason for having every constituent accord pleasantly with every other and with the individuality of the place as a whole: not only the furniture with the architecture, but also the silver, the crockery and the glassware with both. If one of these elements has, at present, to be sacrificed for economic reasons—if, for the moment, individualized steins are simply too expensive—that does not mean that average, mass-produced steins are therefore "just as good," or even, ultimately, good enough. They are not.

And to object to something as idealistic or impossible because it cannot be readily produced under present conditions is to take it for granted, fatalistically, that present conditions can never be changed, and to confess that, for all our vaunted technology, the best we can do is continue living in a world of the average, the second-rate, the never quite satisfactory. It is somewhat like maintaining that because we cannot make by machine the kind of violin once made by hand, we can no longer learn to make by hand a violin that would be better than one made by machine.

TRUE PURPOSE PROMOTES PERSONHOOD

Related to the view of purpose as particular is the view of it as personal. According to this, the extent to which something helps its user to achieve personhood is the measure of its functional rightness. And particularity is of moment here since every person is, as a person, an individual: he has his own unique requirements, which must be met in such a way as to enable him to be fully himself, as himself.

But this means, too, that whatever he uses should likewise enable him to be a social being, since it is in social relations, as we have been discovering more and more of late, that he most readily achieves full and even unique personhood: he is developed into himself as much by how he serves others and is served by them as by how he serves himself. The purpose of a thing well-made is both individualistic and communal: it serves its user as an individual who is also a member of society.

Purpose must also be seen as multiplex. Properly, a thing is made to satisfy, as far as possible, all the needs of man as man: not only his physical, but also his mental and spiritual. To call a thing functional when it does no more than satisfy the needs of the body and some of the lower needs of the mind is simply misleading: it is to suggest that the requirements of what distinguishes man from a lower animal are of little or no importance. It is to sanction implicitly the view that it is legitimate to make things for the satisfying of mere wants, rather than true needs, and that since the satisfying of such wants for a profit is simply good business, it is also legitimate to create them and pander to them unrestrainedly—even when doing so means failing to meet higher needs. In short, it is to vitiate the spirit of technique at its source and to supplant it with the spirit of commercialism.

PURPOSE ANSWERS A NEED

Properly, then, from a technical point of view, the purpose of making something should be seen as that of answering a particular set of needs felt by an individual person; this, in a way that is as satisfactory as possible to his body, mind and soul as he lives a creative life of self-realization in serving and being served communally. Any definition of technical purpose smaller in scope than this is essentially inadequate.

In considering the purpose of a maker, we have also to recognize that it is ordinarily twofold in that he has to produce something that not only functions, but also continues to function. This means that he must inevitably strive to meet at least four, sometimes five or six requirements—at the very least, one of functioning and three of continuing to function. For his product must be made to make something else (like a saw); to operate something else (like a crank or a pedal); to protect it (like a glove); or to conserve it (like a food); and it, in turn, must be operated, protected and conserved. Moreover, a maker must often take into account the similar requirements of the instruments he uses and, beyond them, the requirements of the human beings who work with him as they need to be operated (in the sense of being guided and inspired), protected and conserved. The making of almost anything of importance, therefore, implies the meeting of a whole complex of subsidiary requirements, so that, in a sound culture basic needs must be given prime consideration. Otherwise, we fall into the twofold error of assuming that things, once made, virtually operate, protect and conserve themselves, thereby inevitably freeing their users from all concern with a given need, and that there can never be such a condition as over-production or an inhumane economic complexity, with too many energies given over to the making of conveniences or luxuries.

A DEFINITION OF PURPOSE

This, then, is how a maker or performer thinks about purpose: he sees that it is not a self-regarding end, but an objective one; that it is not an abstract, simple state to be achieved, but a concrete, dynamic role to be played in answering a system of needs; that these needs, since they are of a human being, are fully personal, that is, both individual and social; that they should be not mere wants, but basic human needs experienced by clients trying to achieve full personhood while aiding others to do the same; that the proper answering of them, even in the making of a relatively simple thing, implies meeting a whole set of sub-requirements which are much too complex to be risked unless the product is something more than a gadget or slothful luxury.

Such a view of purpose has, as we shall see, implications for our culture that are virtually revolutionary.

Choosing the right form
and material

The maker's view of form and material is no less dynamic than his view of purpose.

Certainly, he feels that the worst error anyone could make in regard to form is to think of it as static or fixed—as a kind of metaphysical cookie cutter of set figure which is to be imposed on a dough-like material to give this a new shape.

He looks, let us say, at a beautiful rooster and later, as he is making scrambled eggs, at the little black spot of sperm in the yolk. And he says to himself with wonder: "It is here in this tiny particle that there is locked up that flashing red comb, those brilliant and fierce eyes, that swiftly darting neck, those gleaming feathers, that gracefully curving tail, those long, sharp spurs. It is in this small speck that we find that whole system of potentialities which become this form of rooster." And when he makes something, he thinks of the form of it as that dynamic configuration of qualities that he has been able to educe, almost embryonically, stage by stage, from his materials.

Or, to put this a little differently, the form here is that set of specifications which a thing must have, not only to be itself and function, but also to be operated, protected and conserved: the complex of properties required for existence and use in civilization.

Obviously, if a maker were in the true sense a creator, he would have merely to lay out all the requirements of function, to work out the form suggested by these requirements and bring into being the materials that would best embody this form. But although this seems to be a method now made available by modern physics and chemistry, the skillful maker knows that it is a dangerously presumptuous one: it is likely to beget a far too dictatorial attitude.

He is also wary here of the distinction that has been made between primary and secondary qualities. For he knows that the form of a thing is never its mere figure, size, shape, inner geometric structure or any combination of these. It contains these, of course, but not more basically or exclusively than the other qualities we can sense or intuit: color, touch, sound, temperature, taste, smell, proportion, liveliness, resiliency and the like. These are no less *meant,* no less there, no less to be taken into account as manifesting the nature of a thing than are the qualities of spatial pattern. The maker conceives of neither himself nor the Creator as first of all a cubist and secondarily a decorator who, in order to alleviate the coldness of mathematical structure, bedecks it with purely accidental qualities—like so much chrome or costume jewelry or mascara.

MANY FACTORS INFLUENCE FORM

Technically, then, the form of a thing means, in the first instance, the set of specifications by which the patterning is guided and, in the second, that system of qualities taken as a whole which ultimately emerge and prove satisfactory. It is, in other words, a complex resultant of visualizing the requirements that will meet the needs of the client and of solving the claims of each material and each instrument in each stage of production diplomatically and justly, with a due regard for the covariation of all factors. Form is fluid and dynamic since, as any one factor changes, the others must change accordingly. As the purpose becomes clarified, the specifications change; as the specifications are modified, the materials and instruments change; as the materials or instruments prove fractious, the specifications and purpose change; and so on. The most desirable form of a thing can therefore only be what results from the best set of compromises struck between the demands of all the factors; so that often enough it proves as surprising to its discoverer as it does to anyone else.

Nor is even the form taken by the final product necessarily definitive right away: there may still be need of seasoning, a trial run or a shakedown cruise.

Technically, there is no such thing as raw material; there is only an as yet unreleased material. The "stuff" offered to a maker by nature is never a putty-like substance to be molded compliantly into whatever set of qualities may seem desirable. Even putty, indeed, has a strong character of its own, unlike that of mercury, on the one hand, or of resin, on the other. The universe is too nearly organic for that: each thing, expressing itself actively in its own right, helps others to do so, all in accordance with the determining rights of nature and civilization.

THE CONSEQUENCES OF MISUSING FORM

The one thing of which a maker would never wish to be accused is forcing or coercing his material or destroying its potentialities: a dust bowl of any kind leaves him aghast at the unwillingness of men to fit their rhythm of use into nature's rhythm of reproduction, and he shudders at the heedless, tyrannical attitude of those willing to create such a blight.* His view not only of the social but also of the physical order is, therefore, not that of a dictator but that of a democratic ruler: even the rawest of raw material is to be respected for what it is and dealt with, as far as possible, persuasively—as a kind of subperson. For he knows that matter can never be successfully imposed on: if the land that has been callously fertilized and ploughed turns into a sahara, so, too, the silver coin that has been coerced to look like its plaster of paris model ultimately loses its essential imagery: its symbolic details and its very date.

For this reason a maker realizes what the modern world forgets time and time again: namely, that there *are* no substitutes. Nothing can ever really be or do—or, finally, closely enough resemble —anything else. This does not mean that there is anything essentially the matter with artificial materials—with plastics, for instance. But that such materials should never be used as if they were stand-ins for wood, metal or stone. They are what they are and they should be honestly used (or, better, released) to do what they and they alone can do best. Otherwise, we shall continue to live in a faked-up world, in which almost nothing is what it says it is: in which food, for example, even when it still looks like food, tastes like table decor; and almost everything we stop to observe for a moment awakens the vague, disquieting suspicion that materially it is a lie—a technically dishonest substitute, to accept which we have to be, in the worst sense, "sold."

Form, in short, is that which a maker educes diplomatically

---

*See on this point *The Failure of Technology,* by Ernst Juenger, Regnery, Chicago, 1949.

from a particular dynamic material, guiding himself by a set of specifications suggested by truly humane needs.

In sharp contrast to it is what emerges when a certain kind of person "imposes" a pattern on "raw" material for his own selfish ends. Regarding every other being as so much mere stuff, such a man sees it as something he has every right to exploit or control at will. As a result, he has been responsible, without a qualm, for much grim folly. He has transformed fertile fields into dust bowls. He has eliminated or endangered whole species of land animals, fish and fowl. He has confined his schoolchildren to the imprisonment of the desk. He has manipulated his fellowmen by the chicanery of publicity and "image building." As bureaucrat, he has worked on them, not in them. And he has "rehabilitated" criminals by solitary confinement. In sum, because he has not understood what is really meant by form and material, he has blithely ignored the basic rights of all things as subpersons in the ecological system. Unaware of the fact that the cosmos is, in a sense, a kind of democracy, he has dealt with every order of it like a dictator.

Basic principles
of instrumentation

Purpose, form, material: as we have seen, if we are to use artistic method successfully in redeeming our society, it is vitally necessary for us to gain clear and useful notions of these. But so, too, must we gain similar notions of the factor of instrumentation—especially as we are surrounded on all sides today, at all levels, by gravely misleading fallacies about it.

The most important of these are: First, just as we have had to choose, in accordance with an inevitable evolution and progress, between the tool and the machine, so now we are having to choose between the machine and an automated complex of machines. Moreover, since one of our main objectives is the democratic one of trying to see that there is something for everyone, we must aim primarily, almost exclusively, at quantity production. And quantity production implies mass production, which, in turn, calls for the primacy of the machine. Finally, it is a moral obligation for us to take sides here: to line up and be counted either with those who consider the machine to be a Frankenstein's monster or with those who consider it to be an Ariel. We must condemn it as a curse or welcome it as a blessing.

Yet every one of these beliefs is highly questionable, not to say disastrous.

THE FALLACY OF "PROGRESSIVISM"

To maintain, for instance, that we have been forced, in the name of progress, to choose between the tool and the machine is absurd. It is just not true that the mechanical pencil has completely supplanted the wooden pencil; or even that the fountain pen has completely supplanted the quill; or the manually operated typewriter, the fountain pen; the electrically operated typewriter, the manually operated; the electronic copier, the electrically operated typewriter.

Nor is it true that quantity must any longer be our almost exclusive objective; with the vast range of resources now available to us, we can aim at high quality as well. To focus obsessively on efficient quantity production is merely to fall prey to technological infatuation. It is to become so fascinated by our progress in turning out more and more of subtler and subtler, cheaper and cheaper, more and more convenient, products as to sacrifice true quality. It is to overlook, in fact, the very possibility of regarding quality as our primary objective, with quantity and profit real but *secondary* limitations on it.

Finally, to take sides either for or against the machine is as silly as it is to do so in regard to anything else. We should rather try to determine, on the basis of fundamental principles, exactly what each of the means of production really is (what is *the machine,* for instance?) what it, in particular, is best suited for, and how it can be most effectively used in conjunction with every other means.

BASIC PRINCIPLES OF PRODUCTION

What, then, are the principles on the basis of which we can logically arrive at an answer to these questions? As was suggested earlier, they are these: every act of production is essentially an interaction; when one thing changes another, each is affected by the other; as they become one in act, each becomes, or tries to become, like the other and to make the other like itself. It is no crude process of transfer here, but one of complex mutual inter-adaptation and inter-effect. In traditional philosophy, the principles governing this interaction are stated in terms of two complementary formulas: one, "whatever is received is received in the manner of the receiver"; the other, "every agent acts in such a way as to produce something like itself." Concretely, the tennis ball is received in the manner that is permitted by the flat, but flexible, stringing of the racket; and the racket gives it a new trajectory, spin and direction. Properly, therefore, every instrument should be capable of adjusting itself readily to the nature of what it is to operate on and, at the same time, of educing from this certain qualities like its own, qualities desired by the user. And it must maintain a similar relationship with the hand: this must adjust itself sympathetically (or empathetically) to the handle so that the right pressure and direction will be transmitted to the head of the instrument. As an intermediary, then, an instrument is both worked upon (by the hand that plies it and the material that responds to it) and working (on the hand, in offering it the right resistance and control, and on the material, educing from it a new disposition). It must dominate the hand well enough to submit to it desirably; it must submit to the material well enough to dominate it desirably.

Technically, all this means that an ideal instrument is one which submits firmly (resistantly) enough to its user to enable his practiced hand to dominate his material gracefully and tactfully.

Specifically, a good instrument is one that enables the user to control the generation, the modification and the application of its power at all times, as this control is required by each new disposition of both hand and material. And it is this fact that enables us define, distinguish and evaluate the four main types of instruments: the tool, the powered tool, the machine and the automated machine.

THE TOOL

In the light of it, a tool may be defined, quite accurately and usefully, as an instrument the power of which is generated, governed and applied by its operator at all times directly and deliberately. Obviously, therefore, it is a means of production well-suited to the assuring of quality. It can be diplomatically plied in accordance with each particular disposition, favorable or not, of the material it works on. It can be adjusted readily to each special pattern or change of pattern required by the unique needs of the individual client. It can be modified to suit the natural grip, physique, tendencies or talents of the given user. In short, it possesses the flexibility demanded for producing things of the highest quality—things custom-made.

It is limited, of course, in often being no more forceful than its user: it cannot always cope with heavy, large or fractious material; and it may prove toilsome and slow. For these reasons, it may be inadequate or inefficient.

THE POWERED TOOL

The powered tool, as its name suggests, differs from the ordinary tool simply through having its power enhanced mechanically. It is still essentially a tool, because it remains under the direct control of its operator at all times.

The extra power may be given to it for three reasons: to increase the forcefulness with which it may be applied, as with the electric handsaw; to assure its being in the condition best suited to working on its material; and to direct the application of its force, as with the steam shovel, equipped with swivel, levers and pulleys.

It is to be noted that the powered tool does not become any less of a tool because the mechanisms supplying its power are complex. The electric iron, for instance, may be equipped with a fairly intricate system of switches and thermostats, yet become, for all that, not less, but more of a tool. It can be plied more effectively than the ordinary iron because its uniformly assured pressure and moisture enable its user to handle it exceptionally well on various kinds of materials. It is not, in other words, a tool that has been transformed into a machine; it is simply one that has been made a better tool by the addition of machinery.

Size does not change its basic nature, either. The large trip-hammer that is used in shaping great hot ingots; the builder's towering crane that hoists girders and other materials several stories high; the gigantic steam shovel that digs cavernous basements: despite its hugeness every one of these is essentially a tool. So, too, are the ocean liner and the battleship: each is controlled directly by its operator, its captain, flexibly, adaptively, resourcefully.

THE MACHINE

When we come to the machine, we find that it differs, in one respect, from both the tool and the powered tool radically. For it is essentially an instrument that performs at least two operations of change without the direct control of the operator. Hence, unlike either kind of tool, it is an instrument which, by its very nature, is limited in three basic ways: in its adaptability to its material; in its adaptability to the particular requirements of an individual client; and in its adaptability to the personal idiosyncrasies of its user. Obviously, it is best suited to quantity, rather than quality, production. It is very useful, that is, for turning out, repetitively, hundreds of articles like pins or nails that need have only a standard material and a fixed pattern. It is also quite useful in providing an unvarying performance of a relatively simple, uniform service, like that of dispensing a soft drink or of washing dishes. And it is extremely valuable in providing the devices required by the powered tool.

But of itself it can hardly turn out a very good frock, a very good dinner table or a very good dinner.

The distinctions we have been considering here are vital. Unless we appreciate their force and take them into account carefully, we shall fall into the disastrous error of confusing the powered tool with the machine and of attributing the values of one to the other. Furthermore, we are likely to slip into the mistake of regarding tools as only primitive and imperfect machines, and machines as only potential parts of an automated system. And we shall never see clearly why the critics of the machine so often react against it violently; we shall never see clearly to what extent their reactions are, or are not, justifiable.

CRITICISM OF THE MACHINE

Certainly, in the light of the analyses we have just made, it should be easy for us to see why any skillful maker or craftsman (or, for that matter, anyone else interested in quality) is likely to regard The Machine with suspicion. Not only is it, as we have noted, too inflexible for quality production, but it also habituates designer, operator and client primarily to accurate and mechanical, often lifeless, patterns—as against organic and humanly symmetrical. Moreover, it fosters the belief that a product is merely the sum of its parts as put together on an assemblyline—as if this were a normal way of conceiving of a quasi-organism. Then, too, it encourages manufacturers to break the tasks of their workers down into short machine-like motions requiring no imagination or responsibility—all the real designing being done on drawing boards in the office. Granted that the machine and its derivative, mechanized work, can prove mechanically efficient, it may well do so at a heavy cost in boredom and in the loss of the ingenuity that workers might otherwise exercise, as well as of their joy in the normal use of their human powers.

Perhaps the worst effect of the machine is that it not only causes clients to settle for quantity production, with little regard (or hope) for quality production, but also convinces them that the only valid form of quantity production is mass production. Yet that these are by no means identical—that mass production is only one way of assuring quantity production is borne out by the history of architecture. It is only recently that we have begun to have the mass production of buildings, and yet they have always been produced in great quantity. Nor need automobiles have been mass-produced: if fixed homes can be quantity produced without mass production, so can moving homes (which is about what automobiles are to many Americans). These latter could also have been built, in a custom-made way, to endure, rather than to become obsolescent.*

Thinking, under the influence of the machine, in terms of mechanical efficiency has led, moreover, to ignoring a number of ills that are commonly covered up by the boast that we have attained the highest standard of living in history. For such thinking implies measuring the soundness of a product by the difference between what is put into it and what is taken out of it merely quantitatively. And accepting this criterion as decisive leads to our also accepting as normal the requirements it suggests, which are ultimately quite unfortunate. For, to maintain an "efficient" ratio between input and output mechanically calls for keeping a machine, if possible, in continuous operation. Such continuous operation ordinarily requires an ever-increasing, or at least a steady, market. One way of assuring such a market is to make it fashionable for the buyer to purchase a new, quickly obsolescent product (a new car, for example) every year or so. To this end, enormous amounts of money must be sunk into advertising: first, for awakening, each year, sufficient desire for a new model; and then, but no less importantly, for holding on to one's share in the market against competitors. Finally, consumers must be manipulated into incurring the burdens of part-payment schemes.

Obviously, it is fatal to limit ourselves here to the criteria of two lower kinds of efficiency in disregard of an ultimate, higher one; that is, deem a product efficient when the mechanical input for it is low and the mechanical output high; or when the economic input, the cost, is low and the economic output, the return or profit, is high. We must also judge the human efficiency of a product, asking if, or by how much, the human costs of its making and use are outweighed by the human benefits of it.

---

*The problem here is mainly one, not of manufacturing, but of financing. The present writer's house, which cost him about as much as would a Rolls-Royce, is being paid for on a long-term mortgage. Had he been able to buy a Rolls-Royce, or an equally well-built, less luxurious car, on approximately the same terms, he would have done so gladly, spending less in the long run than he will soon have spent on a sequence of quickly obsolescent cars, and assuring himself of superb transportation.

For instance: can the boredom, the resentment and the despair of being treated as an appendage to a machine and literally as a mere hand; can the stultification of the worker through lack of use of his specifically humane powers of imagination, will, intellect and conscience; can the corrupting of a taste for rightness by a lust for fashion; can the high cost of maintenance resulting from hasty manufacture or built-in obsolescence; can the tricky sales appeals to pride of ownership, love of luxury, sloth and show; can the pollution of earth, air and water; can the traffic jams and the death toll—can all these costs, and others as well (the input) be decisively outweighed by the conveniences (the output) provided by at least one car in every garage?

Not the least distressing effect, indirect though it is, of our idolatry of the machine is that on our engineers. Instead of maintaining uncompromisingly their autonomy as professional men, they have sold out to our industrialists. Instead of taking an oath that they would consent to making things only as they were meant to be made—soundly and humanly—they have permitted themselves from the very beginning to be considered, alas, mere employes, hirelings willing to accept any form of pandering which their employers demanded of them.

AUTOMATION

Like the single machine, the automated system of machines is not useful where direct flexible operation is required for the production of quality; but it can readily produce simple, standardized products and services as well as simple, fixed combinations of these. It can also produce the pure power, the electricity, that can be used by both powered tools and machines. Moreover, it can act as a kind of substitute machine-tender: feeding the machine or the system its materials and lubricants; governing its force or speed; stopping it when the feedback "tells" that the materials are running out or that something has gone wrong: making sure, in sum, that it uniformly takes the one course of action which it is meant to take.

Again, automation can afford a relatively simple standard service which requires an extremely intricate cooperation of many machines, as in a telephone system. And, of course, it can provide speedy answers to a range of mathematically determinable problems: of identification, choice, reckoning, etc.

In such ways as these, then, automation can provide auxiliary standardized things and services which otherwise we could not have at all, or could have only at the cost of valuable time and effort. Properly used, it can free and empower us for the exercise of craftsmanship.

THE EFFECTIVENESS OF COALESCENT USE

We must therefore be on guard against the fallacy of supposing that because some men have used machines and automation where they should not be used, or have failed to take proper account of the social consequences of their too sudden widespread use, these instruments are to be condemned indiscriminately. When rightly used, no one of them is in conflict with any other that is being rightly used. Every kind, in fact, ordinarily has its due place in any fairly large institution designed to produce quality. Consider, for instance, a hospital. When well-conducted, it takes advantage of every kind of instrument, from the simplest to the most complex: the simple tool (the scalpel); the powered tool (the electric typewriter); the machine (the push-button elevator); the automated machine (the computer used for accounting and for certain kinds of diagnoses). Clearly, each of these instruments, in being used for what it can do best, coalescently assures quality through fostering the exercise of the various forms and degrees of skill possessed by the members of the staff.

But, it may be objected, a patient is one thing; an automobile buyer, another: the one needs the individual service that cannot be assured by mass production methods; the other does not. Yet such a contention is far too narrow-visioned and pessimistic. There is very little reason why an automobile factory should not aim at qualitative individual service, and therefore resemble the hospital, technologically, much more closely than it does. More specifically, it could well be made up of unitary shops, each run by a team of apprentices, journeymen and masters who together would be responsible for turning out one whole constituent of a product (a carburetor, say) from design to installation—with all the items being under the general team of master builders who would design the product as a whole (the car) just as a group of architects design, for a corps of contractors, a whole building: so as to meet the particular personal needs of each individual client. All these men, like the staff of the hospital, would use, as required in accordance with their various degrees of skill and training, the full complement of instruments, the automated included, as demanded by custom quality production.

TECHNOLOGY IS AN EXTENSION OF CRAFTSMANSHIP

The problems raised by the transition from our present methods to those suggested here are, of course, numerous and knotty. But they will not be impossible to solve ultimately if we keep in mind two determining truths. These are: that technology is less a by-product of science than it is an extension of craftsmanship; and that quality is always a matter of life and death—of the body or of the spirit or of both.

The main reason why technology must not be regarded primarily as a by-product of science is that the scientist is conditioned by his mode of thought to focusing on things as specimens —as general entities quantitatively analyzable. For his discovering and measuring of gravitational pull, for instance, any apple falling from any tree would do. He does not feel it necessary to take into account the individual and quantitatively unanalyzable qualities that make a particular thing or action uniquely itself. Consequently, it becomes second nature for him to approach the manufacturing of a product as if he were concerned with a specimen operation: as if this were to be, primarily, the typical way of satisfying the typical needs of the typical client. Unlike the expert craftsman or professional, he is not inclined to see anything wrong with finding or confecting a standard material, imposing on it repetitively a fixed pattern and having the result adapted later (like a mass-produced suit of clothes) as well as may be to the "peculiarities" of individual clients. As a consequence, he almost inevitably comes to regard mass production as both satisfactory and normal—even when he has sense enough to wear only tailor-made clothes himself. Essential and complete *rightness,* the quality that emerges only from fashioning each new product thoroughly as an individual answer to an individual set of needs— this he comes to consider an extra, something only for those rare, lucky persons who have the money and the taste required.

The true craftsman or professional man, on the other hand, who strives, first and last, to assure the highest degree of quality for his client, regards every product as unique, one requiring not only general but also particular care—one that, in fact, may perhaps never be duplicated.

It is the criterion that is in the mind of this sort of man that should be first in our own when we judge, not only the machine, but every other instrument or combination of instruments. How suited is this, we must ask, to the production of quality? Certainly, any society the members of which become accustomed, through an obsession with quantity, to settling for anything but the best—for anything less than the truly authentic—is doomed to go on wearing shoddy clothing, eating fake foods and remaining content with all kinds of phoniness—and worse still, accepting their fate as inevitable.

This is tragic, for there is no substitute for quality. It is, in the most exact sense of the term a *vital* necessity: a matter of cultural life and death.

CHAPTER 3

THE PLEASURES
OF ENTHUSIASTIC CREATIVITY

In dealing with man as the principal instrument in an act of production, many theorists fall into one or more of three simplistic errors: they think of him as essentially inartistic; naturally slothful; or determinately individualistic. In other words, they think of him as not really interested in skill; as not wanting to do anything more difficult than is necessary; and as always obeying a primarily self-centered motive.

In fact, however, the evidence concerning him turns out to be against all these notions.

MAN, ARTIST BY NATURE

Granted that, once a man has become obsessed by the profit motive and has been brought up to live in accordance with it, he will certainly appear to be as these theorists suppose; still, without this motive, or with it as only secondary, he shows himself to be quite a different kind of creature. When he has invented a new game, for instance, and has started to play it regularly, he inevitably transforms it into an art as fast as he can. He refines the strokes and movements, improves the instrument used, whether racket, club, oar, bat or ski, and even the court or playing field. The rules he makes stricter and more exacting, not only for the sake of fairness, but also for that of virtuosity. In short, he tries to make the play as skillful and artistic as possible.

The great mistake here has been to overlook the fact that man is primarily an artist, a person of technique, in everything he does. He is so because, first of all, he cannot help being so, since, as human, he does nothing in a purely instinctive way;* and, as a metaphysical creature, he has a natural love of the splendor of rightness and a positive desire for the attainment of it.

Moreover, so far from being sluggardly, man is naturally active; he continues to play late in life (as no animals do) and to play as strenuously as possible. Even on a vacation, he wants play that is vigorous and demanding: a good workout. He is simply not, by nature, slothful.

Finally, as anthropology shows, it is absurd to imagine that man as a producer originally thought of himself as primarily concerned with his own individual gain. As a member of a family and a tribe, he would never have known what it was to raise food, to hunt or to fish without reference to the needs of others. The hunt, for instance, which was cooperatively conducted with skill and discipline, was for bringing home the food that was then to be shared by everyone in a communal (usually a ritual) feast, after it had been prepared with a technique that was perfected and made traditional.

Moreover, if there is anything that we have learned in this century, it is that most of our malaise results from alienation, from the sense of not being humanely related to all who are normally concerned with us or with whom we should normally be concerned. The impression that has too often been given, especially by romantics, that the work of a maker or performer, particularly of a great master, is a part of his life that is necessarily sealed off from the rest of his activities—that his work is undetermined by a

---

*An instinct, strictly, is a force which, on a particular stimulation, causes a creature to perform *automatically,* in answer to some organic need, a complex sequence of *unlearned* actions which enable it to answer that need. It may drive the creature through several performances, until either satisfied or decisively balked. A man may be *prompted,* both from within and without, to a useful action; but he has always to *learn* and perfect his human technique, as animals do not. This is the reason why contemporary psychologists made up the word *instinctual.*

whole complex of social and personal obligations—this impression is false. Good work of every kind, no matter how humble or how important, is always determined, far more deeply than is ordinarily supposed, by a network of prudential claims, social, professional, domestic, personal. And the more carefully a man evaluates and meets these claims, the more effective will he be as a producer.

MAN, PROFESSIONAL BY NATURE

The first and most obvious of them is, as we have seen, the claim laid upon him by his client. Clearly, every maker or performer who approaches his work as a man of skill and responsibility—as, in other words, a professional—must regard this claim as primary. He cannot look upon his work as, first of all, a mere opportunity to make money. Nor can he regard it as, in any exhibitionistic sense, at least, a means of self-expression. Caslon, for instance, was a good type designer because we do *not* think of him when, in reading, we scan his type. And if, when we observe a contemporary building, we think first of its being the architect's (Frank Lloyd Wright's, let us say) then something may well be wrong either with us or with the building. For, after all, this does not belong to the architect; it belongs to its owner; and the test of its rightness lies in its suitability to the owner.

The claim of the client is, moreover, a stringent one: it obligates the maker to think about the client's true good—about his true needs. The maker has, in fact, to keep a hierarchy of values at least virtually in mind. As striving himself to foster a humane civilization, he must be particularly heedful of the requirements of those who are also, at least potentially, striving to do likewise. He must try to afford them what they need for leading peaceful, profound and generous lives, treating them as he would have them treat him. Ideally, therefore, his work should be so functional and appropriate as to be *humanly* effectual: enabling men to live contemplatively by freeing them from discomfort and drudgery and by providing them with things that are themselves worthy of contemplation for their intrinsic rightness and excellence.

Since, moreover, there is no such thing as an average person, there is no such thing, ordinarily, as an average client. The maker must be ready, as a consequence, to aim at products that meet unique sets of needs. Usually, as we have seen, except in the making of servile mechanisms or very simple things or parts, he cannot permit himself the luxury of serving his client slothfully through mass production or purely "formula" methods. He must considerately hold himself to the solving of each problem afresh —a requirement which means not that he must strive to be original but that he never must go back on his client and dodge the challenge of what is unique in every problem. He must be respectful of—indeed imbued with—tradition; but he can never be lazily conventional or automatic. To be so is to sin against his client— to treat him as a mere duplicate of another, rather than as a sacredly individual person.

Professionally, the normal maker or performer feels obligated to meet the claims of his fellow practitioners—those of the past and of the future, as well as of the present. He must therefore maintain high standards of excellence for their sakes as well as his own. And he must aid them, both protectively and cooperatively, to maintain a similar high standard. More specifically, not only must he eschew all chicanery, all shoddy, eye-catching glamor, salesmanship, price-cutting and competition, but he must also support loyally all who are of like mind with him, cooperating with them to establish just standards, prices and penalties, as well as responsible franchises. Moreover, through conferences, shop-talk, journals and associations, he will educate them, as well as himself, for the common good of his art.

Moreover, to make sure of the maintenance of it for society, as also to serve younger men in affection and charity, he will feel the obligation of protecting, supporting, guiding, inspiring and training apprentices, helping them to establish themselves as independent masters—even at some risk to his own "trade."

Nor in all this will he ignore the claims of the past and of the future. He will feel obligated to accept his art or profession in the spirit in which it was accepted by his predecessors—as a sacred trust which he must live up to and even, if possible, pass on improved. As its present legatee, he realizes that he owes it to his apprentices to hand the inheritance on to them worthily and inspiringly.

He is also, of course, obligated here to his family. In setting a fair price, he and his fellow masters have to take into account the needs of their dependents, those met in leading humane lives. Naturally, he owes it to his children never to spoil them, taking care especially never to encourage them to follow in his footsteps in a given art simply because he has carved out a safe and profitable niche there. He likewise owes it to them (and to everyone else) to make manifest by his example, the desirability of transforming every occupation into a professional art and of conducting all the affairs of life in accordance with an artistic conscience.

Finally, he must be fair to himself, striking a proper balance between the claims of his artistic conscience and those of his moral or religious conscience. He must, of course, exercise all the virtues that good work inevitably requires: the fortitude needed for resisting illegitimate dictation by clients, for accepting drudgery, for executing many revisions; the humility of avoiding exhibitionistic originality and of recognizing personal limitations; the justice of meeting his client's needs thoroughly and of never forcing either materials or instruments; the temperance of keeping his designs classically and functionally austere. Beyond this, however, he is also never to lose himself so much in his art as to endanger his personal life. He should not have to complain of himself, toward the end, as did Michelangelo, that the arts had been for him the main enemy of the Art (of living). In short, he must try to satisfy the claims both of his artistic and his moral conscience.

THE REWARDS OF THE ARTIST

But if these constitute the obligations determining his work, the meeting of them constitutes his main source of satisfaction.

For his meeting of them affords him the joys of feeling himself to be a part of the past, the present and the future in the upbuilding of civilization; of being a member of a dedicated group; of overcoming the challenges of his work; of acquiring skill and exercising it effectively; of experiencing happy inspirations; of seeing that his work is technically excellent; of realizing that he is leaving his art better than he found it, of contemplating the sheer splendor of masterpieces, his own included; of sharing in that most satisfactory of all fellowships, the fellowship of masters, and that most satisfactory of talks, shoptalk; of educating and being educated generously. He has the deep contentment that comes from having served family, friends, clients, country, all mankind, unstintingly and prudently. With both artistic and moral consciences clear, he can look upon his life as meaningful in the eyes of both man and God—as a dedicated, fully professional and vocational life.

The determining attitude

To be able to produce or perform things enthusiastically and well, a person must obviously appreciate the nature of work, seeing it for both what it is and for what it is not. More specifically, he must gain clear concepts of what is meant by drudgery, toil and labor, as well as by play and recreation. And he must see how all these are interrelated. Otherwise, he will never focus properly on what he is doing and enjoy it as fully as he is meant to.

He must see, first of all, then, that drudgery means primarily work which is performed in a spirit of boredom. It does not necessarily imply toil—exhausting physical effort—though, of course, it may imply this as well as distress and pain. Again, it does not necessarily imply mental anxiety of the kind that results from the inability to cope with technical difficulties. It does imply the distress of having to perform a monotonously repetitive and uninteresting task without letup, unremittingly. In undergoing dry drudgery, the worker usually finds himself challenged both too little and too much: he needs little or no technique, and he must repeat his simple operations endlessly yet urgently. The galley slave, for instance, in driving an oar back and forth dully, hour by hour, underwent drudgery; the oarsman in a modern eight, however, doing externally the same thing, yet feeling the challenge of a technique and not being compelled to row monotonously, enjoys an intense form of recreation, even though it is, to say the least, toilsome.

What, then, at the other extreme from drudgery is meant by play or recreation? Obviously, it is a form of activity indulged in for the sake of immediate enjoyment, without thought of its final productivity or utility. In it, to be sure, the player is given a good mental or physical workout, or both; the more intense, except for strain, the better. But even when, as in crew racing, a certain amount of drudgery is inevitable, this is not felt as purely distressing, but mainly as sharpening the sense of conquest and spicing the delight of final achievement, since no one enjoys playing against a "pushover."

Being a liberal art, play or sport is enjoyed for its own sake, as an activity rewarding in itself, not as a process for producing something useful. It is essentially devoid of utilitarian considerations.

There is a sense, however, in which work and play are not easily distinguishable—in which we can say that work should normally be play, and play should normally be work.

The worst punishment we could impose on a great inventor— on someone like Edison, for instance—would be to ban him from his workbench forever. Even were he to be recompensed with a million dollars, he would still feel trapped and frustrated. The fun would have gone out of life for him; and the first thing he would use the million for would be the mastering of some allied technique or at least a sport. He would still yearn for the best form of play he knew, his work.

And as work, in this sense, is normally play, so play, if it is to be truly recreative, must be a kind of work. As Aristotle pointed out, pleasure naturally results from the strenuous use of one's powers; it is a by-product of normal intense functioning. We are made for action, and play is merely a kind of action suited to the most pleasant "working" of our faculties.

Properly, therefore, work and play should be regarded as coequal, not as subordinate one to the other. We do not work simply in order to be able to play better, nor do we play simply in order to be able to work better. The one activity is not intrinsically superior to the other: eating, for instance, is not essentially better than singing, or vice versa. There would seem to be no reason why we may not enjoy our work as a kind of play or our play as a kind of "good workout," not spoiling either by distinguishing it too sharply from the other.

All sound work is, in fact, an exercise in liberal art. It has to be pursued, paradoxically, as if it were an end in itself and therefore a kind of game. For only then does it become as productive as it should be; only then does it afford the inspiring pleasure of technical achievement and the satisfaction of our innate love of perfection; only then does it enable us to take that form of delight in it that we were meant to take: aesthetic delight in its intrinsic rightness.

The experience afforded the worker by sound work may be, indeed, a profoundly aesthetic one: it may have the unity, variety, vividness and appropriateness that make it intensely pleasurable. The felt unity of aim, the variety of the stages, the vividness of the challenges and conquests, the appropriateness of the solutions and the various techniques assuring them: all these afford the same kind of delight, however subconsciously experienced, as that felt by a spectator in observing another person exercising skill—by a fan or a member of an audience.

All of which suggests what the requirements of enthusiastic and enjoyable work must be. The worker should obviously understand the main objectives of his work. This work should never be so limited, through a mass production division of labor, as to prevent him from seeing its ultimate significance. It should be varied and complex enough to challenge, at one time or other, every one of his powers of mind and will, as well as of hand. It should be vivid in the sense of engaging these strenuously enough to afford them a good workout. For insofar as it does not meet these requirements, it is inhumanely unaesthetic, therefore boring, therefore not nearly as effectual as it should be.

Since mass production methods do not meet these requirements very well, the question arises, what can be done about it? We have already considered one answer to this question—that of dividing every large or complex mechanism into smaller wholes or natural systems of parts and having these designed and produced by teams of apprentices, journeymen and masters. But there is also a palliative method for the making of such simple things as pins, nails, bolts and small parts. It is that of making each worker responsible for two or three processes of manufacture, not merely for part of one of them. Such job enlargement, as it is now being called by those who have found it profitable, may help restore to workers some of the normal joys of versatility and virtuosity.

PART III

IMPLICATIONS

The chapters which follow are not meant to present all the implications of a proper regard for technique. They are simply meant to suggest how such a regard can affect our thinking radically and pervasively in almost every field. Here again, the concern is more with describing a mentality than it is with advocating remedial schemes.

CHAPTER 4

WHAT THE ARTISTIC METHOD MEANS ECONOMICALLY

One of the main values of familiarity with artistic method is that it enables us to put the subject of economics into a proper, that is, a humane, frame of reference, so that we may see it in its widest and deepest ramifications, without crippling our thinking about it through the use of narrow and superficial categories. It enables us to understand, as we might otherwise never do, all the basic forms of economic activity, so as the better to transform and integrate them.

More precisely, a familiarity with the principles of technique or artistic method should enable us to see clearly what the essential elements of making a living humanely are and should be: what we should really be meaning by success, goods and services, remuneration, private property, the consumer, production, competition, labor, advertising, and the like. It should help us to rid ourselves of a certain narrowness by enabling us to see economic activity from a noncommercial, as well as a commercial, point of view.

Just how narrow our thinking has too often become and how necessary it is for us to broaden it becomes immediately apparent to anyone who turns to our ordinary textbooks on economics and tries to find in them any proper treatment of the professions as an intrinsic part of our economy. This segment comprises, conservatively, from one-tenth to one-twelfth of the workers in our civilization; yet their very existence is hardly so much as mentioned in most of our texts. Or, if these men are mentioned, the fact is seldom stressed that their concepts of economic activity are radically opposed to the concepts cherished by the rest of the business world. Professional men stand, in fact, as living contradictions to the popular slogans of the American business world. Here is a class of men who approximate the New Class that Galbraith refers to, in *The Affluent Society,* as the next to become dominant—a class that eighty per cent of our college students say they would like to enter—and yet they are treated by most of our economists or businessmen almost as if they were freaks. Try to suggest to an American audience that rather than transform our professions into businesses, we should transform our businesses into professions, and they will either fail to understand you or think you must be joking.

Yet if an understanding of technique or artistic method implies anything it implies the recognition of just this necessity.

How and why it does so may best be brought out, perhaps, by the two main codes of economic activity that are relevant here: those of the businessman first, and then those of the artist-professional.

It should be understood that in presenting these codes I do not mean to suggest that they are always formulated exactly as I have formulated them here, or that they are always adhered to without deviation. The commercialist will often follow, subconsciously, the code of the professional; and the professional, especially in a highly commercialized society like ours, will often follow the code of the commercialist. What I wish to call attention to is simply the contrast between the code which the commercialist takes for granted that he should follow and the code which the professional takes for granted that he should follow—whether, in fact, they really follow these codes closely or not. I am merely trying to make explicit what is held more or less implicitly—not to write a description of what is actually practiced.

THE BUSINESSMAN'S CODE

First, then, the code or creed of the typical American businessman. It would run, if I am not mistaken, about as follows:

The primary, or basic, reason for going into business is to make a profit; any other consideration is somewhat incidental. For, in the form of money, your profit will assure you of the possessions you need for a high standard of living for yourself and your family, as well as security. It may also enable you to attain social status and independence. If you end up bankrupt, of course, you are simply a failure.

Your primary task is obviously, therefore, to produce the goods that the consumer wants, for "the consumer is king." Just how he consumes what you produce is strictly none of your business; your concern is to make sure that he does so as continuously, and therefore, as conveniently and inexpensively as possible.

First of all, then, you should try to hit, if possible, upon some product that most people want, or can readily be made to want.

In design, it should be eye-catching and "exciting," so as to appeal to a huge number of buyers.

Clearly, the product should be capable of being mass-produced; for this will insure the steady use of machinery at low cost, and the possibility, therefore, that you can sell each unit at a low price and still make a profit. The low cost, moreover, will enable you to give the article a built-in obsolescence to which no one will object: in fact, this condition will help you establish a tradition of a change in fashion from year to year. Obviously, the quicker a product wears out while still affording satisfaction, the more certain you are of the continuous and most mechanically efficient and profitable use of your machinery. You can also feed out each new development as quickly or as slowly as competition dictates.

Low cost and small margin of profit both dictate that you should use the cheapest material available, choosing one that is just good enough to last for the customary period of obsolescence. And, by the same token, of course, you should get the cheapest labor available.

Advertising and salesmanship are to be used for two main purposes: the creating of wants and the holding of your particular market. Your salesmen do not necessarily have to be expert in the construction and the utility of your product, but they must be expert in the arts of persuasion—in moving the prospect to buy through awakening his instinctive drives, the drives to which we are all subject: love of glamor, pride of ownership, amorousness, gregariousness, combativeness, imitativeness, love of play. Once you have established a market, you should use your sales methods to assure it against the inroads of competitors. And, naturally, you should spend a great deal of money on market analyses, to see whether you are keeping up with your customers' changes of taste.

Your work force is to be divided into designers, engineers and production managers, on the one hand, and skilled and semi-skilled laborers, on the other. The brain work will be done by the first group; the manual work by the second—by the "hands." The semiskilled workers will be given small, repetitive tasks, at a tempo set by the requirements of efficiency and the nature of your assemblyline. Each task will prove easy to perform at this speed because not at all complex. Morons can be safely hired to do such work, at a relatively low wage. Even those who are not morons soon get used to it, since it is easy and entails only accuracy, rather than real responsibility.

Most men, you will find, are not very anxious to work; but you can cope with that natural tendency through positive and negative incentives. For the positive, you can offer them shorter hours, high pay, comfortable working conditions, retirement annuities, various fringe benefits; for the negative, time clocks, quotas set by time-and-motion study, threat of layoffs or dismissal, strict super-vision.

The main spur for your executives will be external and internal competition. Their salaries and advancement will depend on how well they do against other companies, but also, often, on how well they can do against other departments and even against one an-other. Beyond that, you can use all the techniques practiced by the army and the navy—with the president of the company treat-ed like the Old Man on a battleship, and the wall-to-wall carpet-ing as the equivalent of the brass on the uniform and cap. If you are skillful, you can build up an Organization Man esprit de corps not unlike that of the Napoleonic army.

You, yourself, will be spurred on by the need, not only of mak-ing money and exercising your powers of authority in keeping the concern progressing, but also by competitors who put out the same kind of product that you do. These kinds of spurs have given us the wonderful industrial system that we now have, the greatest in the world.

The right attitude toward private property and ownership is essentially the natural one that what is yours is yours. You respect the right of others to this attitude; and they, in accordance with the golden rule, should respect yours in turn.

All this does not mean, of course, that you are to be selfish. You should embrace every opportunity that is offered to cooperate with charity drives and worthwhile movements for civic improvement. You owe this to your community as a man of prominence. Besides, these things work both ways: because you are prominent, your name is put on letterheads of good causes; and because your name appears on these letterheads, you become even more prominent. And, while business and sentiment do not mix, still, charity is, in its way, good business: it creates goodwill, and it can often be charged off on tax returns.

THE PROFESSIONAL'S CODE

Now, there is hardly anything here to which the code of the professional man is not diametrically opposed; for this runs about as follows:

Man is to be thought of, first of all, as an artist. The anthropologist is always assured that the bones he has dug up are likely to be those of a human being when he finds near them some artifacts: hammers or bowls. And there is a good reason, though many of us seem to have forgotten what it is, why we still call our colleges colleges of liberal *arts*. For man, as man, is a creature who, in satisfying his needs, wishes to use his powers as skillfully and as creatively as possible.

But he is also, as Aristotle pointed out, a "social animal." He is a person who normally fits into a community of other persons, if only as a member of a tribe.

These conditions imply that it is normal for him to meet needs in a way that is peculiarly human; that is, personally, distinctively and responsibly. A community, as the derivation of its name shows, is a group of persons who are mutually helpful: a group into which one person fits in such a way as to aid others to be more fully human and to be himself aided by them to be more fully human. Properly, then, a maker tries to meet not average, merely animal or subhuman needs, but personal needs. To do so, he must specialize so as to devote his full powers to assuring thorough satisfaction through the excellence of his work. And he risks such specialization because he feels certain that he will not be allowed to suffer as a consequence—that the community will live up to its part of the bargain and afford him the support he needs for such focusing of his efforts.

He does not aim at independence, therefore, so much as at interdependence: an interdependence which helps each person to attain full personhood through helping others to realize theirs. Ideally, this is an interdependence in which all men serve one another in at least a spirit of honor—none feeling that he has a right to step outside the circle of social responsibility.

As Ruskin suggests (in *Unto This Last*), success is not to be measured in terms of ultimate loss to the server, but in terms of his willingness to die rather than serve purely selfishly, as well as by the degree of skill with which he does serve.* The soldier dies at his post; the captain goes down with his ship lest others drown; the doctor risks death in the plague-ridden city; the lawyer dies rather than sanction a concentration camp, and a priest rather than deny his Master. So, too, the man of business loses his fortune before those dependent on him lose theirs. Or, more positively, if a country doctor has maintained the health of his community, or a lawyer has seen justice done there, each at such loss as to end up bankrupt, they are to be considered, of course, in any proper sense of the word, true successes. And, by the same token, so is the grocer who has served his customers well and generously,

---

*As also by the degree of concern he shows for the negative object of his endeavors. If the doctor should be ashamed of, or at least deeply concerned about, the disease in his society; the lawyer, about the injustice; should not the businessman be so about its poverty—none of them leaving these cares primarily to the government?

never stocking the merely profitable items or persuading them to buy what they really do not need, and carrying many of the poor on credit during periods of depression and unemployment, even though he also may end up bankrupted by the unscrupulous competition of a large chain that, by price-cutting and premium-offering, panders to the tastes of his ungrateful, bargain-hunting customers.

In one sense, then, the notion that the customer is king is sound; in another, quite unsound. His needs are certainly to be regarded as primary, but only if they are true needs, not mere wants. Treating him as king does not mean pandering to his wants at all costs. It means that you are to give him what you know will best satisfy his real requirements—just as a good doctor will refuse to prescribe a patent medicine that a patient likes but will instead write a special bitter-tasting prescription or lay down a strict regimen which the patient may not want to follow. Moreover, if, to meet a client's mere wants means that you are to sacrifice the joy of really creative work—failing to meet one of your own main needs as a worker—then, for his sake as well as your own, you have a right to economic *lese majesté,* in accordance with the principles set forth in chapter 14, on the relations of client and maker. In short, you are to satisfy, in a humane way, his legitimate requirements, not his lusts.

Whereas the commercialist concentrates on satisfying average wants of average consumers—these being the kind best satisfied by mass production—the professional never thinks of these as final: he is concerned, first and last, with meeting the particular needs of individual persons. Even when he must make something for a large number of persons, like a state house, he would like to make it peculiarly for them as members of their particular state and their particular capitol. Anything else he would consider to be inadequate. It is in this sense that *the* customer—the single client—may be legitimately thought of as king; that is, as having a royal right to be served as a unique person.

Certainly, the professional's care does not end with his having sold his product. His concern is naturally with whether it will fit into a way of life that enables the client to be the kind of person he should be and to maintain the kind of culture that is humane. He does not think of his products as things to be possessed or used up, but as means for aiding his clients to live, not ignorantly or passively, but alertly and dynamically, and therefore happily.

The contrast between him and the commercialist is readily brought out by the differences in their attitudes toward the following test case: A millionaire collector finds, in an out-of-the-way pawnshop, a very interesting item: a fake Stradivarius that had long been taken, by experts of the past, for a genuine one. He buys it from the honest dealer for a relatively small figure, paying two thousand dollars, however, because it is, after all, a good violin with an interesting history. Later, he shows it to a noted violinist who has been entertaining his guests at a private musicale. The violinist, having examined the instrument carefully and tried it out, convinces the man that the dealer was wrong—that this violin really is a Stradivarius, for which he himself is willing to pay as much as seventy thousand dollars. The millionaire refuses, saying that the instrument has now become a real conversation piece, as well as an excellent investment. The violinist is indignant. And the millionaire considers such a reaction to be quite uncalled for: after all, it is his violin, and he has a right to do with it what he wishes, has he not?

From a commercial and legal point of view, he undoubtedly has. But from an artistic point of view, his action seems almost criminal. For whereas from the one, ownership depends more on possession than right use, from the other, it depends as much on right use as on possession. To the commercialist, ownership does not essentially imply stewardship; to the artist, it does. The one feels possession to be a necessity of comfort and status; the other thinks of it primarily as a source of control and a means of responsible living. The one, therefore, makes products for people to own; the other, for them to employ.

Again, the professional abhors what might be called profit-making methods of production. His natural tendency is to choose, not the cheapest material, but the most suitable, however expensive; not the eye-catching design, but the truly functional; not the least expensive or compliant workmen, but the most competent;

not the highest price, but the fairest; not the merely wanted product, but the truly needed; not the merely fashionable, but the tasteful; not the obsolescent, but the durable.

Moreover, since the artist-professional believes that even what is ordinarily called "raw" material should never be regarded as less than a kind of subperson, a fortiori he does not believe that a person can ever be regarded as a form of raw material, whether as buyer, to be manipulated by hidden persuaders through his instincts to acquire something he does not really need, or as co-worker to be reduced to the status of a part-person—a hand—and made into a "machine tender." For neither of these courses could prove efficient in the long run: the first generates all the uncertainties of whimsical buying-for-fashion-or-fad; the second, all the loss of skilled work resulting from the nonuse of the faculties other than hands.

With Erich Fromm, he does not believe that there is any such thing as a *naturally* lazy human being: such a person is pathological, in need of being restored to normal. And, with D. McGregor, he cannot accept the "carrot and stick" view of the employe: the carrot in the form of high wages, good working conditions, profit-sharing, fringe benefits, even some slight share in management; the stick in the form of time clocks, time-and-motion quotas, supervisors, docking, dismissal. For he thinks of his men, not as employes, but as co-workers, whose rewards are primarily those which he himself enjoys: the satisfactions (as sketched in the last chapter) that come from leading a creatively artistic life. Nothing would appeal to him less than the policy of sacrificing their interests to those of consumer-kings whose sole desire is to lead, through the use of mass-produced goods, lives of slothful luxury.

Basically, he wishes to assure his men of purposefulness in their work: it is the conscious, steady regard for purpose that raises us above all other creatures—that keeps us aware of how, as men, we were from the very beginning given truly human, that is, truly artistic and responsible work to do in filling out that part of the natural world which we call civilization. The termites conduct their colonies with astonishing efficiency and team play; so do the ants their anthills and the bees their hives. Yet, obviously, none of these creatures rises to the level of adopting the artistic attitude, following the artistic method, living up to the requirements of the artistic conscience. For none can consciously choose the purposes it wishes to fulfill, nor hold itself to the discipline of fulfilling these purposes ever more skillfully and conscientiously. None can therefore ever really *mean* its work in its colony as the human being can mean, and normally expects to mean, his work in constructing his equivalent of hill or hive: his city.

Moreover, the professional comes to see the activities of work and play, not as either primarily for the other, but as both essential for normal living—and at their best when affording the most delightfully strenuous exercise of powers.

As for salesmanship, he cannot help being amused at how even those who take its code for granted in the business world find them abhorrent in the professional. Some time ago, there appeared a cartoon in *The New Yorker* in which two men were shown standing at the desk in a doctor's office and the secretary was shown speaking into the intercom, saying: "Doctor, there are two men here to see you from the Medical Association." On the walls are signs reading: "No job too big, no job too small." "Satisfaction guaranteed." "Those with hectic coughs, ten per cent off." "We give green stamps." "Please come again." As the present writer has found, even a good businessman smiles at this situation, though apparently he would find nothing funny in it if the scene were a small business office and the two visitants were from the Chamber of Commerce. And yet why should he not find the two scenes equally funny? What has given him the right to hold the professional man to one standard of conduct while he himself can descend to a much lower one with perfect complacency?

Again, remuneration is not taken by the professional man in the form of profits, but accepted in the form of fees. And a fee is not determined by the requirements of supply and demand, but by what would be just or charitable under the circumstances; so that for the same service (a brain operation, let us say) a professional might charge a wealthy client a great deal, a poor client nothing and the average man the average fee for the given locale.

The professional does not, in fact, ordinarily think of himself as competing on the market at all. Thomas Edison once said that when he sat down to invent, he did not ask himself what he could devise that would bring the most profit, but what it was that mankind needed most. It is this kind of motivation that has given industry its real lifeblood; its very products.

So far as the cult of the Organization Man is concerned, the professional cannot but think it unnatural. For it is on their common aims, their common code, their common training, their mutual respect and affection that professionals, from apprentices to masters, base their esprit de corps, not on techniques of sales campaigns and other pseudo-military forms of motivation. Leadership there must be, and is, of course; but this results largely from obedience to the principle, still in force in the military and in medicine, that no one can command or direct another to do what he has not had some experience at doing himself. He may buy the work of another; but, unless he is an authority in it, he may not in any way control it.

Above all, the professional looks askance at the commercialist as one whose code makes quality almost impossible to achieve. He cannot help pondering: While commercialist A is turning out products for average consumers, with cheap material, eye-catching design, low wages, bored workmen, built-in obsolescence and high-powered advertising meant to prove that the product is perfect, what is commercialist B doing—turning out products for individual clients, with high quality material, superbly functional design and the rest? Where, then, will both of them end up when, having made their fortunes, they look about to buy really good products? Must they not turn away from fellow commercialists to the few men of integrity who still make things in accordance with an artistic conscience? And if, gradually, all these men are driven to the wall by their mass-producing, price-cutting, publicity-powered, acquisitive competitors, will our culture not end in an increasing proliferation of shoddy products that we think are as good as can be?

And while the spread of commercialism could only harm the

professions,* the spread of professionalism could rescue even the simplest of commercial activity; it could do so through developing it into an art and giving it a high code. Take so "low" and

---

*How a great profession, once it has been infected by commercialism, begins to shirk its duties and to degenerate through losing the proper image of itself, is well brought out by the following paragraphs from a letter by Professor John D. Windhausen commenting on an article by Edward T. Chase, "The Crisis in Medicine," in the March 10, 1968 issue of *The Commonweal*:

"Why are those in pre-paid group plans hospitalized far less often than those in Blue Cross-Blue Shield? Why are healthy uteri, appendices and tonsils extracted every year? Why should poverty be allowed to be the third cause of death in New York City, as the acting New York City Health Commissioner said last year? Why do ten other nations have a better record for infant mortality than ours? (We were sixth in 1950.) Why do twelve other nations have a longer life span for males than the richest nation in the world? Why, as Mr. Chase now asks, does the AMA continue to deny the expansion of medical schools when the shortage of medical personnel is so obvious?

"One wonders if any new medical revelation can be shocking. Let me try. Mr. Chase attributes many of the ills of organized medicine to its conception of itself as 'a *business* or *trade*' (his italics), not a profession. Should there be any doubt about this, readers might turn to the AMA's *Report of the Commission on the Cost of Medical Care,* 1964, where the relationship between the automobile industry to the free enterprise system was used to illustrate the operations of 'The Medical Care Industry.'

"The authors of the report insist that the marketplace determines fees for housecalls, office visits, tonsillectomies and annual checkups. Therefore, if doctors (alternately referred to as 'firms,' 'producers,' 'sellers,' and, in this instance, 'entrepreneurs') try to set a higher price, 'buyers' (guess who?) will go elsewhere.

"Or again. The 'patient-consumer' as well as the 'supplier' (recognize him?) plays a major role in the production process, we are told. But the 'patient-consumer' may not always utilize the health services for several reasons, 'including his own unwillingness to accept medical advice, take the prescribed medicines or observe good health habits.' How ironic that in the chapter on 'The Economics of Medical Care,' the authors overlook here the economics of the family in explaining why some patients are deficient in this 'production process.' Enough? On and on the authors ride, desperately clinging to the same philosophy that prevented English statesmen from sending food to famine-torn Ireland in 1847 for fear that the natural laws of supply and demand might be disturbed."

For how this kind of ruination could happen to "the profession of letters," see Balzac's prophetic *Lost Illusions*.

"unskilled" a task as ditch-digging. If a philanthropist were to offer, say $200,000 each year, in a national contest, for the best dug trench of perhaps six feet deep, four across and twelve in length, to be completed within a carefully determined time, it would not be long before many scoffers would suddenly discover how much of an art ditch-digging can be. They might even see that potentially it was quite as great an art as golf. A properly dug trench, therefore, might need one set of spades for breaking ground, another for digging at medium depth, another for full depth, and so on, to say nothing of the analyses of stance, trajectory, types of dirt, types of obstacle, position of digger in relation to cart, and the rest.

Nor is there any reason why masters of the art of digging should not hold themselves to a code, for their apprentices, and regulate themselves for the good of the public as well as their own good—be, in short, a sound professional association, their work consisting naturally of all forms of excavation, complex as well as simple, from that for conduits to that for big buildings, wells, tunnels and even great dams.

But professions can not only transform and elevate, they can also be transformed and elevated: they can be made into true and full vocations in the broadest sense of the term. For a vocation is simply a profession that is followed, not more or less impersonally out of a sense of honor, but as personally as is feasible out of a spirit of love. The vocation *subsumes* the profession. If a sense of honor will ordinarily move one to serve others as well, and therefore as individually, as helpfully and as thoroughly as possible, so will a love of them as persons help us to aid them to achieve ever greater and fuller personhood. Honor serves conscientiously; love serves not only conscientiously but also warmly and solicitously, opening out the natures of both the server and the served, and answering for both their profoundest need: to love and be loved as deeply as may be.

Finally, the professional cannot help wondering if the seemingly inevitable choice between a strictly communist and a strictly capitalist system is really the only choice open. Are the only kinds of motives to be followed either the communist set, "from each according to the materialistic needs of the proletariat; to each according to the will of the all-controlling bureaucracy trying to answer these needs," or the capitalist set, "from each according to his ability to produce profitably what the public can be made to lust for; to each according to his power to strike a bargain and enforce it"? Or is there not a third possibility: "from each according to his talents, one, three or five, as he uses these creatively and generously; to each according to his needs as he does likewise"?

The question naturally arises at this point, what can any one of us do to facilitate the transition from a system inspired by the second set of these motives to that inspired by the third. How can any one person hope to transform significantly a "megamachine" or "technostructure" that is so firmly entrenched as to be taken for granted even by its most prominent critics? Are any other courses open than that of a hippie-like retirement on the one hand or a compromising conformity on the other?

The answer is that there are courses open which, though they may not assure instant Utopia, may nonetheless gradually and ultimately serve to transform our technology and our culture.

To begin with, any person can so imbue himself with sound basic theory about artistic method and its implications that he cannot help disseminating it both correctively and fruitfully. Keeping always before his mind the dictum that "an artist is not a special kind of man, but every man is a special kind of artist," he can explore ever more thoroughly its essential meaning and its implications, especially the economic. Merely by bearing witness casually, as occasion offers, to the motivation and the methods he favors, he can challenge those that are delusive or inadequate and plant the seeds of change.

Concretely, when the remark is dropped casually, at lunch or a cocktail party, "Well, we are in business for profit, of course," he can ask, with Socratic innocence, "Oh? I was a guest at a Lion's Club meeting the other day, and I got the impression that we are in business primarily for service." The fireworks he then sets off cannot help casting some fairly disturbing light on priorities of motivation. And so for the off-hand challenging of similar dogmas of Main Street wisdom. To the remark that "ours is a free enterprise system," one may answer quietly, "I suppose so, but I sometimes wonder: free for what? For each person to pander to or to manipulate every other one primarily for profit, with little regard to social or ecological side effects?" Again, to the statement, "mass production is the key, of course," one may object mildly, "are you not confusing mass production with quantity production?" Or the cliché, "it pays to advertise," one may reply, "if that means tricking the customer—in accordance with the findings of motivational research—to buy your product impulsively, so that you maintain your market against your competitor, then whom does advertising pay? Is not the cost of the competitive struggle passed on to the customer?" Or, again, the dogma, "competition is the lifeblood of industry," may be countered by "but do the scientists—do men like Einstein, Fermi, Heisenberg or even men like Edison and Tesla—really compete with one another? And yet, without such men, where would your technological industries be? Besides, you profess to be a respecter of the Judeo-Christian tradition: how, then, can you rest content with a system motivated by greed and fear? Would it not be more consistent for you to try to establish one based on generosity and love of perfection, as those professionals who have not been corrupted by commercialism hope to do?"

Whoever bears witness in this way may expect, of course, to have to bear the onus of being called a contentious "nut" or a "commie;" but this may be well worth bearing. For the series of tiny shocks that he provides, in season and out, may swell, in the long run, to something like a miniature earthquake—or, to vary the figure, as he makes converts, his impact may spread like that of nuclear fission.

A person can also exert his influences, not only by how he chooses his field of work, but also by how he conducts himself in it. If, for example, he is a freshman in college, he can begin even then to determine carefully if his interests and capabilities enable him to be a professional or a businessman, and then study how he can be either the one or the other as professionally as he should be. It is certainly far better for him to become a good businessman professionalizing his field of endeavor than a fair professional commercializing his.

If a person is already in a profession, he can exert an influence on it by trying to meet its requirements as conscientiously as possible. Negatively, he must do all that he can to prevent his profession turning into a mere money making game. Concretely, he must not think of himself as a "producer," but as an artist; he must not think of the person he serves as a "consumer," but as a client; of his remuneration, not as a profit, but as a fee; of his co-workers, not as employes, but as fellow artists; of his standing as determined, not by his financial success, but by the extent and quality of his service. Nor must he allow the name professional to be arrogated by those who do not truly live up to what it implies (graduates of university business schools, the managerial experts of the technostructure, the well-paid athletes); rather, he must always be quick to point out that the real professional is one who meets a true need of his fellow members of society generously and skillfully, in accordance with a code of honor or charity that he professes.

A somewhat similar influence can be exerted on the world of commerce by the individual businessman, no matter what his special field.

If a manufacturer or a technologist or, for that matter, any member of the managerial class first reorders the priorities of his obligations and then tries, as well as he can, to hold himself consistently to this reordering, he will soon find himself able to make modifications here and there which, through their cumulative effect, may well result in basic changes in the whole industrial system. Let each of these men recognize that, without neglecting any of them, he is concerned with the claims first of his clients, then of his fellow workers, then of his investors, and then of himself. His primary duty is to satisfy his client's needs, rather than pander to his wants, and to satisfy these qualitatively as well as quantitatively. Next, he must be concerned with assuring that all his fellow workers—not merely his fellow executives—may lead generous and creative lives (as fellow artists), taking this requirement into account as an essential determinant of his methods of production. Let him recognize next that he is to aim not so much at achieving unlimited expansion and maximum profits as at a just return for those who are true investors in his firm, who should be mainly his fellow workers. And let him regard his own remuneration not as a skimming of profits but as a just fee.

The union leader or, for that matter, the ordinary worker can also help exert great influence on the industrial system if he too adopts this same set of priorities, and, like our present college students, asks for a share in responsible decision making. He can call for work that is need-serving, rather than merely profit-making. He can welcome responsibility in assuring the quality of what he is helping produce. He can call for changes in methods of production that will make it possible for him to enjoy as creative a participation in it as his given ability permits. If organized efforts have enabled him in the past to win for himself conditions at least as satisfactory as those of a good racehorse, so may they today win for him the conditions proper to a normal worker—those of a true artist.

There are also many opportunities for amelioration open to anyone in the field of exchange. At the very least he can study and strive to promote the kinds of credit-union systems that have been worked out in Scandinavia and Nova Scotia.* For here he will learn how people have discovered a way for cooperatively controlling the uses of money for satisfying communal needs primarily. Thereby, he may also learn how our own credit unions—and we have many—may be better directed, or redirected, toward their social goal. And he will certainly do well to work toward an insurance system like that of New Zealand, which is described later in this chapter.

Again, if a person is concerned with the distributing of goods, he too can exert a real influence on our economic system—at first slowly and slightly, but in the end decisively. Suppose, for example, that he is the owner of a grocery store in a small town. Unimportant as he may seem, he can still lead a comparatively mean-

---

*See *Sweden, the Middle Way,* by Marquis W. Childs, New Haven, 1936; and *Democracy's Second Chance,* by George Boyle, New York, 1941.

ingful life through bringing everything he does in ever closer conformity to a code of professional practice. He can not only gain the satisfactions afforded by it, but also exemplify its validity. Let him spend a little money on a market investigation to determine accurately what his clients really need. Let him come to know them as persons. Let him convince them that he is honestly concerned with their true needs and interests. Let him aid them to buy, not what will make the most profit for him, but will meet their requirements best. Let him educate them in how to resist the chicanery of trick advertising, premium offers and so-called bargains. Let him, as well as he can, "carry" the poor and unfortunate of his neighborhood. In short, let him demonstrate concretely and vividly what it is to conduct a small store professionally; and his impact, in the long run, will prove anything but negligible. His success, however modest, cannot but prove inspiring to his fellow grocers and other small merchants. It may even cause the members of the Lions, the Kiwanis and the Rotary to recognize what is really meant by living up to the code of service they so loudly profess in their meetings.

Last, but far from least, there is the influence that one can exert as a judicious client or purchaser; this, through buying the products and services of right-minded men and thereby, in effect, boycotting those of the primarily acquisitive. In a realm in which "the customer is king," he can exert a powerful influence indeed.*

Obviously, the effect of all these efforts can be multiplied manyfold through the organizing of men of goodwill and sound conscience. These may do well to consider, therefore, such a movement as that described by Erich Fromm in the last chapter of his work, *The Revolution of Hope,* some slight notion of which can be gleaned from the following excerpt:

The first step would be the formation of a National Council which could be called the "Voice of American Conscience." I think of a group of, say, fifty Americans whose integrity and capability are unquestioned. While they might

*For information about such producers and products, write to Tolstoy Farm, Davenport, Washington 99122.

have different religious and political convictions, they would share the humanist aims which are the basis for the humanization of technological society. They would deliberate and issue statements which, because of the weight of those who issued them, would be newsworthy, and because of the truth and rationality of their contents would win attention from at least a large sector of the American public. Such Councils could also be formed on a local level, dealing with the general questions but specifically with the practical questions relevant for the city or state which they represented. One could imagine that there might be a whole organization of Councils of the Voice of American Conscience, with a nationally representative group and many local groups following basically the same aims.

. . . The Councils, of course, do not satisfy the needs which have been mentioned before: the need of the individual to work actively together with others, to talk, plan, and act together, to do something which is meaningful beyond the money-making activities of everyday life. To relate in a less alienated fashion than is customary in most relations to others, to make sacrifices, to put into practice norms and values in everyday life, to be open and "vulnerable," to be imaginative, to rely on one's own judgment and decision, the formation of a new type of social group is necessary.

I propose that this kind of shared activity and interest could occur on two levels: in larger groups of 100 to 300 members who would form "Clubs," and in much smaller groups of about 25 members, which would follow the same principle but in a much more intensive and absorbing way.

Whether one agrees completely with Fromm's idea or not—and it cannot be stressed too much that only the merest indication of it has been given here, and that it should be considered in its entirety—one can certainly strive to attain its goals, using whatever alternative method he may find more congenial.

Finally, not the least important step that one can take in trying to transform both our economy and our culture is that of encouraging a thorough overhauling of our educational system; this, ironically enough, by making it try to live up to its professed aims. Traditionally, our system has been called one of the liberal *arts,* not of science and letters; and what we need do is make it truly artistic in the broadest sense of the term. More specifically, we need to make sure that every child is trained to be consciously skillful in his every daily activity and to be a professional artist in his occupation, no matter what this is. Important as it may be for him to know the chief products of North Dakota, or the capitals of South America, or the recipe for repeating a classic experiment in physics or chemistry, it is more important for him to learn how to walk, talk, handwrite, sing, dance, act, draw, design, plan, converse, confer, philosophize, compose, etc., all as gracefully and effectively as his talents permit. If possible, he should master the various techniques outlined in the second chapter of this book, so that he may lead a well-rounded, a truly professional life—one of generous and creative achievement. Whoever works for an education with these ends cannot help fostering a radical transformation of our whole culture.

But whatever the specific rules may be for trying to assure communal welfare, there are three general rules to be followed for assuring personal well being. These are:

1. Determine what your special abilities are and train yourself to use them as well—as skillfully and generously—as possible.

2. Determine how you can best use these in satisfying the needs of others as they too try to lead such a life.

3. Serve these people, as your clients, wholeheartedly, taking in return the fair fee that will enable you to go on serving them contentedly and effectively.

For, as more than one wise man has pointed out, happiness is not something you achieve by aiming at it directly and self-consciously, but something you enjoy like a beautiful musical accompaniment. It is the *tone* of your actions when you are using your powers normally: intensely, creatively and lovingly.

The requirements of ecology*

As we have come to realize ever more clearly of late, it will not matter very much which system of economics we favor if it does

---

*For a clear view of our ecological condition, the reader could hardly do better than consult the March 1971 issue of the magazine *Ecology Today,* published by Ecological Dimensions, Inc., P. O. Box 180, West Mystic, Connecticut 06388.

not accord with the requirements of ecology; obviously, it could not survive unless we ourselves did. The question therefore arises, which system does actually accord best with these requirements: a ruggedly individualistic commercialism or an artistic professionalism?

We can get an answer to this question fairly readily if we approach it indirectly. We need only consider first what anyone intent on ruining the ecology would try to do and then note how closely one or the other economic system would fit in with his plans.

What, then, would such a person wish to do?

First of all, he would like to make sure that one order of creatures, namely the human, would continue to increase both in number and in range of wants, so that they would consume more and more products the materials for which would be provided by all the other orders.

Next, he would hope that in the processing of these there would be much waste in the form of rubble or residues.

Again, he would like to see the mode of production be such as to pollute, debilitate or poison the environment and all its creatures (air, minerals, plants, animals, fish, human beings).

Then, again, he would like to see elements of the ecological cycle simply tied up or made unavailable or unassimilable as worn-out products or containers.

To gain these ends, he would like to win acceptance for a certain ideology and set of policies. As counter to the fundamental ecological principle that all things are essentially interdependent, he would try to persuade people that their basic economic purpose was to make a profit in order to become "independently well off." He would also try to convince them that, having attained independence, they would no longer have to work (which he would equate with drudgery), but would be able to retire and enjoy life, especially as one or other kind of consumer.

He would, of course, try to promulgate the "principle" that there is no such thing as over-production, the expanding business being the only healthy one: the greater the consumption, the better.

Obviously, he would favor assemblyline mass production for both its direct effects on products and its indirect effects on workers. This method of production virtually requires, for mechanical and cost efficiency, a certain built-in obsolescence on products that ultimately results in vast junk piles. And it inevitably assures the boredom which turns both blue and white collar industrial workers into consumers-for-compensation.

Naturally, he would approve of extensive advertising campaigns as helpful in "creating" limitless wants: those, not only for workaday necessities, but also for recreation—speeding, traveling, vacationing and the like.

It is obvious that all this accords very well with a ruggedly individualistic commercialism. It is the ideology, in fact, which up until fairly recently was taken for granted by both industrialists and professors in graduate schools of business.

On the other hand, it is not something which an artist-professional could ever accept.

For one thing, he would not aim himself, nor would he try to assure for others, an independence that would guarantee a state of aloof luxury. He would aim at an interdependence which enabled all the members of society to serve one another creatively and humanely. For him, the making of a profit is simply a necessary evil, not a primary goal. Private ownership he would justify as merely a basic requirement for the skillful making and fruitful use of products: a person must own his materials and tools in order to employ them properly; and he must own the products made by others for the same reason. He regards ownership, in other words, as primarily validated by the right use of what is owned in the answering of needs, those of others as well as those of oneself.

Since he is mainly concerned with meeting the needs of humane living, he would not be interested in getting more people to use more things; he would try to help them to enjoy all the activities of living (conduct, work, play) as artistic achievements, without having to burden themselves or their environment with a plethora of things. He would certainly not look with favor on built-in obsolescence or slothful, "throw-away" consumption. And, of course, he would forbid the widespread use of advertising, as do our doctors and lawyers even today.

Finally, by understanding functionalism and the needfulness of things, he would find it easy to think in terms of ecological interdependence.

In short, while the ruggedly individualistic commercialist naturally turns to practices that disrupt the ecological system, the artist-professional just as naturally shuns them.

There is another, and very helpful, way for us to look at the ecological system and what it implies. We may see it as the result of a cosmic shakedown cruise that has been seasoning the ship and perfecting the teamwork of the crew for millions and millions of years, until they have attained an astonishing interdependence. So delicate are the mutual adjustments here that if we tamper with them—if we permit any one element, even the human, in this beautiful system to assert its rights individualistically, in disregard of the rights of those of all the other elements—we are risking a catastrophic disruption. A free enterprise, therefore, that is "free" of responsibility for the whole system and a rugged individualism that ignores the requirements of interdependence are nothing short of disastrous.

Security in having the best

The continuous awareness which technique gives us of the requirement of protection is likely to affect our economic thinking in several ways. First, it may cause us to note that the resisting or overcoming of an external "enemy" is no great evidence of a producer's soundness: a cheap-jack manufacturer can slander, price-cut or advertise a good one right out of business. And his very efforts to eliminate a competitor may prevent him from perfecting his product as he should. Conversely, an innocent craftsman or inventor may perfect his product only to have it taken away from him and cheapened by commercial tricksters who use the very patent laws that were devised to protect him for robbing him safely. Again, big companies will spend huge funds on advertising campaigns, not so much to create demand, as is usually asserted, as to protect themselves against inroads into their markets —an expense that hardly lessens the price of their products.

Beyond all this, moreover, an awareness of the importance of protection may alert us to the wise use of actuarial principles; that is, to the discovery of how we may best forestall, for creative purposes, the disruption of personal and institutional destinies through prudent, just and charitable insuring. This awareness will help us to understand how and why a professional association protects its members, itself and the public: its members from price-cutting, false claims, shoddy charlatanism; the association itself from blind, tyrannical regulation from without; the public from deception and poor service.

We shall also tend to overlook, unfortunately, the simple fact that there is such a thing as an insurance-state system which, strictly, is neither communist nor capitalist. Its nature can be brought out hypothetically as follows: Let us suppose that every citizen in a nation took out insurance in a variety of companies against unemployment, old age, sickness, maternity care, tuition for the children's education, and so on: all the main inevitable expenses of life in a family. Obviously, each person would receive these benefits as needed without being dictated to by the insurance companies—any more than our funerals are regulated by our life-insurance companies. Now suppose that all the citizens came together and nationalized and combined all these companies, each citizen promising to pay the necessary premiums to the best of his ability in accordance with his particular earning power. Here, again, the payments would be made with no more regulation than is exercised by private companies. The only people who might be disgruntled would be the selfish who would be called on, because of their higher earnings, for proportionately higher premiums.

To maintain that this system would be so ultra-protective that it would discourage the very initiative required for earning the premiums it needs to be fed with would seem, at first sight, to raise an excellent objection; the only thing is, that the system has actually been working for quite some time now in New Zealand; and it is mainly because of our puritanical fear of coddling that we have unfortunately ignored or under-prized it.

To observe how the system works, let us take the case of a New Zealand worker and his wife and four children, with earnings of $100 a week. He pays no income tax, since this begins only at $5,600 a year. The rate for income tax above this figure ranges from 15% to 60% for the highest incomes.

Our worker would pay 7½% ($7.50) of his weekly wage as a deduction to cover social insurance. This is paid by *all* employees (and also on company income), as well as by the self-employed. He then receives the following benefits:

Family Benefit: $5.25 per child, a total of $21 a week for four children.

Sickness: $65 per week, additional to the above family benefit, after seven days of illness, with no time limit.

Unemployment: Same as sickness benefit, no time limit.

Medical Care: This covers the whole family: almost full doctor's charges, full hospital care, full cost of prescribed drugs, etc., full dental care for children to age 16, full maternity care, ante-natal and post-natal included.

Widow's Benefit: $43 per week (plus the $21 family benefit) for the widow and four children. (See also the Supplementary Benefit below.)

Orphan's Benefit: $14 a week for each of the children to whoever cares for them.

Age Benefit: $35 a week for each person at the age of 60 with proof of moderate need.

Superannuation: $35 a week for each person at the age of 65 irrespective of need. (Both husband and wife may receive one of these.)

Emergency Benefit: This allows the benefits listed above to be granted to those (immigrants, for example) who are in need yet not qualified by reason of non-payment of tax.

Supplementary Assistance: This covers needs not met above, quite flexibly.

Reciprocity: On most of the above arranged with England and Australia.

The dominant motives of the plan are these:

—The elimination of poverty by community action.*

—The redistribution of income from rich to poor; the deliberate aim is to have neither very rich nor very poor. These objectives are to be accomplished through family benefits, large income-tax exemptions for wife and children, and high minimum-wage rates based on the needs of a three-child family.

—The meeting of health care and basic material needs as a community responsibility in promotion of human dignity and as a prerequisite to further growth in initiative, independence and freedom.

Propose this New Zealand state-insurance plan to a group of Americans, and you find yourself in for an intense, but hardly a very intellectual, experience. First comes the conditioned-reflex objection: "Oh, but it would never work!" When you point out that it has worked for years now, you are met with: "But it would never work in America." This objection turns out to mean: "But it would be difficult" (not, observe, impossible) "to persuade Americans that it is not socialistic or impractical." When you call attention to the fact that under the plan the state does not, as in socialism, own the means of production, exchange or distribution, but only runs an over-all insurance company, like any of ours, you are told: "But New Zealand is a small country; ours is too vast." If you counter that objection with the fact that our country is made up of fairly small states, each of which could run its own insurance system, you are met with: "But the plan discourages initiative." If you point out that it does not discourage the priest at the altar, the doctor in the operating room, the lawyer in the court, the scientist in the laboratory, the teacher in the classroom, but only the businessman who wants to make a huge fortune, you meet the final objection: "Yes; and it would never work for that very reason."

In all this the most important objection is not mentioned: the

---

*The interested reader might also look into the cooperative and credit-union movements of Scandinavia and Nova Scotia which have met this problem through taking over the instruments ordinarily controlled by the acquisitive.

plan can work so well as to encourage too much contentment with mere security and a bourgeois level of culture. This objection is no doubt sound—as far as it goes. But the plan is not being proposed here as an umbrella for our present-day economy. It is being proposed as an aid to an economic system in which everyone is following his occupation as a profession or a vocation, using his security to assure *quality,* not mere *quantity,* of service. Without such an aim, New Zealand, or any other country that achieves security, can abuse it as a safeguard to smugly contented, philistine living.

What the client can expect

If it is true that clients should have a right to be served by a good maker or performer, it is no less true that the maker or performer should have the right to serve good clients. He should be able to plan, with some security, to make or perform the right kind of thing—to feel sure that this is the real challenge he is going to have to meet, but no other. He should not be asked to produce what goes against his artistic conscience.

This requirement obviously means that, as clients, we must realize both what we should not ask for and what we should. This twofold necessity, then, is the subject of our next consideration. Precisely, what does it imply?

First of all, it implies that we should be concerned not so much with the appearance of what we are buying as with its reality: not so much with what our senses see *of* a thing as with what our mind sees *in* it. Through appreciating that all products are to be evaluated primarily in terms of their function, we shall be loath to buy them primarily for their glamor, even when this is enticingly enhanced for us by the trimmings of a "gift shoppe" counter. In buying a set of glasses, for instance, we shall not be swayed by their having a strange and exotic tint or unusual lines or proportions; rather, we shall judge them by how well they receive, carry and dispense the right quantity of the water, milk, beverage or liquor for which they were designed. We shall next judge how capable they are of easy, graceful, appropriately toned and pleasant handling, in accordance with the occasion and the mood in which they are to be drunk from: how easy they are to grasp; how hard to knock over; how well-balanced, when filled or partly empty, for being gracefully lifted, drunk from and returned to their place. We should estimate, if only tentatively, how well the designer struck the compromises called for by these various requirements. For it is only then that we may come to some appreciation of the beauty of the essential design. More concretely, it is only when we have felt how appropriately heavy, thick-handled, tall, this glass stein is for the drinking of beer, or how appropriately light and open-handed this champagne glass is for felicitations; or how right for his two-fisted grasp, small mouth, and debonair balancing is this infant's tumbler—it is only then that we should go on to a "tasting," as it were of the qualities of appearance. It is only then that we should gauge how pleasing it would look even to a person who did *not* understand its function and handling. In this way, we may avoid infatuation with a product as with a person and fall truly in love with the one as with the other, not being snared by face and figure alone.

As far as possible, we should buy with the special, indeed the most personal, requirements of the user in mind. A good test case is that of the buying of an instrument for a beginner in a sport or an art. Here, through careful estimating of exact needs, we should avoid two common and costly delusions: one, that because a beginner finds a certain instrument easy to operate, it is the right one for him; the other, that he should not be given a really good instrument because he is, after all, only a beginner.

The first of these notions is most misleading. The skillful movement, the effective stroke, almost always strikes a beginner, when he has yet to become accustomed to it, as cramped and "unnatural." The stance, the swing, the follow-through, all impress him during his early practice, as mysteriously queer and uncomfortable. He often wastes time and money, therefore, in trying, vainly, to acquire the club, racket, tool, brush, that will relieve him of this sense of constraint—always blaming the instrument, rather than himself, as refractory. Yet if and when he becomes an expert, he finds that what at first was an unpleasant movement performed with a seemingly balky instrument has become a pleasant movement performed freely with a responsive one. The making of the right strokes in the right way has become an "acquired taste"; he finds them as delightful and natural as he once found them irksome and strange. And he finally realizes that it is only when he has mastered his technique through obeying its instruments that he can justly evaluate these; it is only then that he can estimate fairly how much he has a right to demand of himself, how much of them.

Those who buy instruments for a beginner, then, will do well to consult instructors or coaches; for these people know that it is as much a mistake to misconceive the beginner's true needs as it is to cater to his false. What is required is an exact knowledge of his needs *as a beginner*. It is absurd to buy him the best if this is the best for experts only. It is equally absurd to provide him with a shoddy or cheap imitation of the instrument that has been found best for the expert. Naturally, a duffer may easily abuse, in his awkwardness, a delicate instrument while making less effect with it than he could with something less fragile. But to use this fact as an excuse for providing him with an instrument which an expert would reject with scorn is to do him a great disservice. Like the expert, the beginner should have what is best *for him*. All of which means that he should be provided with a well-wrought training instrument, one which will prepare him for manipulating the more delicate kind safely, gracefully and tactfully. If it is foolish, let us say, to spend a large sum on a grand piano for a child, it is even more foolish to let him begin on a tinny upright; ideally, he should be furnished a piano which would get him ready for a proper appreciation and use of a concert grand. And so for everything else, from mitts to microscopes.

In the matter of buying, moreover, we have to consider the compromise that has to be struck between the claims of the maker and those of the user and of society in general.

It would seem fair to say that a maker cheats us when his product cannot be operated as it should be, or as its appearance suggests it should be. There is, in fact, a strict obligation for a designer to make something that we, as normal users, should be able to handle *peacefully*—this being a kind of tacit social assumption. We waste enough energy in drudgery, even at best; so that none of us is privileged, in justice, to cause a still greater waste of time in a spirit of vexation: no one has a right to add avoidable tears to avoidable sweat. For a maker to cause us unnecessary disappointment or even indignation, instead of quiet trust and warm gratitude, is nothing less than shameful: it is to poison social life with the venom of mutual suspicion.

On the other hand, the designers of products which pander to our sloth—which coddle or humor us—cannot but harm us, making it virtually impossible for us to achieve results of high quality. They preclude our ever becoming truly expert users. And through making operation unduly easy, they give us a false self-confidence; they encourage many of us to believe that because we can handle complex machines, we are somehow members of the army of science in the great age of progress—as if our use of a slide rule or a Geiger counter proved that we could construct one. They cause us, in other words, to fall prey to the fallacy of instrumentalism, the fallacy of supposing that if we know how a thing is to be worked or conquered for our own satisfaction (the universe included), we know all that we really need to know about it.

In reflecting on the requirement of ease of operation, then, we are inevitably confronted with such questions as these: Do we want a civilization that would be equipped with no more than the number of well-wrought things it requires, which are to be put to effective use by the well-trained; or do we want one filled with over-simplified conveniences to be turned on and off by morons and thrill-seekers, with little or no effort? Is a push-button way of life a good in itself? There is a joy in skilled work to be experienced by us both as makers and as users: is the lack of this joy to be compensated for by the excitement of watching others execute skillful plays, as in football, baseball, basketball, hockey? Is there not some direct connection between the slothfulness of our conveniences and the softening of our manhood—or why are the Outward Bound schools being established to assure that manhood? Is it not foolish, as well as altogether too distrustful of mankind, to suppose that there would not be enough skill to go round, especially in view of the fact that various peoples usually live up to the expectations they have of themselves, producing, as a matter of course, the scientists, the artists or the businessmen they believe they can produce? Will not those who are persuaded that the less skill they have to acquire and exercise, the better off they are, not ultimately turn into human vegetables, content to be the prey or the slaves of those who give them ultrasimplified work and lull them with luxuries? Or, like some teenagers, will they not, resentful of such servitude or surfeited with it, become vandals, since, if they cannot have the fun of putting things together, they can at least enjoy taking them apart?

Finally, as buyers, we may well remind ourselves of the dangers of possessing too many things and of substituting standards of mechanical efficiency for those of human efficiency.

We must learn to prefer a few essential, efficient and durable instruments to a multiplicity of luxurious, distracting, fragile and quickly obsolescent gadgets. For not only do most of even the so-called time-saving devices not make or pay for themselves, but they also need to be operated, conserved and protected; so that they can lure us into too complicated and "tranquilized" a rat race of a life. To fail to recognize this fact is to miss the point of Caesar's calling his equipment *impedimenta*: things that slow down one's progress through getting in "the way of one's feet." We shall fail to see why it is not only religion that sanctions a spirit of poverty (in the sense of having enough, without being encumbered by too much) but also sheer human efficiency.

CHAPTER 5

SOCIOLOGICAL SIGNIFICANCE

Men, like all other creatures, are essentially needful: they too have to be made, operated, conserved, and protected—as do the instruments which fill their needs.

Sociologically, this fact has important implications. It enables us to make out why we have the basic institutions that we have— why we find that a certain set of them is minimally required for maintaining a normal society. It suggests a criterion for judging whether our own society is lopsided or not. It keeps us aware of how institutions tend to proliferate unnecessarily. And it alerts us to the danger of cherishing those which have outlived their usefulness and become ends in themselves.

As the following chart, sketchy though it is, quite clearly indicates, a study of man's making, operating, conserving and protecting of himself physically and mentally gives us a key to the basic complex of institutions which form a society.

SOCIOLOGICAL SIGNIFICANCE

How institutions grow from basic needs

PHYSICAL:

need	implying	requiring
for making man	courtship, marriage, child-bearing	home, social clubs, theaters, etc. maternity hospitals
for operating him	exercise, athletics, sports	clubs, sports mfrs. stadiums, gymnasiums, etc.
for protecting him	housing, clothing	architectural and building firms, clothing mfrs., stores
for conserving him	nourishing, remedying, resting	farms, restaurants, furniture mfrs. drug makers, hospitals

MENTAL:

need	implying	requiring
for making him	educating, training	home, kindergarten, institutes
for operating	study, recreation	publishing houses, libraries, museums, symphony halls, hobbies, theaters, etc.
for protecting him	criticism, guidance	forums, councils, critical journals
for conserving him	mental treatment	mental hospitals, psychiatric institutes, rehabilitation centers

Were we to fill out this chart more fully, taking into account man's moral and spiritual needs, we should find that every normal human society would require as basic only a few institutions: the church, the school, the library, the home, the hospital, the theater, the athletic field and the various business houses called for by the production, exchange and distribution of vital necessities.

Obviously, a well-run society would require, in addition, certain ancillary institutions, particularly the kind needed for controlling justly those which are basic: the meetinghouse, the courtroom, the jail, etc. But even so sketchy and brief a chart as this shows clearly how institutions emerge as answers to man's fourfold needs as a person.

A study of the basic institutional requirements also leads naturally into seeing what criteria we should adopt in evaluating a given society. It is fairly obvious that a society in which the primary physical needs are not very well taken care of—in which people are poorly fed, poorly clothed, poorly housed, poorly cured—is an unsound one, no matter how "spiritual" (as in India) its contemplatives may seem to be. It should be no less obvious that a society in which the best institutions are those for assuring physical comfort and the most philistine forms of mental pleasure is hardly a very admirable one, since it is based on a confusion of a high standard of subsistence and frivolity with a truly high standard of living. And it should also be obvious that only a culture which satisfies the needs of man both as an animal and as a fully human person—a society which assures the conditions for well-disciplined, creative and generous living—only such a society has a right to be considered normal. Naturally, it will not be easily attainable; but that fact is no reason for not trying to attain it.

There are several reasons, of course, why this may be, to put it mildly, somewhat difficult to do. First of all, institutions, no less than persons, are also needy: they, too, have to be aided to operate, conserve and protect themselves—usually with the help of ancillary service institutions. A farm, for instance, would be of little use without a system of transportation; nor would a system of transportation work well without a system of communication. And even these secondary institutions need to be operated, conserved and protected.

Unless, then, the institutions are limited, first, to the basic and their necessary support institutions, and due proportions between them maintained, they will not be in human scale—discernible clearly enough to be readily controlled. Their proliferation will be left to the whims of the powerful and the acquisitive; and we shall drift fatalistically into a demonic complexity. Rousseau, for instance, held that because "the man who thinks is a depraved animal," he was doomed to set up intellectualized institutions that, by their very rigidity, could only defeat him in his purpose. And today, Jacques Ellul would have us believe that man attains precisely the same result through becoming so fascinated with his techniques as to let them run him, rather than he them, for which views, alas, we can see, as we look about us, that there is altogether too much to be said.

In the light of these considerations, we can begin to understand why Aristotle and many others have insisted on the necessity for keeping our typical society small. It needs to be only as large as will assure well-roundedness and depth of living. Athens at its best contained no more than one hundred thousand inhabitants: perhaps every one of our cities of that size could also be satisfactorily proportioned culturally. It may well be that we do not need to choose between Megalopolis and Hicksville as often as we think. We may be able to maintain societies in which the values of both country and city life are blended—as they were, in miniature, in early New England towns, where people lived in close proximity, with their farms and shops spreading out radially.

Certainly, it would seem that if our main human needs are reducible to a few, it would not seem hopelessly difficult for us to maintain a high, though not necessarily very elaborate, culture in every one of our communities; this, by making certain that each community had the handful of institutions essential to a simple but lofty way of life. If farmers were incorporated into the civic structure as a thoroughly professional association of food-raisers, and if every township of, say, twenty-five to fifty thousand contained its full complement of basic institutions, might we not, by spending on them only a fraction of the billions we now spend on recreation and travel "just to get away from it all," avoid the false dilemma of an either-or choice: either town or country? It would seem, moreover, that groups of such communities and of even smaller communities could maintain cooperatively a regional culture of a very high level. In short, when human needs are sanely evaluated and taken care of *proportionately,* and more or less austerely, there would seem little reason for supposing that any modern country must remain one-third civilized, one-third pseudo-sophisticated, and one-third rustic.

If we must be careful to avoid drifting into cultural obesity and lopsidedness, we must also be careful to avoid erecting institutions which, because of their structural inflexibility, do more to hamper than to help. Here is where the attitude of purposiveness, which is a principal determinant of technical method, serves as a vital corrective. For, as recent military experience has shown with striking cogency, it is in purposiveness that we have a key to soundly organic and supple organization. As each new war has made increasingly evident, it is only when a lower officer—or, for that matter, a private—has an adequate notion of why he is being called on to do certain things that he can do them most efficiently. It is only the man, for example, who has some concept of the use to which the information he is about to acquire will be put who can go on reconnaissance as profitably as he should; otherwise, of course, he may disastrously overlook vital facts while collecting impertinent. Ideally, then, as the success of Montgomery's army is pointed to as showing, privates should think, as far as possible, like lieutenants, lieutenants like captains—on up to generals, who should think like a commander-in-chief. So, too analogously, for civil organizations: if there is anything that distinguishes one that is well run from one that is not, it is that the members of the first have a clear understanding of how their work achieves one of the hierarchy of ends dictated by the ultimate purpose of the organization, whereas the members of the second have not.

Moreover, if we have a true appreciation of purposiveness, we are not likely to cherish an organization for its own sake. We are not likely to let Parkinson's Law hold sway over it—the law which says that a department tends to grow and grow even when it has less work to do. Nor are we likely to grant to it the blind loyalty typical of the Organization Man. We shall see it, rather, as an instrumentality that is a quasi-organism, adjustable to shifting ecological conditions, developing naturally, casting off needless organs, reforming itself thoroughly for each new system of aims and requirements. We shall not take as our model the hen that continues to sit on a cracked and leaky egg simply because that is the instinctive, the customary and the loyal thing to do.

Becoming fully developed
—as people and as nations

A major problem engaging the attention of social scientists today is what is called development: just how are we to aid ourselves and underdeveloped countries to become truly developed.

If we are to answer this question at all adequately, we must determine clearly what system of motivation this kind of progress calls for. A crude epicureanism will certainly not do: one that guides or judges itself by the size of the gross national product or by the luxuriousness of our high standard of living.

The gross national product is a misleading criterion for several reasons. For one, it reckons as an economic gain what is often only an economic loss: it counts into its total what has been spent on repair work, whether of machines or men: the money wasted on built-in obsolescence and self-harm. For another, it suggests that we necessarily progress to the extent to which we increase the number of our products each year, regardless of their inflated costs and their ecological side effects. Nor, finally, does it suggest that we balance against it the gross national boredom and frustration, and their deadly consequences.

The high standard of living, as this is commonly understood, is an equally misleading criterion of social progress. For this is taken as implying that, because of our great gross national product, we have attained a high standard not simply of physical comfort and luxurious thrills but also of exceptionally high culture. It leads to the delusion that progress will consist of "more of the same," since we already enjoy, not only the best luxuries (the best shows, the best automobiles, the best television sets, the best phonographs) but also the best staples (the best food, clothing, shelter) and that we really have no cancerous destitution, only a few "pockets of poverty," which are, of course, "the inevitable price of progress."

Nor does either of the two criteria suggest in any way that, to meet their requirements, we have to exploit, though we are only a small part of the world population, an enormous part of its resources.

If, then, our present policy is preventing true progress in both developed and underdeveloped countries, what must we do to remedy this condition?

One of the main answers, if it is not the main answer, given to this question by our social analysts* is that we simply must learn how to exercise austerity.

But how? How are we going to get the members of our society, trained as they are in a profligate consumerism, to turn away from their luxuries and tighten their belts? No one cherishes austerity for its own sake, and few are likely to practice it simply as a safeguard against a remote disaster. The vague visualization of a future evil can hardly outweigh, for most people, a real and present good.

AN ENLIGHTENED EPICUREANISM

One alternative that suggests itself at this point is that of a sound epicureanism, in the carefully thought out, self-regulating form proposed by Epicurus himself.

According to him, a person should aim at experiencing the most intense and rewarding pleasures in life. Doing so rationally would inevitably lead him to prefer the higher pleasures of the mind to those of the body. Moreover, to enjoy either kind as thoroughly as possible, he would need to exercise a certain temperance: it is the appetite kept sharp by slight hunger, rather than that which is satiated by gluttony, which enables one to enjoy the

*See, for instance, *The Cruel Choice,* by Denis Goulet, Atheneum, New York, 1971, p. 256.

dishes of life to the full. And this temperance demands of the mental and physical gourmet the practice of austerity.

There is something to be said for this theory. Several years ago, two experts who had specialized in the psychology of tasting were hired by a big liquor company to test "batches" of their whiskey in order to assure its uniformity of taste—as tea tasters do for tea companies. These men found that it took them some six months of abstinence to restore their taste buds to the necessary state of "innocence"—to the clean, fresh sharpness of response they once had (a sharpness of which all our senses are ordinarily robbed, these days, by our conceptualizing education and our consumerism). Once their taste was regained, however, so that they could learn how to concentrate on the qualities of each sip, they found that it could afford the effect of a work of art. It was no longer a mere stimulant to be slurped down hurriedly for its "kick"; it was more nearly a brief symphony of tastes, the very sequence of which was interesting. And they further discovered, what is in point here, that whereas before they had often drunk two or three cocktails at a party, they now did not always finish one: the carefully limited and spaced sips, fully savored, were so rich as to induce what to other drinkers would have seemed like austerity.

Much the same is true of every other similar method of consumption, of even the most ordinary things.

But greater and far more important than the austerity induced by discriminating consumption is that induced by the pleasures of enthusiastic creativity. These are, as we noted earlier, basically five kinds: the pleasure of mastering a technique; that of exercising it; that of appreciating the beauty of one's product or performance; the pleasure of appreciating the beauty of the technique and products of others; the enjoyment of the satisfactions that one has afforded others.

The number and variety of these can hardly be counted, of course; as creatures who must necessarily exercise in everything we do, we can enjoy the mastering, practicing and appreciating of a great range of techniques. And many actions afford us the delight of serving and being served as well.

The enjoyment of these pleasures can foster austerity in several ways. For one thing they can give us something to do besides occupying ourselves with consuming. For another, they do not ordinarily require that we use things up.

Again, they promote the austerity of asceticism (the term is derived from the Greek word meaning "exercise") inasmuch as all techniques require that we "keep in training" through abstemiousness and practice.

Finally, creativity discourages wasteful consumerism through ridding us of the need for consuming as a form of compensation for the meaninglessness of our lives. When we are leading a life of continuously skillful achievements, we do not need to make up consumptively for the dullness of a routine, noncreative, nonaltruistic "going through the motions."

Are we to say, then, that an enlightened epicureanism (of creativity, as well as of consumption) is all that we need here since it automatically fosters the required austerity? Is it, by itself, enough? Hardly. For we shall always need to exercise an onerous self-control in determining which activities we should concentrate on; what amount of time, money and effort we ought to give to each; what clients we must, in all fairness, serve first, at what cost —and so on. And, in so doing, we shall never find it easy to resist our sloth, gluttony, vanity, and the rest.

Moreover, we must learn to take into account what might be called the paradox of pleasure: if we concentrate on the pleasure which a thing or action gives us—if we focus on this primarily— we shall thereby defeat ourselves. Pleasure and happiness are states that we must *find* that we are experiencing, or have been experiencing; they are feelings of which we are more co-conscious than directly conscious. Just as the man who does not lose himself in watching a game does not get the full enjoyment of it, so neither does the man who does not lose himself in his work, study, conduct or play. To experience pleasure, we must simply become engrossed in doing what we are doing; for then the pleasure will take care of itself.

What we need to realize is that in trying to assure austerity we shall be most successful if we do not try to do it puritanically.

While guiding ourselves primarily by a love of justice and by a warm-hearted charity, we can also enjoy the benefits of a positive austerity: the pleasures that we naturally and rightly come by in leading *artistically* ascetic lives.

CHAPTER 6

TOWARD A HUMANE POLITICS

In a brilliant article entitled "Sources of Public Unhappiness,"* Richard Goodwin has pointed out that a large part of this unhappiness is the result of the narrowness of our past aims, both political and economic. These have been primarily negative. As a consequence, they have fostered institutions that now seem, ironically enough, positively restrictive. Our government has been rigidly organized to assure that no citizen should transgress the minimal rights—those in the Bill of Rights—of any other. Our business structure has been rigidly organized to assure that no individual will be able to prevent another from achieving a physically comfortable "high" standard of living. Because both sets of institutions are run by men who cannot see higher, more humane goals, and because they want to control their organizations despotically, they leave large segments of us hungry for what they fail to assure, and frustrated by our powerlessness to control them. Although they see that the government should promote law and order and that, in justice, it should try to assure certain minimal living conditions, economic opportunities, health care, etc., for everyone, they fail to see that its general, ultimately determinative, aim should be far higher: to foster fully humane, rather than

---

*The New Yorker, Jan. 4, 1969.

merely decent, living. Its efforts to raise up should not become sources of leveling down.* On the contrary, it should foster, in every possible way, both creative work and communal living.

As Goodwin emphasizes, what is now required above all is a group of dynamic leaders moved by a vision of society far less philistine, far greater in the true sense, than the Great Society:

If the forces of feeding discontent are as profound and powerful as I have suggested, then political thinking and ultimately national policy must move toward an entirely new dimension. The last time the American establishment thought seriously about national goals was during the late Eisenhower and early Kennedy years. The formulations from the period of the more enlightened and liberal politicians are already out of date. A strong domestic defense establishment, economic growth, NATO, and so on, though they are still with us, barely touch the principal sources of our dissatisfaction. Other goals of that very recent time —such as the frantic desire to measure every national program, from education to overseas propaganda, in terms of competition with the Russians—are now irrelevant, and some are forgotten. Yet almost all our political leaders seem rooted in the old rhetoric, even if it is clothed in new facts and circumstances, and thus have lost their hold on the popular sensibilities.

The material out of which relevant national objectives can be shaped is at hand in the work of some social critics and a few economists, and even in the insights of a few of the more sensitive politicians. In the process, we must focus not only on solving "problems" as defined in the usual sense—education, pollution, and the rest—but also on the *ways* in which we solve them. This is a familiar idea within a democratic tradition that has, for example, valued many individual liberties above the alluring, if often illusory, efficiency of coercive techniques.

We have always placed certain abstract values—those which cannot be measured or weighed—above economic, logical or physically tangible goals. Confronted with the overwhelming and uncertain complexities of modern life, and informed by a greatly increased awareness of our limited ability to predict or control the forces loosed by our obsessive industry and invention, we must add to the list of such values. They have traditionally included not only the right mentioned in the Bill of Rights and allied civil liberties but equality of opportunity, the freedom to develop individual talent, and, more recently, freedom from starvation and destitution. And all these, imperfectly realized though they may be, still exert a powerful hold on our national thinking and shape our political rhetoric and policy . . . .

*—as too often happens in our schools. See *Coming of Age in America*, by Edgar Z. Friedenburg, Vintage, New York, 1965.

If they are to make out their higher goals as clearly as they should, our leaders need to rid themselves of a certain disastrous tendency to slip into a fallacy of false alternatives: that of assuming the problem always to be that of meeting the claims of individualism on the one hand and of collectivism on the other. How can the rights of the individual be safeguarded against the aggression of society, and how can the rights of society be safeguarded against the depredations of the individual?

To arrive at an answer to this question that is deep enough to be really useful politically, one must be careful not to fall into two semantic pitfalls.

The first is that of identifying the individual with the person—treating individuality as if it were the same as personhood. For by individuality is properly meant only that set of qualities—temperament, attitude, talent, physique—which differentiates him from all other persons. These, however, are not inevitably all good: some of them can be silly eccentricities, the kind of idiosyncrasies that made an ancient Greek call a too-private person an *"idiotes."* They are to be regarded as sacred or inviolable primarily because they determine the idiom in which a given person can best—that is, most freely, generously and creatively—express his personality. The absolute right to his individual style must be assured to a person since it is the only one in which he can most effectively act in accordance with his ethical and artistic consciences.

The other pitfall that must be avoided here is that of confusing a collectivity with a community. A collectivity may be merely a group who find it profitable to live together for the greatest convenience of its members simply as individuals, all agreeing to help one another only insofar as doing so suits the wishes of each and does not harm the others. A community, however, is one which is unified by the desire to cooperate in satisfying one another's needs as persons—ideally, to satisfy *all* the human needs of everyone *as well as possible.* It is a society, not of selfish coexistence, but of mutual helpfulness.

In the light of these distinctions, it seems clear that the society which best reconciles the claims of individualism and collectivism is that which first translates them into those of personhood and community, and then meets them on that level. For, in this kind, every member would be able, not only to develop and use his powers to the full as an individual, but also to do so in meeting skillfully the challenges of serving others and in appreciating their skillful service of him.

Our political leaders might well set their sights, therefore, not so much on the maintenance of a society made up of rugged individuals competing in a struggle to make profits by answering lusts so as to become independent of others, as on encouraging the establishment of one made up of well-rounded persons, each exercising his talents creatively in answering the needs of others in a spirit of interdependence.

Moreover, were our leaders to adopt this latter aim and profess it publicly, they might make a giant stride in winning over to us the underdeveloped or satellite nations of the world, as offering them something which they would really welcome. As it is now, these nations face a choice that they find naturally distasteful. They see the communists as offering them a kind of share-the-wealth program at the cost of dictatorial tyranny. They see us, on the other hand, as offering universal political freedom at the cost of ill-shared wealth. And what they would like to be offered is a system in which everyone would be given the opportunity to attain self-realization as a person and humanely communal living.

Such a system would have an extremely strong appeal for them since they still cherish craftsmanship and the communal life of the family, the tribe or the small settlement. If they were afforded the kind of technology* that is suited to the preservation of their traditional values, they would find the transition to a higher culture a relatively easy and quite congenial one. And we should not have to spend more and more billions on protecting them against communists either within or without their borders. We might win the cold war through having, to use the language of the marketplace, something obviously superior to sell.

Again, were we to reform our technology in accordance with

---

*See Appendix A.

the full requirements and higher aims of technique, we might further reduce the power of the military-industrial complex through
stripping it of some of its glamor and prestige. Anyone who has
come to understand the nature and effects of technology for quality cannot help recognizing its difference from, and superiority to,
technology for quantity. He cannot help seeing that the remarkable efficiency of the mass production of military products is
largely a result of simplicity of aim: the turning out of uniform
weapons for uniform projectiles to gain a uniform simple general
effect—incapacitation. He cannot help wondering, therefore,
whether the mass production and systems analysis methods which
assure military efficiency can be sensibly carried over into the
world of quality production and humane living. He is likely to see
that the military-industrial complex is to be considered a model
for only one thing: a military-industrial complex.

If they are to make the kind of advance which Goodwin has indicated the people wish them to make, then, our political leaders
may well concentrate on fostering a technology that serves the interests, not of the individual and the collectivity, but of the person
and the community.

The relationship between government and client

Since the implications of artistic method in the field of politics
are too many and too varied for all of them to be considered here,
the following set are offered as typical.

First of all, an appreciation of the way in which a maker views
his material should help us very much to clarify our somewhat
hazy notion of authority. For most of us are far too prone to
think of authority as some kind of restrictive force—one that,
being exercised by a superior, must be obeyed. Yet nothing could

be more erroneous than this view of it, as the very derivation of the Latin word, *auctoritas,* clearly shows. This term is from *augeo,* meaning "I increase." It therefore signifies the condition of one who is able to increase the effectiveness of that over which he has charge, whether this a thing or a person. A maker is a true authority in his field when he is able to use his material in such a way as to release its potentialities so well that others call his work "creative" because he seems, literally, to have brought something out of nothing. Technically, as we saw earlier, having authority over a given material means knowing how to deal with it tactfully and persuasively: it means, that is, knowing how to respect it as a subperson, so as to obey it enough not to force it, while at the same time inducing it to realize the potentialities that are needed. A master never cuts across the grain unless he has to do so.

When the "material" is a man, the proper political authority over him is someone who can help him to act freely in the way in which he is meant to act; that is, in answering as well as possible both his own needs and those of others. Strictly, then, the nature of authority is not negative or disciplinarian in the usual sense of the word. The only reason why any one person has a right to be an authority is that he is capable of helping others to be more fully and usefully themselves, more creative persons than they could be otherwise. Like the term *authority, discipline* also can be understood etymologically: by derivation, it means "a condition of learning." A person who is an authority in human affairs, therefore, is always, in a sense, a *doctor,* "a teacher," since he suggests the discipline and the learning that enable his client to act ever more normally and effectively. As an authority, an artist tries to guide and redispose; and the higher up the scale of material he ascends, the subtler and gentler his method and pressure; until, finally, when his material is a creature of intellect and free will, he relies entirely on suggestion and persuasion.

It is in this sense that we may say that the political authority of a nation lies in the hands of its political artists, its governors. When, on the other hand, we say that in a democracy the final authority is vested in the nation (the political clients) we are referring to ability of the citizens to increase the effectiveness of the government either by laying down new policies for it (as by referenda) or by electing or dismissing those who exercise power. And, as was suggested in an earlier chapter (on the relations of artist and client), efficiency requires that there be a careful regard by one kind of authority for the rights of the other, as well as for its own obligations.

Thus, a person should be elected to a position of authority only if, as a master artist, he knows the work of this position thoroughly. For, in accordance with another principle touched on earlier, he should not be allowed to command or direct anyone beneath him to do what he has never done, if only in practice, himself. A doctor does not tell a nurse how to do what he has never done himself; nor does a West Pointer tell a private. So, too, it should not be possible for a man to be made governor of a state (especially one as large as, let us say, California) who will then be called on to direct others in techniques of government with which he has little or no acquaintance. It is only the man who has served a true apprenticeship who has a right to the status of master.

On the other hand, however, once a man has been trained in the science of politics (not that of mere vote-getting) he has every right to trust that his authority will be respected, and that his technique will be evaluated, not by what demagogues and superficial commentators say of it, but by whether it produces the results it is supposed to produce and that are possible under the circumstances. An analogy from medicine is a propos here also. An established physician has every right to expect that a patient will do what has been prescribed—not modifying this by what he reads in health columns or sees touted on television commercials. Naturally, a patient may change physicians; but he has no right to tell any one of them what to prescribe. So, too, for the voter and his representatives: let him change them when he thinks they have proved inadequate; but, once he has put them in office, let him permit them to exercise their authority without interference: no government should rightly be a mail-order government. As Emile Faguet pointed out in a classic work on democratism, *The Cult of Incompetence,* for voters to fail to put a man into office because they suspect him of knowing more than they do, and therefore of being clever and untrustworthy—someone whom they could not readily control—means for them to pay for their security by settling for incompetence. What then happens is that the wily demagogue—the Image—gets himself elected through promising to obey his constituency and goes on, while appearing to do so, to serve the most powerful interests, setting up meanwhile a bureaucracy of "brains" (largely professorial minds) to do his real work for him, even to the writing of his speeches. He keeps his fences mended; he keeps most of his sheep contented; but he could hardly care less for the country as a whole.

If the appreciation of artistic method helps us to think politically by keeping us aware of the normal relationships of artist and client, it also helps us to focus on the main object of political activity by keeping us aware of the requirements of protection. More precisely, it helps us see that government is not primarily for the assuring of prosperity, but for the maintaining of peace and justice. The prosperity of a nation depends essentially on its economic condition: it is the responsibility of its masters of production, exchange and distribution. Granted that the government can eliminate conditions which prevent men of goodwill from carrying on their commerce profitably, still, it is not the main function of the government to guarantee wealth and prosperity. Its primary function is to make sure that no one controls anyone else unduly—that is, so as to prevent him from achieving the serenity and freedom he needs for leading a good life. In other words, the primary concern of government is to see that all citizens and institutions get along together in a spirit of fairness—with as little interference from the selfish and arrogant as possible. It is there "to enable good men to live among bad," not rich among poor—or even poor among rich. It is therefore *basically protective:* from external aggression; from internal disorder; from the private exploitation of resources that belong to the nation as a whole.

Secondarily, it is auxiliary to all individuals and institutions through the carrying out of functions that cannot be performed safely or efficiently otherwise: education, coinage, postal communication, roads, water supply, and the like.

All this implies, of course, that the government is meant to assure liberty—though not in the sense referred to by Plato when he said that to many democracy meant the liberty to waste one's life in going from one idle pleasure to another. This is not freedom but license. For true freedom is not freedom *from* so much as freedom *for;* that is, ideally, the freedom of each individual to lead a life in which he attains ever fuller personhood through enabling others also to do so.

The artistic dictum that needs should normally be met as individually as possible is also to the point here. It implies that the government will not only favor those who serve their clients in this way, but will also try to serve them, its own clients (as citizens) with an equal solicitude for their local and personal modes of living. This requirement suggests that governmental institutions at every level should be kept small enough to be suited to customary conditions—that they be kept on a human scale. Nothing should be done by the central government that can better be known about, and therefore more tactfully handled, by a state government—unless, of course, this latter is being run by bigots or grafters. And, similarly, nothing should be run by the state that can better be known about, and therefore more tactfully handled, by local authorities—provided always that they, too, are real and trustworthy authorities. Certainly, great care should be exercised not to let various programs needing large and central funding (urban renewal, poverty, school subsidy, etc.) fall into the hands of those who regard their "material"—the human beings whom they serve—impersonally. Like every other art, the art of government should be as nearly person-to-person as possible.

To put all this a little differently, the artistic habit of thinking in terms of individual needs can be of far-reaching political importance. It can encourage both maker and client alike to believe that true democracy, as against totalitarian democracy, is based on respect for the *uniqueness* of every person: that it is normal for him to have his particular, not merely his average, needs met. Government should do all that it can to help various states, sections, races, temperaments and talents contribute all their flavors to the melting pot, not simply to increase its liquid content. As far as possible, men should not be allowed to get standardized by their own standardization.

Certainly, anyone familiar with artistic method is likely to feel an instinctive abhorrence of bureaucratism. He cannot help being leery of a system of desk-bound human computing machines who look upon those with whom they deal as specimens to be ticketed or pigeonholed; who, relying on formulas, come to regard persons that are in any way exceptional, even in excellence, as somehow freakish and untrustworthy. For, after all, as artistic method suggests, diagnostic forms and policy formulas, having been worked out for dealing with what is average, are likely to take little account of what is unique, of what makes one thing, person or situation differ from another.

As a result the routine use of such forms and formulas can prove both unjust and uncharitable, especially in social service. Being based on an average which does not exist, they almost inevitably allow some whose needs are above the average to be cheated and others whose needs are below it to be unduly favored. They can tacitly insult each applicant by suggesting that if he is different—or to the extent to which the forms indicate that he is different—he must have something the matter with him. Nothing could be the matter with the form, of course; for surely all men naturally fall into easily identifiable patterns. Finally, the very design and typography of a form is liable to make applicant and examiner both feel that the whole affair is necessarily a coldly probing one, ending in a shame-faced acceptance of a suspiciously doled out sop. Yet both giver and receiver should be feeling the thoughtfulness, the humanness and the true *considerateness* of the action.

Finally, as being an essentially protective agency, the government might well set up, in addition to devices for the checks and balances which protect one department against another, two special offices for safeguarding its citizens: that of the ombudsman and that of the Chief Citizen of the Nation.

The ombudsman, who already functions in more than one nation, is an officer whose task it is to represent a citizen and secure his rights for him when he has run afoul of unjust or hobbling red-tape.* He is a kind of watchdog against bureaucratic tyranny, acting as a continuous reminder to all concerned that governmental relations should be as personal as any other artist-client relations—above all, when the client, the citizen, really needs help.

The other suggested office, that of the Chief Citizen, would serve a somewhat analogous purpose: it would keep the government continually aware of the artist-client relationship that exists between it and the nation. At the moment we are in the absurd condition of having our chief artist, the President, report to us on the state of our country every year as if he were also our chief, representative client. Moreover, although he only represents, strictly, the government, he attends all state affairs as representing America—as Mr. America himself. Not only does such ambiguity make it difficult to focus on his work clearly and evaluate him properly as an artist, but it also keeps us deeply in the dark about our own condition as clients.

What we might well do, then, it would seem, is establish the office of Chief Citizen of the Nation which would have solely these two functions: to represent the nation at all civic and international affairs that were purely symbolic; and to report, at least once a year, on the state of the nation, as this is described thoroughly and factually in the reports regularly issued by our various agencies; so that we could know just how many people were in dire or relative poverty—how rich the rich are, how poor the poor, and whether the rich are getting richer, the poor poorer; just how many of our citizens are on skid row; just what the slum conditions of our country are; how many crimes of various kinds we are committing; how much physical and mental sickness, how much dope addiction, how much alcoholism, there is; how many traffic deaths and injuries; how much is spent on warfare; how much on space travel; how much loss there is through floods, fires, droughts; how our air and water pollution stands; what is

---

*See, on this point, two books by Walter Gellhorn: *Ombudsman and Others: Citizens' Protectors in Nine Countries* and *When Americans Complain: Governmental Grievance Practices,* Harvard University Press, Cambridge, 1966.

the condition of our water table; etc. This report would be in no sense partisan: it would consist simply of the facts of our condition, many of which we blithely ignore when we speak of ourselves as the greatest nation on earth, with the highest standard of living. How otherwise than by a solemn ceremony that forces us to attend to such facts at least once or twice a year are we likely to see clearly where we are and where we are going, and to ask ourselves how our government is helping us take the right path?

The objection that it would be hard to find a suitable person for the office of Chief Citizen or a sound method of appointing him is not a very strong one. For this could be done in one of several ways, of which the following, perhaps, might be the best.

Let a new member be added to the Supreme Court. Then have the Justices choose one from among their members to act as Chief Citizen for, let us say, three years, choosing another at the expiration of his term. In this way, the Court would continue with the same number of members as at present.

As a result of this method of appointment, the Chief Citizen would hardly be suspect as partisan, nor, in fact, could he be, since he would be limited to purely factual documentary reports. And his high prestige and long practice in the writing of reports would make him technically acceptable. As a symbolic personage, he could readily serve to remind us that the nation is not simply the party in power, nor, for that matter, the whole government, but the whole range of Americans, of whom he is a worthy representative.

Through the office of Chief Citizen we should be continually reminded of the fact that the government is the artist, the nation is the client and their relations are essentially the same as those of any other artist and client.

Artistic method can unite all men

Not the least important reason why we must restore art to its due equality with science is that, for the present at least, it is the most unifying of all the forces of civilization, countering, as it does, the divisiveness of commercial interests, scientific disciplines and religious creeds. If we are to foster a humanistic unity that will permit of both diversity of mores and beliefs, we can hardly do better than cooperate as fellow artists in the shaping of our own and of the world's culture. Not only will the artistic attitude and the artistic method aid us then to work and live humanely ourselves, but it will also foster a unity among men that no other attitude or method can, at the moment even begin to foster.

Certainly, commercialism would hardly seem to be much of a force for uniting men firmly. One of its professed basic principles is that of competition: with a straight face, it proposes as a source of unity the common agreement that we all try to get money out of one another so as to support ourselves in otiose luxury. The perfecting of society and its institutions, it would seem, is an incidental by-product of this concerted selfishness. Moreover, the really right making or performing of anything must be a secondary consideration, the primary one being profitableness. Humane excellence in such matters as walking, talking, handwriting, etc. is to be deemed inconsequential, an "external" value. Naturally, we cannot help *trying* to do many of these things "reasonably" well, if only through fear of being thought swinish. But why should we worry about an excellence in which there is no "percentage"? How could such an aim really unify us? We already have a strong common bond of unity in our natural ambitiousness, and we are united in fostering the freedom to satisfy this. Granted that we shall never achieve anything better than a good, comfortable, philistine way of life; still we shall all be alike in our contentment with this condition. Joubert was wrong when he said that men ascend to meet.

If commercialism does little to unite mankind humanely, neither does pure science. It is not a spirit and a method truly accessible to all and it soon begets an aristocracy inside itself. For while science does much to unite scientists, it does not, nor will it ever, do much to unite the rest of us. This is true partly because few of us—even of those who have been to college—have the talent or the training to master and use scientific method fruitfully, and partly because, except for their common ethos, scientific disciplines tend to wall off even fellow scientists from one another. Specialists in diverse fields have little nomenclature or philosophy in common to make for easy and congenial shoptalk. The writer knows: he has been to many a luncheon with fellow faculty members.

Nor, alas, can we look to religion alone for a universal bond of unity, as, God knows, we should be able to. For one thing, too many people are simply areligious. For another, creedal differences, despite the ecumenical movement, cannot but separate men for a long time to come. This is especially true when churches fall into the hands, as too often they seem to have done, of those who would use them to sanction divisive forces of various ethno-socio-economic caste systems. If Berger, in the study cited earlier, is right, the churches do not so much disparage this sort of segregationism as confirm it. The bourgeois have not been taken over and transformed by the churches; the churches have been taken over and transformed by the bourgeois. Too often a sect or congregation attracts its adherents, not by the special way in which it is striving to participate in the revolution which Christ came to promote, but by its willingness to cooperate with those against whom it should be revolting. Many a church building has therefore turned into a citadel for its own ghetto, with its members huddling together in complacent exclusiveness—unified on essentially nonreligious, because nonaltruistic, terms.

All this is not to say, of course, that science and religion cannot or should not unify men; it is merely to say that, because of commercialism, specialism and doctrinal differences, they are not likely to do so very well for some time to come. The artistic attitude and the artistic method, on the other hand, can be a very powerful force for the unifying of men—certainly, powerful enough for us not to take the chance of undervaluing them or, worse still, of overlooking them. For all men, no matter how selfregarding or specialistic they may become, are united in *their natural appreciation of virtuosity.* What athletes are not drawn together as they participate in, or what sports fans as they watch, the breathtaking performance of a champion? Or which of us is not at heart a sidewalk superintendent? Surely, if we all learn, as we all can, to cherish the artistic spirit as we have learned to cherish the scientific, we shall become one in our love of perfection, in our desire to serve clients responsibly and generously, in our delight in skillful achievement and in our satisfaction in the conquest of some general need. Shall we not also, as was suggested earlier, be unified through our common delight in the actions of daily living as we appreciate them as artistic achievements? May not the artistic attitude and the artistic method prove at least as effective in bringing us all together as does any other attitude and method?

It may likewise be suggested here that what is true for the unifying of now separated nations could also be true for the unifying of now separated individuals: it could also apply to the generation gap, the family gap, and the woman's liberation gap. The husband and wife, the man and the woman, the parent and the child—they could all be aided to achieve a soundly objective, sympathetic love for one another through the mutual appreciation of one another's craftsmanship, even when there is only an analogical awareness of this. For all good craftsmen respect and admire all other good craftsmen.

CHAPTER 7

THE AESTHETIC EXPERIENCE

If there is any technique in which, for all kinds of reasons, we need to perfect ourselves today, it is that of focusing on the realities about us—especially the seemingly commonplace realities—so as to gain from them all the delights they are meant to afford us. There is no reason why we must continue to turn aside from the beautiful that lies everywhere about us because we have learned to look only for the true and the good.

But if we are to learn how to set ourselves for the enjoying of this aspect of reality, we must give special heed to what artistic method suggests about the nature of action and of form.

A due regard for action as the most expressive condition of a thing—as the condition in which it is most actual—will aid us greatly in appreciating works of art, as well as works of nature through preventing us from mistaking, so to speak, the skeletons of things for the things in the flesh. It may help realize, for instance, that the first, indispensable step that we have to take in appreciating a poem or an essay properly, as well as a speech or a play, is that of reading it aloud—of producing it, actualizing it. Croceans to the contrary notwithstanding, a printed play is strictly not a play at all—it is a scenario; just as the score of a sonata is not a sonata, but a score. No such work comes alive—is fully itself through functioning as it is meant to function—until it is given the embodiment of utterance, of presentation. To imagine, therefore, that we have had a course in Shakespeare's plays when we have studied only their scenarios, or that we have acquired a fair appreciation of the works of Tintoretto or Van Gogh when we have seen only black-and-white slides of them thrown on a large screen, is about as absurd as to imagine that we have gained a good appreciation of Bach through having analyzed their scores and plucked out their most significant passages on a zither. Unless every element of a work of art has been duly actualized, that work has not come into full or normal being: on the stage the ghost of Hamlet's father is what Shakespeare meant him to be, a startlingly real ghost; on the page, he is a mere ghost of a ghost.

So, too, in the evaluating of other works of skill, from utensils on up, we should keep in mind that we do not know them thoroughly enough to appreciate them rightly until we know them in action. Judging any product on its appearance only is much like judging a pair of shoes without trying them on.

A man buying glass steins, for instance, if he is intelligent, does not think of these as simply "for beer"—or, even, "for holding beer." He studies them estimatively, to see how well cast they are for playing their expected role: of *standing* stably while *holding* and *displaying* beer appetizingly; of being *gripped* firmly and *lifted* steadily; of *exerting the heft* required *to set the mind* for the positive enjoyment of a heavy beverage that is bitter-sour and yet foamy; of *pouring* out this liquid, when properly *tilted,* in suitable volume and weight; of being *set down* forcefully; of being thoroughly washed and dried without too much effort. Unless a stein plays its part satisfactorily, it is not to be considered either a true stein or a beautiful one—no matter how many raptures it may evoke for its proportions, line or luster from nondrinking connoisseurs of glassware.

Moreover, it is only when we appreciate the beauty of action that we can appreciate the full beauty of the social or participative arts: a square dance, for instance, is best known and appreciated by those who execute it; an alma mater song, by those who sing it together. The first is not meant for spectators, nor the second for auditors: the one should not be judged as a ballet nor the other as a chorale.

It is often true, in fact, that even when things are made or actions performed primarily for spectators or auditors, they are likely to be appreciated best by the makers or the performers, who know them from within, intimately and purposively. The delight in the splendid rightness of a neat forward pass that is felt by the real quarterback is far deeper than that felt by a grandstand quarterback. The more nearly the latter can, through imaginative empathy, identify himself with the former, the greater his enjoyment.

If we fail to realize that to appreciate the full beauty of things we must appreciate them as functional, we are likely to fall into at least two serious aesthetic errors. One is to suppose that the essential beauty of a thing is purely external. The other is to assume that you cannot have a truly beautiful thing unless you have one the parts of which are individually pleasing.

The first of these errors leads many of us into misprizing as ugly whole realms of nature, like that, for instance, of the insects. All too frequently, those of us who are entranced by the beauty of a spider web are equally horrified by the "ugliness" of the spider. Understandably enough, too; for unless we see how beautifully the spider executes the actions for which he was designed (from spinning the web to anesthetizing the prey) as well as how marvelously he has been wrought for executing these actions, we may believe that because he is repulsive to the senses, he is ugly to the mind. We may fail, in fact, to see that this very repulsiveness of his to the senses is one of the beauties of his design, since it frightens us away, his otherwise most powerful enemies. What is true of spiders is no less true of other things, whether they be jellyfish or elephants: their external appearance is not to be confused with their essential beauty.

Moreover, a thing can still be very beautiful when no one part or quality of it can be isolated and enjoyed for itself alone. The blade of a scalpel may seem ugly in its shortness and keenness; its handle may seem unsightly in length and pattern; but these distinct appearances should not distract from its overall beauty as an instrument suited to a marvelous act of skill: they should not blind us, in other words, to its wonderful maneuverability and precision, its splendid rightness as a cutting instrument, its true beauty. Again, the separate pieces of glass of a stained-glass window may well leave us cold, while the window as a whole, in full act, ablaze with sunlight, may warm us through with its meaningful splendor.

Certainly, if we wish to appreciate drama, whether on stage or off, we need especially to keep in mind the beauty of functional action. Otherwise, we may fail to see that a play or a happening can produce, through its thematically plotted unity, an integratively or a compositely beautiful effect even when its separate elements or stages, considered in isolation, seem to be nothing much, or even positively ugly. So it is that more than one Italian motion picture (like Fellini's "La Strada" or "Nights of Cabiria") comparatively crude as they are in wardrobe and setting, have proved far more beautiful than most of Culver City's "super-specials," the elements of which have been heedfully glamorous. The crudities of the one (like the crudities of the stained-glass window) coalesce into a compound of harshly real splendor; the refinements of the other form, not a compound, but a mixture: a soft blend of mutually self-defeating prettinesses.

Further than this, a proper regard for action should aid us to see that appreciation itself is an action: as sound courses in the appreciation of art, music and literature (to say nothing of gastronomy) all imply. If we are to respond to something as appreciatively as possible, we must learn to focus on it, grasp it and meditate on it actively—so much as a matter of second nature that we are not even aware of doing so. In the strictest sense, there is no such thing as passive enjoyment that is the fullest kind of enjoyment—even of a comedy skit or a glass of wine.

As assuring the general morale of a culture an appreciation of the excellence of actions can hardly be overvalued. Such a sensitivity should aid us to enjoy life far more continuously than we ordinarily do, or even imagine we could do. It should help us gain much the same delight from a performance outside of sports as inside them; so that, just as we rejoice in or admire the beautiful putt, the beautiful serve or volley, the beautiful double play or forward pass, we may do the same for all the ordinary tasks of daily life.

Too often we cheat ourselves of this kind of enjoyment because we do not visualize clearly the normal patterns of these ordinary tasks and have therefore no standards for appreciating them. The beauty of skillful dishwashing, for instance, is not that it comes to an end quickly or that it results in clean, shiny, well-stacked dishes. This sight is, to be sure, one of the main rewards for the dishwasher. But it is altogether too bad if this is thought of as the only reward: the beauty of the *action* here is like that of any other action of skill: it has a certain splendor of its own (a certain good form) regardless of ultimate results. Unfortunately, we Americans will spend thousands of dollars and hours watching someone else perform skillfully, enjoying the splendor of the rightness with which they execute plays of one kind or another, yet overlook the similar delight to be found in the "plays" of daily work. To the experienced cowboy the events of a rodeo are as enjoyable on the ranch as on the fairgrounds. But most workmen, alas, are hardly in the same situation.

In fact, as was pointed out earlier, it would be hard to think of a greater philanthropy than that of establishing rodeo-like contests for all the so-called menial tasks of daily life (with mere speed, incidentally, a secondary consideration); the artistic interest that might thereby be fostered might ultimately have the effect of transforming chores into something like games. We might rid ourselves of the delusion that life consists of rounds of drudgery punctuated by sugarplums of skill-watching—even leaving a note for the milkman might offer the challenge and the reward of calligraphy. Perhaps we could even become the performers and the fans of life itself.

THE BEAUTY OF FORM

Akin to the failure to recognize the beauty of action in its fullest sense is the failure to recognize the beauty of form in its. The great error into which most people wander in dealing with the factor of form is that of considering it to be both static and visual. It becomes for them the equivalent of mere shape, as is shown by their tendency, in discussing it, to use sculpture as the main source for illustrating their theories. It has even been said by an

eminent philosopher that there could never be an art of fragrances; this, not because—as he could rightly have maintained,
the olfactory nerves tire too quickly—but because, as he says,
fragrances are "formless." What a parfumeur would say to this
can readily be imagined: how, if perfumes are formless, can one
distinguish hundreds of different forms of them?

The important thing, then, is to see that "form" does not mean
"figure," and it certainly does not mean "geometrically set figure." The form of a rooster in an egg means the red in his comb
as much as it means the sharpness of his spurs—even when these
are still locked in the tiny speck of life there. In short, as was
pointed out earlier, form means *all* the qualities that characterize
a thing as they emerge stage by stage.

The failure, in aesthetics, to recognize this full meaning of form
has often proved disastrous. There are still college art courses in
which students are taught the appreciation of Greek sculpture
without being shown that, or how, it was colored. There are still
college administrators who think that a plaster of paris statue on
the campus or in the chapel serves some reasonable purpose, ignoring the fact that its significance is destroyed by part of its very
form: its ghastly white color. There are still gardens, public
squares, lawns, full of such ghosts of sculpture. There are still
courses in art appreciation given in black and white slides. There
are still hosts of bearded young men filling canvases with what
they call abstract forms—to which they surreptitiously lend
meaning and glamor by giving them poetic, often melodramatic,
but seldom abstract titles: stealing from literature to enrich painting. There are still teachers of poetics who, anti-Platonic as they
profess to be, are under the influence of a certain kind of aesthetic
Manicheanism or Puritanism; so that they speak of the beauty of
a lyric as if this were simply the beauty of its quasi-mathematical
or quasi-musical "plot." There are still courses in drama in
which, as was pointed out earlier, the students get the impression
that they are studying Shakespeare or Sophocles when they are
reading, silently, the scenarios of their plays and visualizing the
story line of their plots. And how often do our theorists in aesthetics illustrate their points, not with examples drawn from the

dance or the drama, but from those from sculpture and painting, in which latter arts the "form," as they would call it, is easily discernible: it is much easier to deal with the shape of a Greek urn than it is to deal with the form of a Greek play.

A truly good appearance

Thus far we have been considering the intrinsic requirements of things well-made or well-performed. But since these are to be appreciated as elements in human conduct—as in accord with human tendencies or dispositions—we have now to notice the seemingly extrinsic requirements of humanly acceptable appearances, and what these imply.

Through our earlier considerations we have incidentally been prepared for a theory of aesthetics which is basically philosophic. In traditional philosophy it is said that insofar as a thing has fullness of being, it also has fullness of beauty; and now we can begin to make out how true this formula is. For it does seem that the higher a thing is in the scale of being, the more it fulfills the requirements that have been laid down for a thing of beauty; that is, the greater is its unity, its variety, its vividness and its appropriateness. A rock, for example, is unified in a relatively simple physical and chemical way; it manifests a variety of qualities and principles; it has the vividness of tremendous locked up atomic forces, and is perdurable; it is appropriate to various kinds of action, from crushing to gleaming brilliantly or affording the substance for sculpture. A vegetable has a remarkable organic unity; a variety of living as well as nonliving principles or elements; the vividness of life; and the appropriateness to the performing of many actions far beyond the capabilities of the rock. The animal is superior to both rock and tree in all these qualities. And man rises far above the animal.

Moreover, the care for real, as against empty, appearance that we are concerned with here has certain ethical and cultural implications of great importance.

For the main, the sound motive for such care is not pride or the desire for admiration, or even for affection; it is not primarily to make ourselves attractive, but to aid ourselves and others to live humanely. If, as the old adage says, politeness is to do and say the kindest thing in the kindest way, then we are merely being polite when we make sure that what we produce or use accords with the highest norms of human behavior or decorum. True style, in other words, does not come from a desire to show off, to express ourselves or to gain praise and liking; it comes from a desire to communicate with and to serve others as pleasingly as possible: it is the quality of conduct (hence of the things that play a part in conduct) which makes everyone glad to be human.

It may be neglected, ordinarily, for one of two reasons. A designer may feel that if the parts of a thing are objectively in due proportion, that thing will be beautiful—overlooking the fact that, as St. Thomas points out, its parts must be in due proportion to the knowing mind. He may fail to realize, for instance, that an arch which is perfect mechanically might seem too balloon-like to those who behold it or walk under it—that it is fully itself and therefore fully beautiful only when it is so shaped as to forestall this impression, since, after all, its main function, psychologically, is to welcome or celebrate. To adjust proportions honestly to the requirements of the normal client is not, as we have noted, an act of hypocrisy; it is an act of courtesy. And to ignore this necessity, to consider it negligible, is to be less than primitive (primitive people make no such mistake); it is to be philistine, not to say barbaric. Yet how many Americans have ever thought of their streetcars, their factories, their hot-dog stands, even their schools and hospitals, as in this sense barbaric?

We need only consider, as was said earlier, what it would be like to live in a culture in which everyone moved as if to unheard music; where it was a pleasure merely to watch someone walking down the street; where everyone spoke clearly, resonantly, melodiously; sang easily and surely; wrote a beautiful hand; wore clothes both fitting and expressive—we need only daydream thus far to realize keenly how valuable a sound regard for appearances can be. The problem, then, is to learn how to treat them properly as reflecting the realities that underlie them and as satisfying our need for humanness in all our affairs.

A system of education that trains us in everything but this may, to be sure, produce a fair number of men of culture, but it will never produce a culture; and it is about time that our educators awoke to this fact, as great oriental educators have done long since.

The fine arts

There is another doctrine of artistic method that is worth calling special attention to as being rich in implications here: it is the doctrine that *all* works of art are properly called forth as normal answers to human needs. For this doctrine may keep us healthily aware of several facts which, in our philistine culture, we are much too prone to overlook; namely, that, as answering normal needs, the masters of the fine arts are also basically professional men, with their due place in society; that they satisfy needs with services which, lasting down the ages, cannot be paid for in a strictly commercial way (who could ever have paid Michelangelo adequately for his *Moses*?); that their works are meant to provide a kind of experience not provided for in any other way, the aesthetic experience, which is not to be confused with the hortatory or the purely pedagogical; that the realizations they afford us are communicated through profound visions of reality which can only be suggested: they are not to be confused with assents to conceptual truths that can be given strict formulation.

We may also be led to see that we need both the critic and the scholarly teacher to help us focus on works of fine art, since these were not always meant for us as their main appreciators, but for other peoples in other eras.

Maybe we shall come to see that an aesthetic experience is no mere escapist experience; that, normally, a poet, a painter, a composer, is not an isolated, delicate soul, moaning to himself esoterically; that the fine arts are not merely fringe benefits of a wealthy culture which cannot produce them, but can only buy them from "primitive" people or from social outcasts. Maybe we shall begin to ask ourselves such questions as: What is it that the fine arts can do that the sciences cannot do? What would happen if, one by one, the fine arts were eliminated from civilization: so that we should have no stories in books, on the stage, on motion picture or television screens; no music; no pictures; no statues; no dances? What hungers for what experiences would be left unsatisfied, what needs unmet? And how long could we stand this condition? Maybe, if our politicians and our college administrators could understand how essential the fine arts are to the answering of deep and normal human needs—maybe this could save us from becoming yahoos.

CHAPTER 8

SCIENTIFIC KNOWLEDGE ALONE IS FUTILE

The value of a familiarity with artistic method to many of us is that it may help rid us of a certain scientism that can cripple our thinking in several ways.

First of all, it should help rid us of the delusion that there is only one really worthwhile knowledge, the precisely scientific. Next, it may help us realize how futile purely scientific knowledge can be either for the devising of a new technique or for the understanding or the mastering of an old. And, finally, it may show us how, if science can be used to cast light on technology, technology can be used, perhaps equally well, to cast light on science.

All too often in trying to be scientific our educators give the impression that it is good to be only scientific—to cherish only such truths as are universal, testable and clear; they encourage the falsely Platonic view that what is changeable and sensory gives birth, not to well-founded belief, but only to opinion, which does not matter. It is as if they presumed that a graduate student who had been assigned to write a thesis on the psychology of the dog, even though he had no liking for dogs, would ultimately know dogs better than would a man who had grown up with dogs affectionately and still had two or three of them as pets for his children. In one sense, of course, the first man would know dogs better than the second; but he might have little understanding of what caused the gloom to permeate the other man's home when one of the pets was run over. He might understand very well what is meant by the biological death of a dog, without in the least understanding how Gabriel Marcel's philosophy of death might apply here. His poetic sense of the uniqueness of a given dog might well have been deadened by his methodical ignoring of this uniqueness: he might have little awareness, in other words, of the "replacement value" of a dog (or of any other creature) or, rather, of its value as irreplaceable. For him, "conatural familiarization" would be an interesting subject to analyze, but hardly a method to be practiced very often: spending time in loving contemplation of a thing for its own sake would seem like stealing time from the laboratory.

Certainly, many of us seem to have forgotten the very existence of what can be called, in the broadest sense, experiential knowledge.*

Too often we neglect this type of knowledge and go in for a kind of rarefaction of it "that is no substitute for direct intuition of the living individual. 'As if,' says Newman, unconsciously echoing St. Thomas, 'as if any number of abstractions would, by being fused together, be equivalent to one concrete. To know a person by his qualities is not to know him exactly as he is. *To know Socrates as the son of Sophroniscus'*—the example is not without humor—'*is not really to know Socrates.*' Notions are manageable, but real and complete substances are for the present felt to be fugitives to our thought. Scientific knowledge does not directly deal with singular things, for they are not definable. . . . Man is no longer what he really is, an individual presented to us by our sense, but . . . he is attenuated into an aspect,**

---

*For which St. Thomas (as Gilby points out in *Poetic Knowledge*) has no less than seventeen names: "(a) *per connaturalitatem;* (b) *per modum inclinationis;* (c) *cognitio affectiva;* (d) *notitia experimentalis;* (e) *per affinitatem;* (f) *per modum naturae;* (g) *per viam voluntatis;* (h) *per contactum;* (i) *per unionem;* (j) *per amorem;* (k) *ex intimo sui;* (l) *per deiformem contemplationem;* (m) *ad modum principiorum;* (n) *sine discursu;* (o) *ex instinctu;* (p) *cognitio absoluta et simplex;* (r) *quasi ex habitu.*"

**As when he is called "an intellectual" or "a liberal" (my note).

or relegated to his place in a classification. Thus his appellation is made to suggest, not the real being which he is in himself . . . but a definition. If I might use a harsh metaphor, I should say that he is made the logarithm of his true self, and in that shape is worked with the ease and satisfaction of logarithms.' "*

Reflecting on these facts may help keep us clear on why science may not always take the place of art. The need which the scientist satisfies primarily is that for unusual certitude about the general and specific laws of nature. The needs which the maker or artist satisfies is that for a particular product for an individual. There is nothing, therefore, in science itself which automatically produces technology; nothing in technology itself, as now understood, which automatically produces craftsmen; nothing in craftsmanship itself which automatically produces scientists or technologists—though craftsmen may and do take advantage of the discoveries of science and the instrumentation provided by technology. It is about time for us to cease thinking of science as having, of itself, given us technology, or of craftsmanship as only a rudimentary form of technology.

Science is one thing, then, and art is something else again; and neither has the right to boast of the products of the other. Certainly, anyone who has solved one concrete problem of making after another soon comes to realize that a knowledge of general principles does not of itself dictate which principle or set of principles it will be best to follow in any given situation. A knowledge of the principles of electricity did not of itself enable its possessors to hit upon all the inventions (more than two hundred) that were required for setting up the first lighting system for a city block; to do that took the art of an Edison, who neither then nor later was a noteworthy scientist.

The scientific attitude may often, in fact, prove prejudicial to the artistic. The scientist's habit, for instance, of searching for a single cause for a single effect may well prove, from the point of view of an inventor or maker, dangerously *simpliste;* it may cause him to think of invention as merely devising machinery to turn

---

Op. cit.

out, quickly and inexpensively, thousands of products exactly alike: pins, bullets, screws. And this way of thinking, while consonant with that of the technologist, perhaps, is hardly consonant with that of the craftsman or artist. As our educators fail to see, alas, they do not automatically turn out liberal artists by turning out liberal scientists—or even, for that matter, by turning out liberal technologists. On the contrary.

Again, whereas by the scientist perfection is associated with the readily predictable, and by the present-day technologist with the readily duplicable, by the artist it is associated (as its derivation would suggest) with the thoroughly satisfactory—that is, with the filling of particular users' needs as completely as possible. Consequently, the artist cannot help asking himself many questions which do not always plague others. Which kind of civilization do we want or, rather, ought we to want: one in which everyone has many things, especially luxuries, none of them quite satisfactory; or one in which everyone has the basic essentials and a few luxuries, all satisfactory? Which kind will give the greatest happiness, or even the greatest pleasure? Which kind is likely to foster a love of perfection and a delight in things right and appropriate? Which is likely to be a civilization of "substitutes"; which, of the "genuine article"? What happens to a culture that has lost the memory —hence the expectation—of using things that are custom-built?

If the scientific attitude is not always the most helpful for the devising of a new technique, neither is it for the understanding or mastering of an old one. Science is likely to rule out almost automatically a thorough consideration of purpose, and especially of particular purpose, although these are the main determinants of most techniques. Yet it is only when we have a due regard for them, the kind that is habitual with every sound maker or performer, that we can ordinarily find the key to what may otherwise seem to be a bafflingly mysterious technique, as the following examples, the one hypothetical, the other drawn from common experience, both make abundantly clear.

Let us suppose, then, for a crucial instance, that a great Martian sociologist were sent down to earth every Saturday for several years during the fall season to study, surreptitiously, the typical

American college football game, with the aim of discovering as much as he could about the customs of this planet and the character of its future leaders. Let us suppose, further, that he would not know our language or our particular system of Arabic numerals, but would be equipped with all kinds of photographic and computing devices of great precision. The amount of information that, as a good scientist, he could collect, classify, define, order, measure mathematically, formulate and interpret theoretically would, of course, be staggering. But how futile all his work would be until he came to know exactly what the purpose or object of the game was and what function it served in American life, above all in American collegiate life. He could be a Martian Einstein and occupy a chair of Human Athletics in their greatest university, yet know less about the real nature of college football than a freshman drum majorette.

Or, for a more useful example, consider the "problem" of punctuation. Here, incredible as this may seem, is an art that is entirely logical and sensible; yet it remains forever a mystery to most of us simply because, instead of being shown why we do what we do in practicing it, we are trained to follow a set of conventions unthinkingly, conventions derived from a pseudo-scientific analysis that ignores the factor of purpose.*

Proceeding on the assumption that science collects specimens, observes their habitats, their similarities and dissimilarities, and then formulates general laws based on frequency and uniformity of occurrence, the investigators sought out and classified typical instances of the appearance of the various marks, noted when they appeared before and after certain grammatical constructions and then formulated "laws" accordingly. As a result, they have handed on to us hundreds of descriptions of *how* punctuating is done, without affording us the enlightenment of a single *why*.

We are told, for instance, that "words in a series are customarily set off by commas." And we ordinarily learn to accept such a statement as if it were a true principle. Yet it would be hard to find anything sillier. For all words are in a series, it being

---

*For other examples of which, see Appendix B.

obviously impossible to utter two of them simultaneously. Nor can the formula be saved by being changed to "words of the same kind, with the same use are automatically set off by commas," for even then it still does not apply to many expressions, such as "the Glen Ridge Charity Drive Report," with its four nouns in succession, all used as adjectives. Nor does it give us any inkling why, on the other hand, we should normally use commas to set off words, in a similar expression: "He was tall, handsome, witty, dashing and brave." The word "customarily" in the formula is no help; after all, it fails to indicate the reason for the custom.

The student who is "well-drilled" in obeying this sort of rule without any view of purpose has not learned how to punctuate thoughtfully; he has merely learned how to respond to a variety of grammatical stimuli. He has acquired, not skill, but a set of conditioned reflexes—like Pavlov's dog.

On the other hand, had grammarians investigated punctuation primarily as an art; had they focused on it, first of all, as something designed to fulfill a certain set of purposes; had they then proceeded to observe how these same purposes were fulfilled in other arts; and had they considered, finally, that our punctuation took a special form in accordance with the particular dispositions of the users of English; they might then have been able to show a student how strictly this art is governed by a clear inner logic—by true principles which could be mastered consciously and followed creatively.

For consider how well the method of analysis by purpose would work here.

In accordance with it, we ask first: what is it that any mark of punctuation is designed for—what is it meant to do? Clearly, just as any letter was designed to signal that we should make a sound, any mark of punctuation was designed to signal that we remain silent for a moment.

Why, then, should we be given such a signal?

We can arrive, or at least begin to arrive, at an answer to this question by looking about and observing other media of expression, to see whether they too have punctuational devices and, if so, why. We soon discover that all the so-called "time-arts" certainly have such devices, sometimes a whole range of them: the motion pictures have the fade-out and fade-in, the iris-out and iris-in, the dissolve, the wipe; stage plays have their "curtains" at the ends of acts and sometimes in the middle of them; the symphony has its pauses at the ends of movements, as well as a wide range of musical rests.

The next question obviously is, why do all such arts afford us these various moments of intermission? The answer, as a little reflection shows, is that time-arts feed out their impressions piecemeal; and if we are to assimilate these as orderly sequences, as units, we must be granted an occasional interval in which to do four things: unify the impressions; grasp their significance; appreciate this; and prepare to correlate it with what follows.

If we turn now to a sampling of texts of all kinds, from the earliest handwritten on, to observe how these requirements have been met, we are startled to discover that often they were not met by the use of marks at all: the first form of punctuation as we know it was white space. Then, if we stop for a moment and ask ourselves what this use of white space enables us to do, we see, on a little reflection, that it enables us to do four things: stop and collect the letters of a given word as a unit; grasp the meaning of this unit; appreciate it; and get ready to correlate it with the meaning of the word that follows. We see how much white space helps us to perform these operations as we space out such a text as:

AFTERTHEYHADMARCHEDASTHEYDIDWITH
ASTONISHINGSPEEDFORALMOSTTENMORE
LEAGUESTHEARMYSUDDENLYCAMEUPONA
GREATLAKESEEMINGLYBOUNDLESSWHICH....

into the following:

AFTER THEY HAD MARCHED AS THEY DID
WITH ASTONISHING SPEED FOR ALMOST
TEN MORE LEAGUES THE ARMY SUDDENLY
CAME UPON A GREAT LAKE SEEMINGLY
BOUNDLESS WHICH . . .

Turning now, with this experience in mind, to modern publications, so as to observe whether we now use white space punctuationally, we may be somewhat surprised to discover how often we use it: very commonly, of course, in outlines, but also in solid texts, between sentences, paragraphs, sections and chapters, as well as between outer title and inner, and inner title and first page.

When we read over the text as we have spaced it thus far, however, we discover that our spacing does not help us to pause normally between phrasal units. And when we try to assure such pauses by the use of extra large spaces, we get:

AFTER THEY HAD MARCHED   AS THEY DID
WITH ASTONISHING SPEED   FOR ALMOST TEN
MORE LEAGUES   THE ARMY SUDDENLY CAME
UPON A GREAT LAKE   SEEMINGLY BOUNDLESS
WHICH . . .

A glance at this layout shows us, however, that such spacing would be costly, ugly and spotty. We now realize that it is as a substitute for these larger units of space that scribes devised the several different marks of punctuation: we see that these are, in their way, musical rests indicating silences of different length. They signify, in other words, the various kinds of "time-outs" needed by a reader for adjusting to the different degrees of difficulty he experiences in collecting, unifying, grasping, appreciating and correlating fairly large units of expression. The sentence, at the one extreme, requires a four-beat time-out, indicated by a period; at the other extreme, the small phrasal unit which is in some ways unexpected, either in ordering or in form, requires only a one-beat time-out, a comma; the clause which can be correlated with its successor to form a whole sentence requires a two-beat time-out, indicated by a semi-colon; and the large unit which can be so correlated only when kept in mind carefully all the way through the reading of its successor requires a three-beat time-out, indicated by a colon.

This, of course, is only an outline of a theory which has to be developed, as the author has done elsewhere, in detail. But sketchy as it is, it is still highly illuminating, for when we see why the marks have been devised, what their common and particular purposes are, we find the simple inner logic of punctuation emerging clearly and beautifully.

What is true of the art of punctuation is no less true of the arts of making ships and shoes and sealing wax. In pursuing, as well as in mastering, all of them, we must obey the habit of adverting continually to their determining aims. We must work out the inner logic of every technique as this is dictated by its ends; we must see it, that is, as the always deliberate, never the merely routine, way of attaining its clearly visualized system of purposes.

We may thereby be prevented from unduly cherishing immediate or secondary objectives and their fixed routines. True purposiveness prompts us to make our choices inventively, adoptively and adaptively—never merely slavishly. It helps, therefore, to rid us of conformism, thus indirectly affecting our whole lives, moral as well as technical. In short, it helps us acquire an alert artistic conscience, which never lets us rest content with solutions via formulas. We shall continue to be creatures of habit, of course, but of *meant* and *supple,* of deliberate and resourceful choice. And we shall be continuously rewarded with the joy of *fresh* achievement and of a growth in a technique—a growth that results from seeing goals ever more clearly and devising new methods accordingly.

The habit of thinking in terms of purpose should likewise help us to learn more, not only about the devising and the following of techniques, but also about subjects investigated primarily by science itself. It should help us to realize that, as was suggested at the beginning of this chapter, if the findings of science can cast light on technology, those of technology can often reciprocally cast light on science and even suggest new patterns of investigation. By seeing how a creature was made so as to perform and function in certain ways, we can begin to see it as *necessitated,* as having to possess its constituents and structure. And this kind of knowledge is no less scientific than that which we acquire by observing, classifying, defining, analyzing and tracing out evolutionary and genetic origins. If it is good ornithology, for instance, to observe and classify birds and to study their anatomy, their physiology, their genesis and evolutionary development, it is equally good ornithology to study them technologically, as creatures that have been basically determined by the requirements of aerial navigation and ecology—a truth vividly illustrated by the following passage from a work by a famous aviator:*

Can you imagine any better example of divine creative accomplishment than the consummate flying machine that is a bird? The skeleton, very flexible and strong, is also largely pneumatic—especially in the bigger birds. The beak, skull, feet and all other bones of a 25-pound pelican have been found to weigh about 23 ounces. Yet, the flesh too is pneumatic, and in some species there are air sacs around viscera, muscles, and, where balance and streamlining permit, immediately under the skin. The lungs are not just single cavities, as with mammals, but series of chambers around the main breathing tubes, connected also with all the air sacs of the body, including the hollow bones. Thus the air of the sky literally permeates the bird, flesh and bone alike, aerates it entirely. And the circulation of sky through the whole bird acts as a radiator or cooling system of the flying machine, expelling excess humidity and heat as well as exchanging carbon dioxide for oxygen at a feverish rate . . .

The main flying motors . . . are the pectoral muscles, the greater of which pulls down the wing against the air to drive the bird upward and onward, while the lesser hoists the wing back up again, pulling from below by means of an ingenious block and tackle tendon. This extraordinary halyard which passes through a lubricated pulley hole at the shoulder is necessary because the heaviest muscles must be kept at the bottom of the bird so that it will not fly top-heavy. Just as the motor may weigh half of a small airplane, the powerful wing muscles of a pigeon have been found to weigh half the whole bird. These pectorals, by the way, are the solid white meat attached to the breastbone or keel, a location insuring the lowest possible center of gravity—just forward of such other low-slung ballast as gizzard and liver, and well below the very light lungs and air sacs . . .

Did you ever notice how similar are a feather and a sail? The quill, though it can be bent double without breaking, is stiff enough for a mast. The forward or cutting is narrow as a trimmed jib, the aft or lee vane wide like a mainsail. The barbs correspond to the bamboo lugs of a Chinese junk, strengthening the sail, enabling it to stand the full typhoon of flight. The primary feathers of some sea ducks, however, can be as jibless as catboats, having virtually no vane forward of the quill, which thus itself becomes the leading edge. The cross section of such a feather is rather like an airplane wing and highly efficient in lift . . .

It is time that many of us recognized that information of this kind is every bit as scientific, every bit as vital—even if it is not

---

*Song of the Sky, by Guy Murchie, Houghton, Mifflin, Boston, 1954.

the kind that appears in textbooks—as that which enables students to place a bird in its proper genus and species, or identify it by its coloring, shape, warble or song. Guy Murchie may not be a member of the Audubon Society, but his understanding of birds is no less profound or scientific than theirs. For if descriptive and causal science tells us how a creature inherits, as it were, its characteristic powers and structure, teleological science based on technical necessities affords us an understanding of why it has just this combination of powers and just this structure. If science equips art, art enlightens science. The one supplements the other, each being indispensable.*

Technology and technique

One of the most intelligent readers of this book while it was still in manuscript form was a technologist who said that it seemed to have little to offer to anyone other than a craftsman or a sportsman. After all, he observed, there is hardly any mention here of purely engineering problems and methods—none at all, for instance, of systems engineering; and while such a study might be useful to others, it could hardly be so for men like himself.

Yet, although this objection seems quite valid at first sight, it does not prove so when it is analyzed carefully.

For it is based on the notion that, properly, technology must be conceived of as a by-product of science, while, in fact, it is an extension and refinement of craftsmanship. The sound technologist is the maker who uses science to refine his methods and materials circumspectly and creatively. Like a good doctor, especially a good general practitioner, he sees himself as primarily an artist in his field who needs science to perfect his art, his technique; he is

---

*Students of biology will find interesting here *The Directiveness of Organic Activity,* by E. S. Russell, Cambridge University Press, 1946.

not primarily a scientist (any more than Edison was) who incidentally uses some art in applying his science.

Unless, in fact, he gives himself enough training in some basic form of making, some basic craft if you will, to appreciate the implications of this fact, he will simply never be the technologist he could be. He is likely to make habitual several attitudes that can only impede him.

First of all, he is in danger of becoming fascinated by mechanical efficiency, by the ratio of work input to product outgo. So obsessed can he become with this consideration (which is in accord, of course, with the employer's need for reducing labor costs) that he comes to prize a machine as excellent when, because of its complex harmony of parts, it turns out a huge number of products quickly, all of average quality for satisfying average needs.

His tendency to think in these terms means that he finds desirable the use of a purely homogeneous material which the machine may therefore process mechanically, "imposing" on it the desired average (minimal standard) "form."

And this dictatorial tendency is fostered by his using chemistry, not to find a suitable material and then obey it, but to confect his own "raw" material synthetically: for this kind is most suitable for repetitive machining. Nor will he find it abhorrent to force a synthetic material to "substitute" for a natural traditional one, even in an obvious imitativeness in appearance. Obedience to his material may strike him as a sign of incapacity, rather than of tactful skill.

These attitudes may seem natural to him for another reason as well. He may come to feel that the "form" of a thing is primarily, as mathematics suggests, the system of its so-called "primary qualities": its size, shape, volume, density, etc. To be truly efficient, a machine need therefore assure this basic form. The beauty of the product will be basically cubistic; and once this has been assured, we need only "add" some external beauty, mainly by ornamentation: coloring and chrome.

Certainly, we need not worry very much about whether the form is organic, personalized for a particular client, and culturally harmonious with the environment. These are fringe benefits not always compatible with standardized parts or production for the average needs of many people.

Moreover, since the aim of mechanical efficiency is that of getting things done without having the product "touched by human hands," an engineer, unless he is on guard, can easily come to misprize, not only hands, but tools and powered tools, treating these as if they were merely almost-machines, rather than instruments in their own right essentially for assuring products of the highest quality. And there is also the temptation to treat the worker as an appendage to the machine, at best its babysitter, certainly not a person who is continually challenged, all day long, to work inventively with others in turning out ever better products.

But what is perhaps most disturbing of all in the technologist who has too narrow a view of his profession is that he is content with averageness in the service of democratism: to him a vast quantity of things that are "good enough" is the be-all and end-all of technology. Whether he admits it or not, he seems to be convinced, deep down in his heart, that we can never hope to aim, for all our vaunted productivity, at quality for all, but only at quantity. From his point of view, therefore, it is simply "idealistic" to suppose that we can ever make our factories, as was suggested earlier, more like our hospitals, using *suitably* everything from the simplest tools on up to the most cybernetic mechanisms. Rather, it is merely "realistic" to say that the hospital is doomed, in the name of progress, to become more and more like a mass production, highly automated factory.

I am not for one moment suggesting that engineers give up being thoroughly trained scientifically (I could hardly be using an electric typewriter for saying so if I were); but I am suggesting that a philosophically grounded course in technique made cogent through experience in mastering a basic craft is indispensable to every one concerned with making—even to the systems engineer.

Such a course might awaken the technologist to the fact that he is a professional man responsible, both positively and negatively,

for the reasonable comfort of his nation. It might make him realize that he must therefore think not only of the quantity but also
of the quality of what he helps produce. Further, he must make
some effort to determine the kind of civilization the products he
designs are meant to fit into and foster. And further still, he must
be heedful of the side effects of his work: the polluting of air and
water; the dirtying of buildings and clothing; the traffic conges-
tion and mortality toll; the crazy obsession with speed; the callous
disregard of technological unemployment; the meretriciousness of
"exciting, new" products; the chicanery of built-in obsolescence;
the mental strain of dull, monotonous work; the exhaustion of
natural resources, arable soil, wood, coal, oil, even water; the
adulteration of foods; and all the rest—to say nothing of the
ruination of taste which his work, if it does not positively second,
does little to control.

Certainly, it would seem to be time for at least the future technologist to realize that in entering an institute of technology, he is
not training himself to become the hireling of an industrialist. He
will not be able to excuse himself from the consequences of what
he obsequiously invents by pleading that he is a scientist and
therefore responsible only for the discovery of the truth, not with
its social or economic consequences. (After all, he is *not* a scientist primarily, anyway; he is an inventor.) Rather he must see
himself as a professional man with a sense of honor: one who
provides clients with the designs, the methods and the instruments
they need, but always for qualitative, not simply quantitative,
production. He must no more be a slave of the industrialist than a
doctor should be a slave of the patent-medicine maker. It is largely his task to safeguard the *humaneness* of our standard of living.
For, if he goes back on this duty, he is no more than a co-
panderer with his bosses, all the worse for being a scientifically
trained one.

His aim should therefore be to help us go from a technology

THAT IS	TO ONE	THAT IS
a by-product of science developed by engineers		an extension and refinement of technique
who are employes of industrialists		carried out by autonomous professional artists
using whatever art is necessary		using whatever science is necessary
for turning out products in great quantity, of adequate quality		for turning out products of high quality, in adequate quantity
primarily for making a profit		incidentally for making a fee
to meet the largely created wants		to meet the legitimate needs
of "prospects"		of individual persons who are fellow members of society

Creating a humane environment

Most people when asked how we are to bridge the gap between our present condition and a properly humane one would reply, of course, "through an ever-increasing refinement of scientific method and an ever-broadening application of it to all our cultural problems."

Yet such an answer, for all its common acceptance by laymen and authorities alike, could hardly be more erroneous or tragically misleading; this, for several reasons:

—Scientific method, at least as we now understand it, has not been vitally necessary in the forming of highly humane cultures.

—It is only one of several methods required for dealing with

127

problems of any size or importance.

—It does not of itself train us in the use of the method we now need most: the artistic, or technical, method.

To rely on it exclusively, therefore, is foolhardy, especially in view of our need to take full advantage of any resource we may have available.

SCIENCE NOT INDISPENSABLE

History shows that the perfecting of the ordinary, as well as the fine, arts has not depended very much on the use of purely scientific method. The men who have shown us how to move gracefully (Pecourt, Zorn, Fokine); how to write a beautiful hand (Arrighi, Johnston); how to cook pleasingly (Brillat-Savarin, Escoffier) could hardly be considered scientists. Nor could thousands of other makers and performers whose work was of the highest quality, quality often beyond our duplicating today; the famous tapestry weavers, goldsmiths, cathedral builders, vintners, cabinetmakers, shipbuilders, wrought-iron workers, stonecutters, explorers, formal gardeners, violin makers, to say nothing of poets, singers, actors, painters, dancers, dramatists or composers. And surely no one thinks of those who give direction to our governments and social institutions—men like Washington, Jefferson, Lincoln, Ghandi, Pope John XXIII, Churchill, Kennedy, Martin Luther King—as strictly scientific. Undoubtedly, a thorough training in modern scientific method might have benefited these men; but they do seem to have gotten along fairly well without it.

FOUR METHODS NEEDED

The main reason, however, why we should not rely on scientific method exclusively or obsessively is that when we deal with any problem of far-reaching ramifications, we ordinarily find, as the chart on the following page makes clear, that we must have recourse to at least three major methods, all under the guidance of a fourth. More specifically, we find that we must follow, not only the scientific method required, but also the moral and artistic methods, all under the guidance of the prudential method.

128

NECESSITIES OF ANY ACTION ANSWERING A NEED

KNOWING
what the action
really is

SANCTIONING
whether or how it
ought to be done

PERFORMING
it as it *should*
be done

(TRUTH)

(MORAL
GOODNESS)

(PRACTICAL AND
AESTHETIC GOODNESS)

SCIENCE

ETHICS AND
MORALS

"TECHNOLOGY"

(sapientia; intellectus;
scientia)

(justice)

(art)

requiring
investigative

requiring
judicial

requiring
technical

CERTITUDES

theological, axiomatic, syllogistic, moral, statistical, experimental, phenomenological; to be attained by the use of:

METHODS

of: exegesis; contemplation; dialectics; demonstration; rhetoric; poetics; technology; logistics; casuistry:
learned by "experimento, . . . doctrina et disciplina."

These certitudes and methods being prescribed, insured and used by:

PRUDENCE

in its eight integral parts:
memory; intelligence; reasoning; foresight; docility; inventiveness; caution; circumspection

Take, for example, an important surgical operation. This calls for the use of all these methods. The surgeon needs scientific method in order to determine exactly what kind of disease or lesion he is concerned with, as well as what resources he has available for dealing with it. He needs moral or ethical method in order to determine whether, under the circumstances, it is morally right for him to perform the operation or to charge the usual price for it. He needs artistic (technical) method in order to perform it as skillfully as possible.

And he needs prudential method to guide him in following each of these methods rightly. For, properly, scientific method is only the *prudent* way of discovering the truth about a thing or an event; ethical method is only the *prudent* way of determining the moral rightness of an action; and artistic method is only the *prudent* way of executing it skillfully. More precisely still, prudential method traditionally dictates that whichever of the other methods we are following, we must do these things: learn the facts; determine the underlying issue they raise; reason logically; foresee consequences; consult with experienced authorities; use our own resourcefulness in arriving at the final decision or plan; proceed cautiously, step by step; and take all factors into account. The scientist meets these requirements by observing, classifying, hypothesizing, experimenting, verifying, measuring, formulating and tracing out theoretical implications; the ethician, in judging the legitimacy of an action in accordance with the traditional norms of experience, the natural use of faculties, the universal validity of the principle to be obeyed, the assuring of the greatest good for the greatest number and of a sound hierarchy of values. The artist (maker or performer) meets these requirements by determining his client's needs, estimating potential materials and means, designing, working out sketches, mock-ups, rehearsals, fixing the stage or fashioning the performance, producing, revising, perfecting.

To treat these various methods as if they were only one, or at least were properly reducible to one, is to fail to gain from each of them what it, and it alone, has to offer. It means, particularly, to fall prey to the delusion that if we adopt the scientific attitude and follow scientific method at all times as if it were the only or primary one, we are automatically adopting the right technical method and attitude. Yet we could hardly make a greater error.

For the user of scientific method is primarily concerned with taking things apart to discover, as with a Geiger counter, what makes them "tick"; whereas, the user of artistic (technical) method is primarily concerned with putting them together so that, in the meeting of a need, they "click." The one sees a thing chiefly as a specimen, the concrete embodiment of a principle; the other, chiefly as a means to an end. The chemist, for example, looks upon a pinch of salt as a specimen of sodium; the chef as a basic source of flavoring. Granted that the scientist must be an artist as an inventor of hypotheses and experimental methods, and that the inventor or performer must take advantage of whatever scientific method or finding will prove useful to him; still, there is little in the primarily abstract-analytic training of the scientist which, *of itself,* perfects the concrete-synthetic habit of mind of the artist. There is good reason why Einstein's name is not to be found on the roll of great inventors, or Edison's name on the roll of great scientists.

The point to be appreciated here is that although technology (as the derivation of its name suggests) is both scientific and artistic, it is primarily artistic. Properly, it is to be viewed not as a by-product of science which uses art when necessary, but as an extension of art or craftsmanship which uses science when necessary.

CHAPTER 9

THE NATURE
AND PURPOSE OF EDUCATION

Educationally, the implications of artistic method are so manifold that they would require a whole book by themselves. Here, therefore, the treatment of them will be limited to a consideration of a few basic principles.

Familiarity with artistic method is especially valuable in helping us focus clearly on the nature and purpose of education. It makes us keenly aware of two basic facts. One is that education must be regarded primarily as an action or set of actions. The other is that it must be regarded as itself fostering a set of actions.

Focusing on education as a set of actions enables us to identify its elements, or factors, rightly and with a helpful precision. It helps us see that the form of any act of education is one of interchange, that is, of teaching-and-learning; the material is that which gets informed (the student); the instrument is that which acts upon that which gets informed (the teacher); and the purpose is that of raising the student to a new condition of competence. This analysis shows us that we cannot properly speak of the material of a course, therefore, as the textbooks and the lectures (which are essentially only part of the instrumental cause); nor must we think of the teacher as simply the purveyor of information and the student as merely the absorber of it with hardly any interaction.*

But if this analysis of the form of an act of education is valuable because it is dynamic, so too is the analysis of the purpose of this act when it is also dynamic.

For, the first thing which such an analysis suggests is that education should be aimed, not merely at acquiring knowledge, but also, and above all, at developing skill. This aim does *not* mean that we are faced with an either-or choice: that we must settle for acquiring *either* knowledge *or* skill. It does not mean that we must aim at knowledge and neglect skill—or that the only skill worth acquiring is that for gaining more knowledge or greater certitude. Nor, on the other hand, does it mean that we must aim at acquiring skill to the neglect of knowledge—as if it were possible for anyone to gain the highest degree of skill without knowing the principles underlying it. We must never let ourselves forget— as too many of our educators seem to have done—that we can be very "learned" without being very skillful, but we cannot be very skillful without being, in the best sense, really learned. We can amass a huge store of intellectual *impedimenta,* and still not be well-educated—there being no greater bore on earth, as Whitehead says, than the merely well-informed man.

If our system of education has suffered from anything, it is the delusion that knowing all the facts about something is much the same as knowing how to appreciate it and deal with it; or that knowing how a thing is done is the same thing as knowing how to do it. We still call ours a liberal *arts* system (one in the liberal training of various forms of *skill*) when these are the last things we aim it toward or test it by.

What all this suggests, then, is that we should use the same general criterion in judging the "products" of education as we use

---

*The student is, of course, an active part of the instrumental factor. Just as the member of an athletic team acquires skill mainly through his own work, with coaches and athletic facilities as the means thereto, so does the academic student regard the acquiring of academic skill mainly as his own work, with administration, teachers, fellow students and community facilities the means to this end. He is at school not to be processed but to develop himself by all the aids afforded him there.

in judging those of any other art. If we should ask, "Can this spoon stir, dip, measure or carry as it should?" maybe we should also ask, "Can this student do all the kinds of things he is meant to do as he should?" This criterion may help us see that the graduate who can reproduce from memory some hundreds of facts, his main ability being that of knowing how to take notes, collect opinions, compile bibliographies, follow instructions of laboratory manuals and fill bluebooks, hardly deserves to be called well-educated, no matter how good his grades or how quick his answers on television quiz programs. The real test is not how much inert knowledge (to use Whitehead's phrase) he has mastered, but how many forms of skill he has acquired for living humanely;* that is, how well he can invent, plan, make, experiment, philosophize, contemplate, communicate, worship. For, surely, it is not enough that he should know how these things can be, or how they have been done by others; he must have learned through self-disciplined and hard practice to do them himself both habitually and gracefully. The student who has memorized all the principles of logic, without having practiced assiduously the arts of classifying, distinguishing, defining, syllogizing, detecting fallacies and so on, is no more a master of the art of sound thinking than is that person a master of truck-driving who has memorized the traffic laws and a driver's manual and then watched a few truck rodeos. Mastery of any art, liberal or not, is finally proved by one thing: performance.

We must not, however, fall into the common error of identifying education for action with education for utilitarian action, as if contemplation, for instance, were both static and useless. Education for action means education for every kind of action; it is guided by the belief that working out a theorem in pure mathematics, meditating on the beauty of the cosmos and discovering the meaning of a psalm, are all actions ultimately quite as useful as testing out a system of lighting, interpreting a new tax form or making a good sales talk.

In the final analysis, we do not face a choice between a liberal

---

*As indicated on the Chart on page 129.

state of inaction and an illiberal one of action, simply because there is no such thing as a choice between inaction and action. Even in sleep a person is far from a state of complete repose: recent studies have measured the amount of twisting and turning he does and have shown the dangers of dream-deprivation. Even on a vacation, one is likely to be continuously active, whether in reading, conversing, pursuing a hobby, playing cards or enjoying a sport. Certainly, a game of tennis or golf, when it is a good game, can hardly be called a passive affair; the more challenging and strenuous the workout, the happier the player.

The choice, then, lies not between education for action and education for ease and passive enjoyment; it lies between education for actions that are essential, recreative and noble and education for actions that are luxurious, lazy and selfish. And the test of a school is the range and value of the actions which its students perform throughout their lives after graduation. Marks, degrees, titles, honors, possessions—all these are, by comparison, negligible.

Student unrest

Of all the forms of unrest agitating our society today there is perhaps none so bewildering to most people as student unrest. Because it has generally been treated as if it were primarily a kind of political rebellion, people cannot help wondering why, on that score, the students really have to be so violent. It is hard to see why such a privileged class could suddenly start acting as if they were the oppressed members of a ghetto.

The fact, however, is that student unrest is not simply or basically political, and we shall never begin to understand it until we appreciate it as educational. To deal with it effectively, we must learn three things about it: first, what educational ideology is behind it; second, what changes we must make in our methods if we are to help students define, correct and carry out that ideology; and, third, what problems are posed for the academic world by these changes.

Meeting the first of these requirements—that of defining the educational ideology behind the student movement—is not, of course, very easy, because here we get relatively little, if any, help from the students themselves. They could hardly state their aims more vaguely. They seem, in fact, to define these aims, not positively, but negatively: as simply the opposite of what our society, especially our military-industrial-political leaders—our "megamachine," as Mumford would call it—holds as patriotically inevitable and even sacred. Such a definition is, for practical purposes, almost useless: its natural effect is not constructive action, but violence.

Yet what the students are positively asking is not too difficult to discern if one does not fall prey to the fallacy of limited alternatives. For they do not wish to be either capitalist or communist; they wish to be personal and communitarian. They are not interested, that is, in a system based on the principle, "from each according to his ability to produce profitably what the public can be made to lust for; to each according to his ability to protect his own interests;" or in one based on the principle, "from each according to the materialistic needs of the proletariat; to each according to the will of the all-controlling bureaucracy trying to serve these." Rather, they are aiming at a system based on the principle, "from each according to his talents, one, three or five, as he uses these creatively; to each according to his needs as he lives in this way."

Moreover, as the leisurely folk subculture of the hippies indicates, another aim of our rebellious students (who are, in a sense, hippies who want to change, rather than withdraw from, our society) is to live life artistically, doing everything, even dressing, as imaginatively as possible—and therefore as enjoyably both as performer and appreciator. For them, the goals of the self-centered—power, success, profit-making, status, luxury—are not so much objectives as dangerous will-o'-the-wisps. Their desire is simply to lead lives that are generous and creatively satisfying.

Feeling such a desire, it would hardly be less than miraculous were they not to react violently against not only the socio-economic system which seems to them to frustrate it but also the educational structure that either fosters or does nothing to change the system. They strike out all the more wildly because they have been blinded by the very education they want to change. They suffer from the great delusion they have absorbed that a college is a convenient assembly place for the study of science and letters, rather than a leisurely, but dedicated, community for the cultivation of the liberal arts.

What they therefore fail to see is how cripplingly everyone is controlled by a certain scientific academicism today. Most teachers, and ultimately, therefore, most students, are guided by the notion that the essential function of a college is the conveying of scientific knowledge and the fostering of scientific habits of mind; this, as detachedly, disinterestedly and uncommitedly, as possible. To ask them even to begin to regard its function as also the developing of intellectually grounded, philosophically interrelated and socially valuable forms of *skill* is to expect an openness and breadth of mind that is rare indeed.

Naturally enough, for the typical faculty member is a person with all the limitations of a strictly trained scientist. He has been trained, first of all, in a special style of analysis and discovery—not of synthesis and invention. Moreover, he has ordinarily limited himself to acquiring the kind of knowledge that is, if possible, mathematically or exactly definable and testable. Knowledge of a lower degree of certitude does not concern him very much—certainly not that of opinion or experience on the basis of which most practical action has to be taken. Above all, as a scientist, he is trained to stay scrupulously inside his own field.

As a result, his teaching conveys only unexceptionable truths that can be stated precisely and systematically. He does not feel called on to correlate these with the truths of any other discipline, nor to help the student make such correlations for himself. And the last thing he would ever think of doing is suggest to the student how to use the findings of the field to reform, or cooperate with others in reforming, the present society. When it comes to trying to work out an overall view of reality or to devising a technically sound plan of action for fostering the good life, he literally leaves the student to his own devices.

His teaching is also limited in two other ways: by his allowing scientific knowledge to usurp the rights of artistic, and by his confusing of "liberal" with "useless."

Because scientific knowledge is unusually certain, precise and, when properly applied, quite productive, because it seems a *sine qua non* of technological advance, the academic mind becomes subject to a very harmful confusion. He comes to suppose that knowing how a thing is done—indeed, most often, merely knowing the general laws governing the elements of an action—is much the same as knowing how to do it. The "authority" in most subjects, therefore, is the man who simply knows most of the facts and principles of it, as these can be stated precisely. He is not the man who knows not only the facts and principles but also how to correlate these and apply them inventively. It is because our teachers are scientists first and last that they have permitted the sacrifice of a cultivation of skill to a cultivation of knowledge.

And nothing, as our students subconsciously feel, could be more disastrous in the long run. Presumably, it is as if one could study a hundred books (or hear a hundred lectures) on the theory of the automobile, consult another hundred on the art of driving, and then venture to drive through New York City, blithely confident that, on the basis of one's bluebook answers, one knew all that was necessary about this art. Even the dullest undergraduate —and the typical college protester is hardly that—would find such a method of education absurd. And he cannot help looking askance at the analogical equivalent of it as he meets it in classroom after classroom.

The other unfortunately limiting misconception is that if a study is practical, it is for that very reason illiberal, since truly liberal knowledge is that which is pursued for its own sake, with no utilitarian aim in view. The mistake lies in assuming that the spirit in which knowledge is best acquired necessarily implies that its practical value must be ignored once it has been acquired.

It is certainly true that if a person is ever to master a subject properly, he must not approach it calculatingly, testing it continually for its probable utility. He must lose himself in it as if for its own sake, taking no account of its ultimate application. Thus, unless an accountant, let us say, falls in love with accounting, and forgets everything about it but its fascination as he studies it, he will never be as good, and therefore as practical, an accountant as he should be.

But all this does not mean that this or that branch of knowledge, this or that combination of studies, should not have been selected for its ultimate utility. Nor does it mean that once a subject has been mastered theoretically, it somehow becomes degraded and less liberal when its findings are applied to vital concrete problems. It does not suddenly become tarnished at that point, while having remained straight and pure up until then. It does not become less valuable, but more. And failure to realize this fact allows experts to rest content with inert knowledge.

The resentment of our students, then, does not seem too hard to account for. It is that of young men and women who see the world falling apart and feel themselves unable to do much about it; who want to transform our bourgeois, manipulative, superficial, violent, philistine society into one that is at least humane; and who therefore want a training that will enable them, not only to acquire and appreciate knowledge for its own sake, but also to use it generously and creatively in solving our common problems.

In short, what our students are rebelling against is the academic, scientistic *narrowness* of our system of education.

They want not only well-ordered, carefully delimited lectures and texts, with discussions and laboratory practice, but also a philosophic correlation of the branches of knowledge, a relating of these to viable ideals and commitments and a development of required forms of skill through case-method apprenticeship. They want, in other words, not one-third of an education, but three-thirds. They want a full, dynamic education.

Are they asking too much? Perhaps. But even a relatively simple change in the ordinary curriculum might bring startling results. Suppose, for instance, that every student were required, as a freshman, to work out his own Utopia or Great Society; then, perhaps in his sophomore year, to study the nature of man as this is made clear by all the major disciplines—biology, anthropology, sociology, psychology, theology, etc.—and, finally, in his senior year, to work out once again his concept of a sound society, revising his freshman attempt, and to determine his commitment in the light of it. Such a procedure could make a vast difference in student-administration relations since it would afford students what they feel has been lacking thus far: challenge, integration and commitment. Naturally, this plan is no panacea; but it does suggest the kind of thing that we must do if we are ever to channel our student unrest.

The role of the artist

Not only does a familiarity with artistic method enable us, as we have seen, to focus on and aim our education properly, but it also helps us to develop the right moral attitude toward our work.

Too often, theorists have made out that the artist is, as such, inevitably amoral: it would seem that it is not up to him to decide on the right use of his product; this decision is the client's or the patron's. As artist, one is simply expected to turn out a good job; the morality of the whole affair is the burden of the person commissioning the work. Yet nothing could be more over-simplified than this.

To do any good work, an artist must be humble, setting aside any desire he may have to show off; he must be charitable, filling his client's needs generously; he must be temperate, resisting all useless decorativeness or "technical effervescence"; he must not be avaricious—not pandering to the lusts of his client in order to make money; he must possess the fortitude to accept legitimate correction from an apprentice, and to work patiently, slowly and thoroughly, meeting the demands of his artistic conscience meticulously, never "playing it safe" and lapsing into conventional and thoughtless routine.

But there is another way as well in which a knowledge of artistic method determines our moral attitude. By generating in us the habit of regarding things dynamically, by seeing them as most truly themselves when in a state of intense normal action, it rids us of niggardliness of spirit, of the miserly hoarding of our energies as if these were not given us to be spent. We come to realize that all things (and the very cosmos itself), since they are what they are because of the sequence of actions they were designed to perform, can be thought of as, in a sense, clocklike mechanisms which are wound up and then released, at appointed times, into these actions. Or, more Augustinianly perhaps, they can be thought of as seedlike, spending their locked up programmed energies cooperatively in growing, flowering and bearing fruit— the whole drama of their coalescent activity being, in the eyes of God and of those men who have the vision for contemplating it (men like Teilhard de Chardin), a single play. Since the discovery of the atom bomb, our sense of being alive in a world the deadest minerals of which are potential explosives locked in mutually helpful check, has been intensified a hundredfold. We are becoming accustomed to viewing all things as bundles of energy, of an energy which they spend either in what the philosophers call "first act" (in maintaining themselves as themselves) or in "second act" (in spending themselves in operating according to their natures)— a notion related to the physicist's that matter may be thought of as energy and energy as matter. Certainly, we would seem to be less and less in danger of regarding the cosmos, to quote a famous phrase of Bradley, as a "ballet of bloodless categories." And we may therefore find it easier to cooperate enthusiastically with all others (with men and things alike) in the vast *commedia del arte* of history.

Such a view may help us realize that we are meant to be both heroic and generous—that we are meant (like electrical workers) to deal confidently with the high voltage of reality, and that we are never meant to exercise a miserly, apprehensive economy in spending ourselves. To be convinced that all things are meant for action is to gain in a sure trust that generous self-donation is normal and that cautious self-coddling is not; it is to see that rusting is not resting; it is to realize that recreation differs from work mainly in how it is oriented and savored, a good workout in a gymnasium being, as its name implies, a desk man's substitute for a good day's labor at the forge. What if our powers, like our muscles, become sore when over-used; underused, they atrophy.

The habit of thinking in terms of dynamic finality, then, should prompt us to suspect the futility of all forms of pure withdrawal and passive disengagement, all attempts to escape action or to try to find a Nirvana-like heaven on earth. It should make us wonder whether there really can be any such thing as a truly happy *retirement*—even after sixty-five—if there is no really engaging activity to retire into. No philosophy, whether epicurean or stoic, would seem to be able to make such a course of action positively desirable.

Certainly, it should strike almost anyone who prizes fullness of action that epicureanism is questionable. For this philosophy, like its contrary, stoicism, is based on the belief that since all physical activity is in the end functionally pointless, we had best steer clear of all involvement in it. The epicurean feels that to observe, as a spectator, the drama of its accidental harmony is, of course, wise and pleasant enough; but to lose oneself in one's role as a member of the cast, under the delusion that the cosmic drama means something, is fatal. Atoms, it would seem, came into being for the sole purpose of forming, by their chance coalescence, whole substances, the functions of which are merely those of working together in accordance with certain principles (nowadays determinable through experiment and mathematical measurement) of attraction and repulsion to form a system of nature which will finally pass away in an event of self-destruction, a cosmic conflagration. If this system of nature has any purpose, it is simply that of ticking away until, having gone through all its phases, it runs down and explodes; and the life of man, since it is only a sequence of movements among the other movements of the system, has no ultimate significance: it is something merely to be gone through. The wise man, then, is the one who, acknowledging these facts fearlessly, makes the best of his predicament. Seeing that human affairs have no ultimate significance, he stays out of them as much as he can (in his own homemade Shangri-la) tasting life, as it were, but never drinking so deeply of it as to have a morning after. The best life consists, not in dissipation, but in a detached, temperate relishing of all things, especially in the savoring of "the higher things"; for these prove, in the long run, both the most enjoyable and the least harmful: taken abstemiously, they afford the most intense delight and leave the fewest bitter dregs.

The stoic would assent, in a way, to most of this theory. But he would quickly add that there is simply *no* pleasure without its pain, and therefore we should spare no effort to achieve a state of imperturbability. The most that the wise man can hope for—and this is not inconsiderable—is the sardonic calm of self-possession: the tranquility of somehow keeping in the "eye" of the storm or of not being swept into the maelstrom of enthusiastic activity. To vary the figure, he might say that we must never step on to the meaningless merry-go-round of life except under compulsion. By preference, we should stand aside and contemplate, with a smile, the grown-up children who are under the delusion that they are getting somewhere, especially when they hook the brass ring that gives them another ride for nothing.

Beliefs of this kind (which hardly died with Epicurus or Diogenes) are not likely to attract anyone who has come to feel that, like man-made things, creatures are given existence so as to spend themselves, and that man, as their epitome, needs to enjoy spending his powers as intensely as possible.

If, then, the attitude of the artist is essentially neither epicurean nor stoic, can it be said to accord with what are the two highest forms of motivation of our culture? The answer is that it could hardly accord with these more, agreeing with them, as it does both in their diagnoses of our ills and in their prescriptions for remedying them.

Consider, for instance, what a leading humanist like Erich Fromm has to say of our present industrial organization and its effect on man, in his work *The Revolution of Hope*:

> What is the effect of this type of organization on man? It reduces man to an appendage of the machine, ruled by its very rhythm and demands. It transforms him into *Homo consumens*, whose only aim is to *have* more and *use* more. This

society produces many useless things, and to the same degree many useless people. Man, as a cog in the production machine, becomes a thing, and ceases to be human. He spends his time doing things in which he is not interested; and when he is not producing, he is consuming. He is the eternal suckling with the open mouth, "taking in," without effort and without inner activeness, whatever the boredom-preventing (and boredom-producing) industry forces on him— cigarettes, liquor, movies, television, sports, lectures—limited only by what he can afford. But the boredom-preventing industry, that is to say, the gadget-selling industry, the automobile industry, the movie industry, the television industry, and so on, can only succeed in preventing the boredom from becoming conscious. In fact, they increase the boredom, as a salty drink taken to quench the thirst increases it. However unconscious, boredom remains boredom nevertheless.

The passiveness of man in industrial society today is one of his most characteristic and pathological features. He takes in, he wants to be fed, but he does not move, initiate, he does not digest his food, as it were. He does not reacquire in a productive fashion what he inherited, but he amasses it or consumes it. He suffers from a severe systemic deficiency, not too dissimilar to that which one finds in more extreme forms in depressed people.

Man's passiveness is only one symptom among a total syndrome, which one may call the "syndrome of alienation." Being passive, he does not relate himself to the world actively and is forced to submit to his idols and their demands. Hence, he feels powerless, lonely and anxious. He has little sense of integrity or self-identity. Conformity seems to be the only way to avoid intolerable anxiety— and even conformity does not always alleviate his anxiety.

Fromm then goes on to explore the many measures that must be taken if man is to be inducted into a condition of truly human living. This study represents, in a way, the supplementing of an earlier one, *Man for Himself,* in which he had shown how, from a psychological-ethical point of view, the transition required man's developing from a nonproductive to a productive kind of person. More specifically, man must go from being a primarily receptive or consumptive creature to being a dynamic and creative one; from being an exploiter to being a cooperator; from being a hoarder of possessions and powers to being a fruitful spender of them; and from being a marketer to being a server. The key to his transition from his present state to one that is humanly normal lies in productive living inspired by a spirit of love, care and responsibility.

In such close agreement is the philosophy of art with these

positions that it could almost be considered a direct supplement or corroboration of them.

And if it is in accord with the humanistic view of things, it is certainly no less in accord with the Judeo-Christian. As one of the main parables suggests, man is not meant to hoard whatever talents he may possess—one, three or five—but to spend them as productively, as fruitfully, as possible. Nor is he to be judged at the Last Judgment by how much he gained for himself thereby—how many thrills, how much money, status or power—but by whether he has developed and applied them generously in answering the needs of others—the hungry, the naked, the homeless, whom he is to regard, no matter how unimportant they may be, as sacred and holy, as other Christs.

The man of religion might also suggest that to produce as effectively as possible, an artist should, ideally, be in a state of positive peace; and this state he can most surely attain when he can most fully admire, hope and love, for as Wordsworth said, "Man lives by admiration, hope and love."

Insofar, therefore, as he can admire the infinite skill of an omnipotent and loving Creator, an artist may well be inspired by it, imitating it and corresponding with it as a kind of apprentice. Insofar as he can rely on having whatever he does, provided it is the best he can do, prove meaningful to a supremely generous appreciator, he can rejoice in a firmly founded confidence that frees him for fully dedicated effort. And insofar as he can love and be loved by, not only his fellows, but also by one who is the Spirit of Love, he can attain a peace and respond with a grateful love that will enable him to act as generously as possible.

The humanist may say that all this is wishful thinking. But it cannot be denied that even for those who do not believe it to be so, it proves to be not so much a contradiction of humanistic motivation as an extension of it.

CHAPTER 10

THE NEED TO BE LOVED

To understand why there has been growing up in the United States a huge army of malcontents, we need to recognize the motives for their attitude—namely, their hunger for self-assurance and for meaningfulness—and the fundamental psychological reasons for these. Only then shall we begin to appreciate how and why a proper cherishing of technique may prove remedial here.

The fundamental reasons for the two hungers may be summarized briefly as follows: Everyone needs to love and to be loved. But this requirement means that he must be able to love himself. He must not suffer from a congealing doubt about his being worthy of affection. Therefore, he must know himself objectively as reasonably "adequate."

But this requirement in turn means that he must have the opportunity to find out from experience how good he is: what kinds of things he can do naturally and do well. He has to learn about his own nature in much the same way as he learns about that of anything else: by observing the actions it performs and then inferring what powers it must therefore have. Hearing himself sing on key, for instance, he comes to know that he has a sense of pitch; hearing himself sing melodiously, he comes to know that he has a good voice. And so for the discovery of every other one of his capabilities.

Furthermore, he should have, ideally at least, the opportunity to discover how well he can perform the inevitable activities of daily life after he has a fair amount of training in them—especially as guided by a philosophically grounded technique.

Beyond this, he should have a similar chance to discover his capabilities in artistically meaningful work; that is, he must come to respect himself as doing work that is meaningful in several ways. First of all, as was noted earlier, it must be such as allows him to "mean" as consciously as possible every one of his choices of purposes, materials, forms and methods. It must enable him to see himself as acting responsibly, deliberately and creatively—rather than slavishly, unthinkingly and unimaginatively. Then again, he must feel satisfied that his product means something to his client —that he is happy with it as aiding him to lead a fully human life. It must also mean something in the eyes of fellow masters, as even, perhaps, making a real contribution to their common craft or profession. So, too, should he feel that it means something to society as a whole, as fostering the common good of a humane culture. As religious, he should be able to feel that his work seems meaningful as being in accord with nature and the will of the Creator. Finally, it should also mean something as a source of sustenance for himself and his family.

In the light of all this, it is not at all difficult to see why malcontents are multiplying in our society; for, obviously, very few of the requirements of contentment, as indicated here, are being met for them. Few American children, for instance, are being afforded proper, indeed any, training in the artistic performance of the various basic activities of life. Almost all that our students become sure of is that they are acceptable when they are "good enough" at these, since they are, after all, relatively unimportant in our society.

Nor have they, as young adults, the chance to feel sure of themselves as doing meaningful work. Unless they can enter a profession, their main hope, at the lower level, is to become a "hand" and, at the higher, an organization man. In either case, they hardly look forward to work that is artistically meaningful.

Clearly, then, technique as described in this book has virtually revolutionary significance. Unless this fact is understood, we shall continue at a loss about coping with our seemingly perverse malcontents. We shall continue to be bewildered by the rejection of our culture as normative by the black, by the "new Indian," by the rebellious college students, and by hippies. (Nor, for that matter, are we likely to understand why underdeveloped nations may look upon our offers of industrialization with grave suspicion.)

For what sensible black, conscious of his nature, really wants the pallid flaccidity of our present white ways? What true Indian would give up a reservation for a worse slum, or his land for suburbia? What thoughtful student is really satisfied with an education in liberal arts, so-called, that leaves him incapable of doing anything skillfully except, at best, memorize, perform laboratory experiments and hold seminar discussions? What hippie or "freak" can be expected to cherish the pseudo-mystique of the "little boxes"—of the Organization Man in search of sales or profit-making efficiency, or would willingly endure the boredom of repetitive, mass production drudgery for the rewards of tavern life or TV stultification? It is no wonder that we have withdrawals of all kinds, positive as well as negative, by those who feel that they are offered no chance either to find themselves or to act creatively—the alcoholics, the psychedelics, the vandals, the sex-obsessed.

Maybe it is high time that we realized how legitimate are the basic motives for our mass withdrawals and to rescue our malcontents by asking them to help us turn our culture away from its gross, quantitative, inhumane mode of life toward a graceful, qualitative, humane one.

Technique and self-integration

One way of coming to appreciate how vitally important from a psychiatric point of view technique can be is that of observing what happens to the natural tendencies of a man when that of craftsmanship has been blocked or starved.

Conventionally, these different tendencies—sometimes wrongly called instincts*—are broken down into the following: flight, pugnacity, gregariousness, craftsmanship, curiosity, play, amorousness, parental love, ritualism, subordination. More specifically, a man normally wishes to maintain his own privacy through dissent and "getting away from it all." He enjoys overcoming something difficult and dangerous. He likes to feel himself one of "the gang." He likes doing things skillfully. He enjoys doing them ritualistically—even as part of an anti-ritualistic movement. He is naturally playful; he likes doing things "for the fun of it." He delights in a love affair, even in the lifelong one of marriage. Despite its headaches, he takes pleasure in parenthood. He rests content in a system of sound authority, of clear-cut command and obedience.

What may happen, then, when any one of these tendencies is not given normal exercise is that a person may over-respond or respond wrongly to one or more of the other tendencies: it is not the love drive alone that can make for inner maladjustment or disruption. Certainly, the balking of craftsmanship—which, after all, is exercised in most of our activities—may well bring about unfortunate compensations all down the line. First of all, it may cause a person to indulge in the various kinds of withdrawal described in the previous section (flight). It may cause him to become pugnacious in the wrong way—to rejoice in a fierce "spirit of competition." It may encourage him to make a mystique out of club life or "togetherness." It may lead him to take, as a relief from boredom, an almost absurd interest in the latest scientific or technological discoveries: in flights to outer space, and the rest. Because he cannot enjoy craftsmanship in his work, he may be driven to becoming a do-it-yourselfer—or an avid sports fan who enjoys performing vicariously. His lack may cause him to become subject to an interest in sex that is a perversion of

---

*As we saw earlier, man has, strictly, no such thing as an instinct: no tendency to go automatically through a fixed pattern of responses to a given stimulus. He has only a general impulse to do so, one that he can channel consciously and reasonably.

creativity. Parenthood will become a bore because it is not visualized as an art or achieved artistically. And for the normal camaraderie of craftsmen he will substitute the false loyalism of the organization man.

On the contrary, when the "instinct" for craftsmanship is duly satisfied, every other one is aided. For craftsmanship calls upon him to make his final decisions *alone* (flight). It challenges him to overcome difficulty after difficulty (pugnacity). It offers him the happy fellowship of fellow artists and coworkers (gregariousness). It raises problem after problem, puzzle after puzzle (curiosity). It makes of his work essentially a form of recreation (play). It puts love in its place and makes it more enjoyable as a technique (amorousness). It makes parenthood also enjoyable as a technique. It helps a person achieve and enjoy the humanly appropriate formal pattern of humanly necessary action—a pleasing etiquette (ritual). And it aids in the acceptance of organizations as authoritatively necessitated instrumentalities and working clubs (subordination).

Without technique, then, one is liable to the disruptions consequent on compensatory use of the other tendencies; with it, one may follow these normally and proportionately.*

---

*It is interesting to note here that "The Place" in Cambridge, Massachusetts, an institution set up to help young people to return from withdrawal and find a meaningful life as integrated persons, offers training in the crafts and the arts.

CHAPTER 11

A QUESTIONNAIRE RESUME

Perhaps the best way in which to gain a summary view of the various implications of artistic method that we have been considering is to try and answer for ourselves the following set of questions:

Is it not true that man, as a creature, is basically needful, but that, as an intellectual and imaginative creature, he is called upon to meet these needs creatively? Is it not true, therefore, that he is, by his very nature, essentially an artist: is it not true that "an artist is not a special kind of man, but every man is a special kind of artist"? As God-like in another sense—spiritually—is he also not, by his very nature, meant to act generously: to answer the needs of others unselfishly and to have them serve him unselfishly in return?

But if he is to answer needs as generously, and therefore as skillfully, as possible, will he not have to specialize? But can he ever specialize with any success unless he sets up institutions (in the broadest sense) for answering each specific set of needs—institutions that in turn have their own needs and together constitute an interdependent communal structure? Should we not, then, have artists in investigation and teaching affording knowledge and skill; artists in invention using their knowledge and skill in the making of things and performances; artists in exchange and distribution seeing that these are passed on to those who need them; artists in governing who assure the peace, justice and general welfare necessary for enabling all to live together harmoniously and cooperatively; artists in communication who afford men vision and dispose them for the heroism for living up to it; and artists in helping all to attain earthly and ultimate salvation?

But will any man specialize unless he feels that by so doing he is not jeopardizing his future? Must he not be sure that he will not suffer through limiting himself to one kind of work? Do not the members of a society feel, therefore, that they have made a tacit contract with one another that specialization will not result in technological unemployment—unnecessary suffering to the specialist? Cannot this assurance be achieved through some such insurance-state method as that of New Zealand, with the family unit the primary one to be insured?

Will not all artists in the same kind of work normally constitute a profession; that is, an association of men who publicly profess an oath of honorable and charitable service to others? Will not each such association establish a code of effective and just relations between artist and client: one which makes it possible for the client to lay down reasonable specifications but grants to the artist autonomy in meeting these? Should not the artists normally be granted such autonomy insofar as they know their materials and instruments and have manifested their inventiveness: that is, have shown themselves to be true authorities, "those able to increase" the power of things or persons under them?

Should not artist-professional associations be granted the privilege of devising their own code of self-regulation for banning poor work and assuring good? Should they not be able to bar from practice, therefore, all "masters" who are interested in pandering to the wants, rather than the true needs, of their clients; who are interested in profits, rather than fees; who either overcharge or pricecut in order to monopolize the market; who rely on cheap material, eye-catching designs and moronic help; who have recourse to trickily motivated advertising and persuasion; whose prime motives are self-aggrandizement, greed and fear of competition; who treat their helpers as mere commodities, appendages to machines who would best be made machine-like; who ultimately gain economic and political control through subsidies, bribery and influence, rather than supereminence in skill?

Will not true artists do all they can to insure the highest quality in their products and services to others? Will they not try to provide others with the means for living rightly and nobly in accordance with their abilities and social demands? Will not every association of these artist-professionals (including the governmental) establish training schools for apprentices, so that these may take over what is handed down to them by masters and carry on the profession expertly? Will they not share among themselves all the "secrets" of their profession, and not try to patent or monopolize them for their own advancement? In addition to what the state may do, will they not take care, without remuneration, of the general needs of society and of the special needs of associates?

Does not all this apply, not only to medicine and the presently recognized professions, but also every occupation; since every occupation, from ditch-digging on up, when carried out artistically and dedicatedly, can become a profession—indeed, a vocation? Should not the economy, therefore, be thought of as a complex of interdependent artist-professional associations?

Governmentally, does not all this imply that there should be one body of representatives, along with the other bodies, to be elected by and from such associations—masters well-known to their fellow masters—and that these representatives should constitute an agency for the overall self-regulation of their services to society; so that no one economic group may be able to dominate or disrupt the system? For if such men, who would know one another through a common tradition of craftsmanship, and be united through a common profession of service, could not regulate their affairs mutually with justice, what reason is there to suppose that administrative courts or other boards would be able to do so?

Again, if authority is the ability to increase the power of those who are under one's control, should not positions of political authority be granted, not simply to those who can get votes, but rather to those who have proven their expertise? Should not our governmental officials, therefore, be trained in their work as artist-professionals?

And if they are to be thought of as artists in government, are not citizens to be thought of as clients? Should they not have, then, a Chief Client, a First Citizen, to represent them and to report to them on the state of the nation, not factionally, but factually? Should not this chief client, as representing the nation-clientele, have the sole functions of attending all patriotic affairs, all welcoming of foreign national heads, all launching of ships, and the like, as well as the special function of reading aloud at regular intervals during the year the main reports of the various departments of the government? Cannot these be purely factual reports (such as are even now available to anyone who has the time to look them up) on conditions of slums, ghettos, crimes, dope addiction, unemployment, usury, levels of culture in motion pictures and television, etc. so that, without taking sides, our First Citizen could make known to us exactly what our cultural state was?

If it is man's basic needs that dictate what institutions he should have to be fully human, should not *every* city of any size have the handful of these institutions required for truly civilized living: the churches, the schools, the hospitals, the theaters, the library, the forum, the athletic fields and houses, the museums? Must we continue to depend on a few centers in big cities for our cultural life, letting all other communities remain philistine or rustic? Is the cultural cleavage between country and city inevitable?

Are our schools properly artistic? Are they mainly concerned with developing the various kinds of skill we need for humane living—or with getting students to memorize scientific doctrines with some light experience of experimental method? How well are our students taught to enjoy the performing of all the ordinary actions of life—walking, talking, etc.—as artistic achievements and to delight in the similar performance of them by others? How tactful, persuasive, urbane, considerate are they trained to be?

How well can they solve original problems in economics, politics, history, philosophy, etc.? How well can they conduct a discussion, especially an intellectual one? How skillful are they in dialectics? How well can they conduct themselves socially? How many of them are inspired with the desire to lead dedicated lives of skillful service?

Finally, is there not a value in regarding religion as an art—the art of leading a dedicated life in serving, delightedly, creatively and generously, the needs of others (while not neglecting one's own) out of love for them as persons and in worshipful gratitude to God for having been given the chance to lead such a life?

PART IV

THE METHOD IN DETAIL

Thus far, we have been considering the necessity for artistic method, its general nature, and the implications it has for our culture. The rest of this work is somewhat less theoretical, and therefore possibly less interesting to the general reader, since it is concerned with showing the specific principles that should be kept in mind by anyone trying to master a new technique, whether of conduct, of work or of play.

CHAPTER 12

PURPOSE IS
THE PRIMARY CONSIDERATION

As we saw earlier, the question which confronts us immediately in the study of technique is which of the four determinants of an action of making or performing should we turn to first. Which of them is of chief importance both in itself and in its controlling effect on the other three?

The answer, of course, is purpose.

The following example, simple though it is, illustrates this fact fairly cogently.

A manufacturer of canned goods decides that spaghetti would be a profitable food for him to put up since he sees it sold in hundreds of Italian restaurants throughout the country. Without asking himself what this food is for, what special needs it satisfies, how it is normally served as part of a meal in an Italian home (fresh, *al dente,* with an antipasto, red wine, salad, etc.) by whom it is normally eaten, in what quantities, he merely has several batches of it made up, samples them, and plumps for the one which he, his advertising men, and his office staff like best. This stuff he then mass-produces in large orders, to be served, not *al dente,* not with an antipasto and the rest, but under American conditions as part of a hastily prepared American meal. If, under these circumstances, he manages to turn out anything that tastes like the food he is trying to duplicate, he will be performing a feat little short of the miraculous.

On the other hand, suppose that, instead of simply trying to copy a dish of spaghetti, he had begun by asking himself what this kind of food was especially for and had visualized the typically American conditions of serving and eating a meal. Then, taking into account the particular culinary effects he could achieve in producing a *pasta* in large quantities, he might be able to produce a fairly delicious one. It might not taste very much like spaghetti, but it still might be something that even an Italian would not reject.

What is true here is also true of the arts of making ships and shoes and sealing wax: in all of them it is well for us to cultivate the habit of thinking at all times of the determining aims. For a steady, careful regard for purpose calls forth the *inventive* way of making or performing, not the merely fashionable or conventional way.

We may then avoid both a nostalgic conservatism of the past and a present-day radicalism that opposes it blindly. We are not likely to fall prey either to the habit of assuming, for example, that the new home we are about to build must be early mission or New England Colonial; or, what is equally silly, to the counter habit of assuming that it must be late Bauhaus or even later ranch house. If it is beside the point to be automatically period-piece, it is just as much beside the point to be automatically its opposite, or split-level.

But the greatest value to be derived from respecting purpose as primary is that it disciplines our thinking creatively.

In inventing, for example, it helps assure us of the freshness of vision, the free and responsible use of our powers, the determination and the optimism that spur us to work resourcefully and enthusiastically. Freeing us from subservience to past and present modes, it incites us to use all powers of mind and will, and to use them with address. Merely to make a calm, thorough analysis of our purpose is of itself to challenge ourselves to *aim* our powers clearly and resolutely and, as it were, to warm them up. As we bring into ever sharper focus the outlines of our goal and its inevitable requirements, we automatically become more and more absorbed in designing the ways for attaining it.

Moreover, this thinking out of each new problem afresh in the light of purpose has the double value of piloting our cogitation and of accustoming us to obey the principle of economy of means. When we make out clearly just what it is and what it is not that we are aiming at, we find it not too difficult to visualize both the kind of thing we are to devise and the simplest form of that thing. It is partly for this reason that almost every modern invention, from typewriter to television set, goes through a sequence of simplifications. It is frequently simpler in the end, when fulfilling a complex purpose, than it was at the beginning when fulfilling a simple one.

Certainly, the habit of adverting to purpose continually helps us discern and focus on the unifying, the organizing, principle of our product, aiding us to make *all* our choices deliberately and responsibly—so that we could even stand a cross-examination on them. It accustoms us to constructing our models, and even practicing our five-finger exercises, inventively, rather than routinely —as themselves works of art. And it affords us a key to a freeing, rather than a crippling, imitation of the masters.

Finally, the law that "technique follows intention" is in large part based on the fact that an ever clearer focusing on purpose seems to aid, not only the conscious, but also the subconscious mind in mulling a problem over and in bringing to light the hidden stores of the imagination. The sudden flash of insight that often enlightens both scientist and inventor is not the result of pure accident: as many have testified, it is called forth only by a continual adverting to the end being striven for.

The first of the effects is clearly in the nature of things. It is inevitable that the person who regularly asks himself: "Why am I making this choice rather than that? What should each of the parts or stages here contribute to guaranteeing the total effect to be achieved by this product or performance? Can any of these be substituted for, reordered, amplified, simplified or eliminated without loss to this total effect?" It is inevitable that such a person can hardly help insuring the unity, coalescence and overall efficiency of his product or performance. So it is, for instance, that, as soon as he could make out clearly what is implied in the easy and safe cutting of stubble from the face, King C. Gillette was able to hit upon the organizing principle of the safety razor; or that, as soon as Maurice McLoughlin visualized the exact purpose and requirements of the serve in tennis—as soon as he saw that it was to put a high, twisting bounce on a ball which had gone through a long arc—he also saw how the ball would have to be stroked so as to go up before it went straight out or down and would have to be hit fairly high in the air. McLoughlin was then able to work out at least the basic exigencies of such a stroke, from stance through follow-through, and thereby give it a new and dynamic pattern.

The habit of thinking in terms of purpose trains us, then, to think *responsibly*: to *mean* our choices, holding ourselves answerable for every least one of them and to realize that our right to the title of maker or performer depends primarily on this intentionality. Not that we are called upon to foresee all contingencies or to hope for no "good breaks." When, in painting a watercolor, for instance, a person accidentally achieves a pleasing effect, for which in his heart he knows that the paint and the brush are more responsible than he is, he must humbly confess this fact to himself; but there is no reason why he cannot then adopt this effect if it suits his general purpose. The point is that (like every other sound maker or performer) he must mean this adoption—choose to commit himself to both the given effect and the method for achieving it. He must rest content, that is, only with things that are done at least this much "on purpose."

Purposiveness is also essential to sound practice or training. As any coach will testify, one moment of thoughtful exercise is worth an hour of mechanical drill. The latter can, in fact, prove positively harmful. It may, to be sure, accustom nerves and muscles, for a while at least, to certain routine motions; but it may also accustom mind and body to acting independently of each other. They may be conditioned to work, if not directly, at least indirectly, against each other, since their failure to cooperate may set up, with repetition, a habit of noncooperation. By "faithful practice" is really meant, therefore, fully intended, *deliberate* practice; it implies that, whether at blackboard, piano or workbench, the learner must advert continually and thoughtfully to his purpose. He must even learn to regard his completed works or performances as, in a sense, practice pieces, judging them in part by how well they have taught him to deal with a similar set of purposes.

Not the least value of purposiveness is that it enables us to take advantage of the experience of others—to make it, as far as possible, our own. It is a key to the workshop of the masters, enabling us to enter and look over their shoulders profitably: through understanding what they are aiming at, we come to appreciate why and how they follow their particular methods. In this way, we avoid slavish, and profit by free imitation. For whereas the one consists in copying products and following routines automatically, the other consists in determining purposes and observing how, to fulfill them, these men followed brilliantly certain principles. More specifically, we imitate the masters with profit when we take the following steps: determine clearly the purposes they were trying to fulfill; determine the problems which these raise; work out our own best solutions to these problems; compare our solutions with theirs, noting what principles they were guided by, and for what reasons; and consider how we may best follow these principles adaptively or analogically in our own work. And purpose, of course, is the primary determinant.

It is now also possible, in the light of this discussion, to distinguish between spurious originality and genuine. The first is achieved by the man who sets out "to be original"; the second, by the man who lets originality, in the sense of uniqueness, take care of itself. The maker or performer who tries to be original ordinarily slights the factor of purpose and concentrates on making the form unlike anything that had been devised by an earlier master. As a result, he produces something that is more like a negative of another man's work than like a positive, so to speak, of his own; more like a contradiction than an assertion. The truly original maker, on the other hand, knows that if he faces his problem for exactly what it is, he cannot help being original. For one thing, his purposes. cannot be exactly the same as those of previous makers, since the needs he is trying to answer are in some way unique. For another, he will not have available exactly the same materials, patterns, instruments, methods, imagination and technical skill, as they had. Let him simply strive to control all these factors as well as he can, and he must inevitably turn out something "original" in the best sense of the term. Facing the job afresh and doing the best he can—here is the key.

Purpose and act

If it is fairly obvious that we must concentrate on purpose as primary, it is not quite so obvious how we may best visualize this factor. It is this question, therefore, that we consider next.

Briefly, the answer is that can best visualize purpose dynamically, regarding it as an act, rather than as a condition. We must never merely name it or define it abstractly. We must picture it concretely. And we must do so in terms of actions.

To ask ourselves, for instance, what the purpose of bread is, and then to rest content with a general term, like "nutrition," is almost to waste our time. It will certainly not help us very much to gain an insight into breadmaking. We should do much better to visualize bread as a food in loaf form which can be sliced, piled, toasted, buttered, broken easily into firm morsels, pleasantly savored, masticated and digested for assimilating carbohydrates, vitamins, etc., as a kind of obbligato-food for most other kinds. For even such a view of its purpose, vague as it is, tends to awaken inventiveness through focusing our minds on the exigencies of producing something that will play a part in a whole sequence of acts.

We must realize, in fact, that nothing we ever make will be simply an end in itself. We never make a thing merely to be a thing. We make it to be an instrument, to be something that has a role to fulfill in answering a system of needs. And the clearer we see what that role is, the better we can design the thing for playing it.

When, for example, we make a forensic speech (as in a political assembly or a policy meeting) we must think of it as aiming, not simply at persuasion in the abstract, but at catching attention, allaying suspicion, arousing desire, evoking and guiding careful deliberation, inciting to a definite decision and stirring to a resolute line of action. Or, again, when we design furniture, or even make an arrangement of it, we must think of this, not merely as insuring livableness, but as affording comfortable sitting or reclining which enables those who are doing so to keep warm, to read, to listen to others or to the radio, to observe pictures or television, to converse pleasantly and listen attentively.

Our learning to think in this way is facilitated when we realize that an act, as well as a thing, can be broken down into the four factors we have been considering. It, too, has its material, formal, instrumental and intentional determinants, as we see clearly when we analyze some of the functions for which the things we dealt with earlier were designed. A barbecue oven, for instance, is made to act (as instrument) on meat (the material) through cooking it to one or other degree of thoroughness (the form of action) in order to assure a tasty slice or patty (purpose). A toolchest acts (as instrument) upon the tools (the material) encasing these and holding them in order (the form of action) in order to protect them and keep them readily available (purpose). And so for what might be called the purpose-acts, or functions, of all other things made; these too can be profitably analyzed in this way—causally.

This fact is important since every full-fledged maker, being both craftsman and inventor, is concerned, not with one kind of act only—making—but with two kinds: making and functioning. These interlink since the act of making results in producing the thing which plays the central role (of instrument) in the act of functioning. In other words, everything is made so as to function, and to function means to play the part of instrument or agent in an act of use. And as acts, both kinds can be analyzed in terms of the same inevitable four factors.

This interlinking and essential likeness is made clear by the chart-like analysis of a housewife's pie-making:

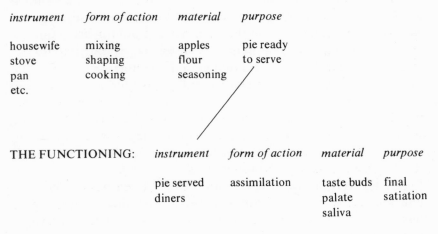

THE MAKING:

instrument	form of action	material	purpose
housewife	mixing	apples	pie ready
stove	shaping	flour	to serve
pan	cooking	seasoning	
etc.			

THE FUNCTIONING:

instrument	form of action	material	purpose
pie served	assimilation	taste buds	final
diners		palate	satiation
		saliva	

A study of this chart should help us identify clearly the elements and aims of a full act of making.

For one thing, it should prevent us from falling into a certain common form of over-simplification. It should cause us to see that as makers we are always concerned, not with one kind of material, but with two kinds: not only with the material of the object we are making, but also with the material that is the client on whom it works. For example, it should keep us from assuming that the determining material of education is the textbooks and the lectures; for medical treatment, the medicines; for architecture, the stone, wood, etc. used in the building; for the law case, the facts and arguments of the brief. It should help us to recognize that this determining material is the client for the educator, he is the student in a state of indifference, ignorance, awkwardness and selfishness to be transformed into one of enthusiasm, knowledge, skill and dedication; for the doctor, he is a patient to be transformed into a healthy person; for the architect, a creature susceptible to the elements into one protected against them; for the lawyer, the judge and jury in a state of indecision to be transformed into one of just decision. It is the person served as needful who is thus, in the technical sense, the final material of the act of making.

When we say of a man, then, that "he knows his material," we mean that he knows the material of the thing he is making above all in relation to the requirements of the material (the client) whom he is serving by the functioning of that thing.

The chart may also help us to see that in making we are ultimately concerned, not so much with producing a thing, as with *staging a performance* requiring that thing—a performance determined by the system of needs it answers. We have therefore to take into careful account the normal conditions of operation, estimating their various contingencies. We must think of ourselves, that is, not only as craftsmen and inventors, but also as impresarios or managers. And through studying just how we are analogous to these men (promoters, stage directors, coaches, generals, executives) we may learn to profit by their experiences, carrying over into our own work as much of their technique (particularly in logistics)* as may be applicable to it. For, in making a thing with which to carry out an action, we too are staging a campaign, if only in miniature. At the very least, we are serving as our own property man (in the theatrical sense). By thinking of our work in such terms, we may learn to take advantage in small projects of methods that have proved effective in large.

If nothing else, we shall acquire the invaluable habit of looking upon whatever we are making as *necessitated:* as something that would not have come into existence but for the exigencies of a certain form of functioning. We shall learn to judge it primarily by whether it is well cast for its part.

Certainly, the habit of regarding things as if they were actors playing roles will encourage in us a professional sense of having to satisfy clients much as actors feel obliged to satisfy their audi-

---

*In the broad, not purely military, sense of the science of having what we need when and where we need it.

ence. It will keep us keenly aware of the fact that, for a user, a product is not a product at all unless it provides the service to him it was meant to provide—no matter how stylish, streamlined, expensive or well-wrought it may be. The conscientious maker will hardly boast of his guarantee that his product will do what it is supposed to do. And certainly he will not boast of his providing a multitude of service stations. Any tailor who would advertise that he had a large chain of shops where the seams of the clothing he has made would be conveniently resewn, or the buttons economically replaced, would seem strange indeed; and so should any other maker who prides himself on his repair shops.

There is also a useful derivative habit to be considered here: that of evaluating things for their potential. When we read that one of the first acts of Napoleon, on landing at St. Helena, was to make an inventory of what it contained that might offer a means of escape, we may be inclined to smile at the strength in him of this habit of looking on all things as possible resources; but we may be a little less inclined to smile when we remember that, after all, he did escape from Elba. And the long record of famous escapes from prisons and prison camps, which have resulted from the patient weaving of ropes from odd scraps of cloth, the making of files, the fashioning of makeshift spades, gives us some measure of how practical it is to visualize things functionally. Often enough, indeed, this habit has been the source of marvelous inventions, as well as scientific discoveries, to say nothing of the economic. salvaging of otherwise wasted by-products. Technical progress has so frequently resulted from the resourceful turning to account of apparent mistakes or oversights or accidents that sometimes the art of invention seems to consist of not much more than this. The Edison effect, unused by Edison, gave us, when used by De Forest, the radio tube; and what is called crepe paper was originally a batch that was about to be thrown away because it had become accidentally crinkled—until the manufacturer saw how useful it could be for the purposes of decoration. Similarly, as Taton has pointed out in his work *Reason and Chance in Scientific Discovery,* it is the habit of alertly taking advantage of what may seem a negative result that has proved a main source of scientific discovery.

In short, if it is good to develop the habit of asking what thing can be used for this purpose, it is no less good to develop the habit of asking what purpose might this thing fulfill.

The purpose is to answer needs

Next in importance to the habit of thinking of purpose as an act is that of thinking of it as an act in answer to needs.

We must test our product searchingly by asking ourselves the questions: What set of requirements, what system of needs, was this thing designed to answer? How well does it answer each of them? For, obviously, unless it passes this test, no matter how progressive or scientific it may appear to be, it is deficient. The streamlined automobile, for instance, that loses through weight what it saves through streamlining and is so closed in that it has to be squirmed into and parked by dead reckoning, is a monstrosity. So, too, the house that does not assure the air, the light, the space, the temperature, to say nothing of the privacy, required by those who want a real home is not worthy of the name, no matter how interesting its split-level flooring or how spacious its picture window. Nor is an *Ave Maria,* even one by Schubert, good music when it is played as an obbligato to a radio program. For none of these things meets properly the needs it should be meeting.

The questions to be considered next, then, are these: Exactly what kinds of client are there? What kinds of satisfactions are to be afforded them?

CLASSIFICATION OF CLIENTS

In answer to the first of these questions, we can classify clients, at least at the outset, in two ways: first, by whether they are the immediate or remote user of the given product; and second, by whether they are simply the users of it or the users who are also the makers.

It is helpful to classify clients into immediate and remote since,

by so doing, we remind ourselves that things are to be judged by
their ultimate, as well as their immediate, satisfactoriness. A pen,
for example, is to be judged, first of all, not simply by whether it
pleases the penman, but also, and above all, by whether it makes
letters that are pleasing to a reader of taste—letters that are truly
calligraphic; just as the final test of an article in a magazine is not
whether it pleases the editor, but whether it really enlightens its
readers. Unless, in short, a maker succeeds in pleasing and serving his ultimate client, it matters little whom else it pleases and
serves.

The other distinction—between the client who has something
made for him and the client who makes it for himself—keeps us
aware of two facts: one, that there is no such thing, strictly, as art
for art's sake, or the making of a thing for no one, since the very
act of making implies at least one client, the maker himself; the
other, that the more a maker becomes one with his client—the
more he can feel his client's needs sympathetically—the better
will he be able to satisfy those needs.

Once we see, in fact, that every artistic action implies at least
one client, the artist himself, we begin to discern the folly of pure
self-expressionism—certainly its limitations. Like the man who
plays a game of solitaire, the scholar who dallies with a theory he
does not trouble to publish, the poetaster who sweats out verse
that only he can understand, or the dauber who fills his closets
with abstractions—even this man still has a client, himself: a person whose need is satisfied for a systematic use and release of
powers, energies, talents, realizations. The artist who proudly
proclaims that he works for no one merely betrays the fact that
he works for no one but himself—as a Narcissus of the workshop.

Even when he feels that he is his own best client, he will do well
to work for the self that he is, not at the moment of making, but
at the moment, sometime later, of using. To become a truly
sound judge (or appreciator) of his work, he must stay away from
it long enough to be able to see it for what it is, rather than what
he thought it was while he was making it. It is primarily for this
reason that men as different as the poet Gray and the painter Ti-

tian kept some of their work from the public for years—until they themselves could see it clearly, as the persons for whom it might have been produced.

Ordinarily, of course, the maker has to respond to a somewhat different challenge. He must make an accurate estimate of the kind and quality of the product he is called upon to turn out, and of the limitations of time and money under which he has to work, and then decide how, in the light of these considerations, he may operate most justly and efficiently. It is only when he knows that under the given conditions it is better, let us say, for everyone that he make many shoes quickly rather than a few shoes slowly; prepare a plain meal hastily, rather than an epicurean one meticulously—or vice versa—it is only then that, enjoying peace of conscience, he can estimate freely and comfortably what test of skill he is facing and act accordingly: determining, with some exactitude, the amount of time, expense, thought and effort he is able, in justice, to devote to each task and its stages, and fixing upon what materials, instruments and technical processes he must settle for.

Obviously, because he has an artistic conscience, he will try at all times to live up to his own highest standards, even when his client would be content with lower.

The satisfactions which the maker may aim at for both his client and himself are these: that of enjoying a product directly, through consuming or assimilating it directly (as in eating a pie); that of enjoying it as an instrument (as in using a barbecue oven); that of enjoying it as a manifestation of skill (as in appreciating the workmanship of a good toolbox). The maker can also justly aim at affording himself the pleasure of the full, intense and disciplined exercise of his skill; the delight of overcoming difficulties; and the satisfaction of realizing he has served his client (and therefore society) justly and well.

The habit of translating purpose into the satisfying of needs tends to improve both our morale and our technique.

It tends to improve our morale by encouraging an attitude of unselfish, humble, thorough, and, as it were, soldierly craftsmanship, inducing us, from the outset, to concentrate on what our client needs, rather than what we profit most by, or most enjoy making. It causes us to realize that it is his verdict on how well we have served him that we should respect primarily (even when we may have later to reject it). It helps us, in short, to become "good troupers," eager to do what is needed, regardless of risk of failure or embarrassment; to accept the discipline of professional standards at all times; to be divinely discontent; to be truly dedicated to our art, however secondary or obscure this may be.

Technically, this habit both challenges and inspires. It challenges inasmuch as it suggests that, to be worthy of his craft, a maker should be able to stand a cross-examination on everything he does: be able, that is, to tell exactly why he fixed on every beam or stone, valve or cog, line or color, as being the only one really adequate under the circumstances for answering properly the needs of his client. And, by the same token, through knowing that this is his primary responsibility, he is freed from having to design either conventionally or unconventionally, popularly or academically, so long as what he produces attains its due effect. He finds that his technique, through being aimed by the unique requirements of his individual client, is thereby, paradoxically, freed by them.

THE RESPONSIBILITY OF THE MAKER

A habitual regard for needs inevitably sharpens the maker's sense of *final* responsibility. Clearly, his responsibility does not end with the sale of what he has made; for he cannot be sure that this really does what it should unless he follows it up, not merely in laboratory testing, but also in general use. The maker of golf clubs who does not study how well his clubs meet the requirements of various kinds of golfers as they execute typical strokes under typically diverse conditions of confinement, wind and visibility, can hardly sell these clubs responsibly; nor can he improve with assurance their shaft, head or grip, giving it better heft, balance, resiliency and strength. Furthermore, he and every other maker or inventor should, as far as possible, make a complete study of the history of his products as they have functioned under all kinds of conditions: he should be able to write authoritative "biographies" of them. He should have regular recourse to both a bureau of standards and to common criticism: to the one because laboratory tests can be made extremely stringent; to the other because no laboratory test can duplicate exactly the contingencies of actual use. If a product does not satisfy properly the needs for which it was made, the man of professional honor welcomes a thorough report of this fact, tries to meet the challenge of it, and even to make amends because it is the right thing to do, *not* because of fear of competition.

We may now take a step further and suggest that not only must a thing made play a part in an event so as to answer systems of needs, but it must do this comprehensively and humanely. There is a human need to have things function in a human way. This requirement means that, as man is composed of body, mind and soul, the manner of meeting even his bodily needs must be, not only physically, but mentally and spiritually satisfactory. Men are not beasts one moment and angels the next, but whole men always, whose natures need to be satisfied by all three aspects of reality: by the true, the good and the beautiful. Eating, for instance, would seem to be a fairly animal occupation. But a man in a restaurant who orders an apple pie and is given one which, while good, still does not taste like an apple pie, will be rightly enough disappointed because it is not a *true* apple pie. Or if it leaves him hungry for dessert, it will not strike him as a *good* one, either. And if it is soggy, saccharine or harsh-tasting, and served sullenly and sloppily, it will hardly seem a satisfactorily *beautiful* one. His desire, as a human being, is to relish all three of these transcendental aspects of being, and unless he can do so, he will remain dissatisfied, no matter how nutritious the pie will have been or how delectable it would have tasted to a goat.

A designer, then, if he is to fill all the needs of his client as a human being, is required to make sure that his product will fit into the pattern of fully human behavior—that it will accord with the *style* of human life. When the thing he plans is not to be used in isolation, he must make sure that it "rhymes" (kinesthetically as well as visually) with its fellow instruments in the large function in which they all play a part cooperatively. In a set of silver-ware, for instance, the spoons must accord, in size, general proportions, pattern and weight, not only with the knives and forks of the set, but also with the plates, cups and saucers that will be used with them; and all must be no more and no less formal than is necessary for the occasions in which they are to figure, those for an ambassador's banquet being somewhat different from those of an ordinary meal. Moreover, if they are to bear any inscription or decoration, this should be unobtrusively, but appropriately, symbolic. And since the normal client will wish to live at all times integrally, by a code in accordance with which his every action will be both civilized and, in some way, sacral, the designer tries to make his product honest, suitable and religiously expressive: in the fullest sense befitting a profoundly human way of life.

The primitive craftsman found it natural to make a bow, let us say, that was at once efficient, pleasing and sacral: that would shoot accurately, delight the eye and the arm and bear an image on it of the Farshooter. It is only a certain kind of modern man who considers two of these qualities to be of no account. And it is only when we begin to think once again that these qualities do matter that our megalopolis will become as truly humane as the tribal village.

Four kinds of purpose

At first sight, the number of needs we might aim at satisfying, hence the number of considerations we might try to keep in mind in designing things, appears so vast as to stagger the imagination. Yet, if we classify all the various functions which they may be made for, we shall discover that these can be reduced to four general kinds: to make, to operate, to protect and to conserve.

By the first of these, to make, is meant, of course, to transform. A chisel, for instance, is obviously designed to make in the sense of transforming the stone or wood on which it operates.

By the second function, to operate, is meant to set something in action or to govern it when set in action: as by a lever, steering-wheel or fuse.

By the third, to protect, is meant to act as a guard or shield, as does a shoe, a bumper or a coat of paint.

And by the fourth, to conserve, is meant to maintain something intrinsically, to help it sustain itself as itself, as by food, a replacement part, or recharging.

Naturally, a given product may be so designed as to do more than one of these things; but it must be designed to do at least one. We can be sure, in fact, when we examine a new product, that if it is clearly not meant to perform any one of three of these functions, it must have been designed to perform the fourth—whether we can make out exactly how or not. If, to cite a very simple case, a savage were to come upon a saw for the first time and to discover that it was not being used (like a bow) to operate something, nor (like a blanket) to protect something, nor yet (like a piece of bread) to conserve something, he could safely conclude that it must have been designed (like a hammer) to make something, since there would be no other function for it to fulfill.

We turn, then, to a study of each of these functions, so as to distinguish them clearly and to observe how they determine a maker's design. Concretely, let us consider how they determine the making of a simple article, the ordinary teaspoon.

And, for this purpose, let us note first what the ordinary teaspoon is *not* primarily designed to do.

Obviously, it is not designed primarily to conserve something, since it neither nourishes nor repairs. Nor, again, does it protect: it does not act as cover, guard or box. Nor does it make anything: it does not act like a hammer, saw or plane. Therefore, it must be designed to operate something.

Thinking in terms of act, we then observe that its main function is that of dipping a certain amount of liquid from a cup or bowl, carrying it gracefully to the mouth and depositing it there safely, transporting each time only so much as provides a fair sip of what otherwise might be too hot if taken in larger amounts.

It is clear that if we go no further in our analysis than this, we have already begun to make out how the design of the teaspoon is determined by its mode of operation. We see how it must be of a certain shape and size that will assure the dipping out of a small quantity of hot liquid and the gradual diffusion of it without any burning of tongue and lips. There must, in other words, be a bowl large enough for the amount dipped to afford a fair sample for indicating the heat and sweetness of the liquid; and it must be so shaped as to have this engage easily the taste buds at the front and sides of the tongue, which register sweet and sour respectively.

Even this much analysis, short and incomplete as it is, would also prove helpful to the maker in determining the materials that should be used for a teaspoon. It suggests that an instrument designed primarily for the transporting of such a substance as hot tea must be made of only certain kinds of materials: those which do not absorb liquid; that are not easily warped by heat; that would not splinter, corrode or flavor. These necessities limit the teaspoon maker from the outset, therefore, to a few materials: certain metals or plated substances.

The pattern and the material become even more clearly inferable when we go on to analyze the secondary functions of the teaspoon. We then see that this instrument is commonly to be used in at least three other actions: that of stirring; that of shovelling; and that of measuring. As a consequence, it may be patterned, subordinately at least, to perform these functions as well as may be without interference with the principal function. The need for stirring may thus suggest that the spoon be given something like a point, which will permit the liquid to slip by easily and not spill over the edge of the cup. The need for shovelling may suggest that the lip of the spoon be given a slight flatness for digging into soft foods, cereals and the like, and also that the handle be made a shovel-like shaft. And the need for measuring will require that the bowl of the spoon be of the size that has become more or less fixed by medical convention (so as to contain "one teaspoonful"), and that the bowl and the handle be easy to hold level before the eyes. A visualization of the stirring, digging and measuring, then, as well as of the dipping, transporting and pouring, will aid the silversmith to make out quite clearly the general preliminary and tentative pattern and material for this instrument; as will, of course, a similar process of analysis and visualization for all other products.

Naturally, a primary function must never be sacrificed to a secondary. An instrument may be expected to play several roles, but it must play them proportionately.

Sometimes it is better, as experience (like that of golfers) proves, to design one-purpose instruments (a different club for every essentially different shot). But this choice must be made deliberately. We should therefore learn to think in plurals, asking ourselves not "what function is this thing to perform?" but "what functions?" Otherwise we may not be able to make an intelligent choice between the making of a single versatile instrument and a set of them that are specialized.

The realization that there can be only four general functions should help us, then, to fix quickly upon those with which we are mainly concerned, to evaluate these, and to design for them systematically and proportionately. It should also help us to appreciate the beauty of someone else's product through judging it in the light of the system of functions it was made to fulfill and in the light of the tact with which the necessary compromises were struck.

It is a sign of supreme skill, of course, when diverse functional requirements are each so well met as not to seem the result of any compromise. Take the claw hammer, for instance. So well does it pull out nails that as it does so, we hardly think of this function as determining in any way its primary one of driving nails in. And although the human hand is primarily for grasping, it can be hardly said to have been limited thereby, since from it have come all the other instruments of the world.

A purpose
is a particular purpose

If we wish to make anything well, we cannot aim at serving merely some person in general or even an average person; this, for the very good reason that the average person simply does not exist. A tailor cannot make a suit for *a* boy, since a boy may be anyone from five to fifteen years of age: and so on. Undoubtedly, a mass production tailor could make *a* suit for *a* boy of ten that would be so shapeless, colorless and unsymbolic that it could be adapted fairly easily by a store tailor to almost any boy of that age and general size. But to maintain that a garment of this kind is satisfactory merely because it is inexpensive, not too queer-looking and readily available to absurd. Nor does it become any less absurd for our having got used to maintaining it.

A thorough maker tries to visualize as exactly as possible the particular needs he intends to fill: he tries to meet them in all their uniqueness. Even when "the" client turns out to be a group of clients, he tries to define them as a particular group, not exactly like any other. When Lincoln planned his Gettysburg Address, for instance, he planned it for the American audience that had lived through the Civil War and would be present on the battlefield. He made this speech brief, therefore, because he knew that his audience would already have sat through a long one by another orator. And he made it a summary of the significance of the occasion since he realized that his audience would by then need no more than this. As a result, he could legitimately use long words of Latin derivation, as being those best suited to a solemn summary ceremonial in tone, measure and cadence. Visualizing the needs of his particular audience exactly, he was able, in answering them, to use his resources with astonishing aptness.

The habit of meeting the unique requirements of individual clients has the effect of awakening a maker to the complexity of every task, no matter how simple this task may appear to others; it challenges him with multiple possibilities. He learns to rejoice in his work as a kind of conquest. Like the surgeon or the general, he becomes accustomed to looking on it as, in some sense, a dangerous operation, feat or expedition: an undertaking that calls for painstaking diagnosis or reconnaissance; for careful estimating of possible accomplishment, of means available, of effective employment of these means, of chances of failure and withdrawal for readjustment; for the scheduling of processes; and so on. The more particular the requirements are, the richer they are likely to be in contingencies; hence the more of a campaign they will call for—and the pleasanter will be the victory.

The efforts to satisfy the needs of a particular client will also help to keep a maker straight on the question of originality and imitativeness. If no two human beings are ever alike, obviously no two clients are: the needs of one are never exactly those of another; so that the thorough answering of the needs of each cannot but produce originality. The maker who sets himself to answer individual requirements as a matter of course cannot help coming to realize that a slothful conformity to established styles and methods is just as reprehensible as wanton rebellion against them. Conversely, it will not be long before he begins to see that it is just as stupid to be afraid of not being original as it is to be afraid of not being traditional.

Certainly, he comes to suspect that because a style of thing was satisfactory to an ancient or a medieval, it cannot, *for that very reason,* be wholly satisfactory to us today: that the architecture of a Greek temple, for instance, is no more suitable for a modern bank or stock exchange than that of a Spanish galleon is suited to an oceanliner. He will see that, although he must never fail to study the best methods of the past, he will use them rightly only when he translates them into present-day terms idiomatically and analogically, saying to himself: "To the extent to which this or that master whom I am studying had clients very much like mine (as well as materials and instruments) I may be able to learn something from his solutions—but to that extent only."

Just how unfortunate it may be for a maker to leave his objective too vaguely defined is well brought out by the following excerpt from an article entitled, "What Do You Mean—

Legibility?"*

Legibility? What do you mean—legibility?

Do you mean (1) easy to read fast, (2) easy to read at a distance, (3) easy to read in a dim light, (4) easy to read when you haven't your glasses, (5) easy on the brain, (6) not tiring to the eyes, (7) possible to grasp in big gulps of meaning, (8) pleasant to read, (9) inviting to the eye, or (10) something else?

. . . Specifically, although there is some degree of relationship between them, that which readers most like to read is not necessarily what they read most easily. "Attractive to read" and "easy to read" are not the same thing.

It all depends. Do you want to read newspapers? Or billboards? Is your reading done on the porch in the moonlight? Have your eyes been "refracted" lately? Do they tire easily? Would you like to collect beautiful works in Sanskrit? How often do your eyes blink as you run over the pages of the latest Book-of-the-Month Club selection? Do you turn away from unattractive, books however interesting in content? Legibility? What kind of legibility?

The Gutenberg Bible is one of the most *inviting* books ever printed. Do you like to look at it? Would you like to read it? Is it legible? (All right, so you're a Latin student. Do you know all the contractions? And while it's been proved that Germans read text type faster than roman—antiqua to them—can *you*?) The Gutenberg Bible,—inviting? Attractive? Readable? Or legible?

Tinker and Paterson's *How to Make Type Legible,* the work of two psychologists and in format based on their findings, is about the ugliest, least attractive, and most uninviting book ever printed. The Harpers designers must have died a thousand deaths putting it through the press. Only someone who had to know what was in it would read it. But *it can be read fast,* which is what Tinker and Paterson were after. Readable? Or legible?

The Gutenberg Bible: beautiful and inviting, but unreadable. Tinker and Paterson: easy to read, but who wants to!

What do you mean,—Legibility?

YOU.

*By Irving C. Whittemore, in *Print,* the Magazine of the Graphic Arts, Vol. 5, 1948.

CHAPTER 13

ALL PRODUCTS ANSWER NEEDS

The design of a thing is determined intimately, not only by its having to function in various ways so as to answer needs, but also by its having its own needs. If it does not bring itself into existence (if it needs to be made) neither does it operate, protect or conserve itself.

For our present discussion we may define the necessities of having to be operated in terms of the requirements of being plied or used. And these are the requirements, ordinarily, not of one action only, but of several. For a pocketknife, for instance, they would be those of: picking up, opening, setting, hefting, adjusting for a firm grasp, adopting a proper "stance" in relation to it, etc. They are the requirements, in other words; that must be met if the thing is to be operated gracefully and effectively under normal conditions, rather than clumsily or harmfully. Positively, they call on the designer to give careful study to the exigencies of preparation for use, application and manipulation. Negatively, they raise such questions as: what kind of foolproofing should the designer provide, and how much may he modify his design for the sake of this? Should he, for example, broaden or weigh the base of a drinking glass or an ink bottle, to insure against its being knocked over too easily; add a guard to a carving knife or fork to prevent the accidental cutting of the hands; put fenders on parts of a machine that are dangerous? In short, since nothing made can be expected to move itself into position, start and operate itself properly, the designer's work is not finished until he has determined carefully the requirements of these actions and modified his pattern accordingly.

Nor can he neglect the requirements that a product has for protection. It is often of great importance that a thing be so designed as to be easily painted (or repainted), plated, sheathed, stacked away and housed: guarded against the elements and collisions, as well as stupid and even malicious use. These necessities, too, may affect its design radically.

Finally, the designer has also to take into account the requirements of the actions of conservation. These differ from those of protection as having to do with inner, rather than outer, enemies: with the guarding of parts against one another, the replacing or restoring of old or damaged parts, the recharging or strengthening of them. A thing is well-designed for conservation when its hood has to be lifted comparatively seldom.

Now, it is fairly obvious that to meet justly all the claims of these various requirements, the designer will have to exercise no little ingenuity. They demand that he aim at simplicity, closeknit structure, the blending of vibrations, impulses and interactions, the use of recoil and feedback, the accessibility of parts, economy of means, frankness in exposing parts that can be left exposed and some customary standardization of replaceable elements.

Consider, for instance, how some of these kinds of requirements may affect the design of a simple instrument like a pocket-knife.

The requirement of ease of operation would, of course, determine its design basically. A knife has to be so made as to fit into the hand neatly and balance gracefully when it is put through the various actions of being picked up, opened, pressed into paper or wood, directed firmly and precisely for straight-line slitting, manipulated accurately in whittling or carving—to say nothing of its having to be closed safely and carried conveniently in an ordinary pocket. The necessity for its being operated both gracefully and effectively will dictate many things: the curve of the handle; its length; breadth; flatness; roundness; weight; its proportioning in relation to the blades and to the best stance of the operator; the breadth and flatness of the top of the blades; the nick for the fingernail to fit into, as also the number, sizes, weights and proportions of the blades.

The need for protection affects the design of a knife both in form and material. All the parts that might rust dangerously have to be covered when not in use, or made of stainless or plated metal. The handle must similarly be of some noncorrosive substance, such as silver, bone or plastic. Naturally, the whole thing should be sturdy enough to withstand being treated roughly—as by being dropped on the floor.

Ease of maintenance also affects intimately the fashioning of the knife. For it must be so designed as to be easily sharpened—the shape, thickness, resiliency and friability of the blades being suited to quick, effortless, even and frequent honing. Internal protection implies that hinges may be oiled readily. And full repair would imply that the knife could be easily taken apart and put together again, its elements realigned or replaced and the whole thing tightened or trued up. Granted that the designer may not need to take all these considerations into account, limiting himself mainly to those of honing, since users may prefer buying a new knife to repairing an old, still, he may well concern himself with them when designing more complex instruments.

Finally, all the requirements of being operated, protected and conserved must be visualized (like the main functions of the instrument) as concretely and particularly as possible.

Once a designer has visualized in detail how a product is to function, how it is to be operated, how protected and how conserved, he is more or less ready to determine which requirements of these various actions are to be most tactfully sacrificed to which. How much, for example, should efficiency of function be sacrificed to ease of operation; how much should ease of operation be sacrificed to thoroughness of protection; how much should any of these be sacrificed to exigencies of conservation? Concerning the knife, for instance, the designer might ask himself: are the functions of whittling sticks or sharpening pencils to be considered more important than those of cutting paper or cord; are the sizes of the blades to be determined, as they once were, by the sizes of vestpockets; and so on.

And even this system of compromises he may have to change if he finds that he lacks the particular material it requires.

He may not, of course—in fact, he almost never does—think as systematically as these analyses suggest; but sooner or later he is likely to "check back" on all the requirements mentioned here, if only for safety. And he may use them in training himself or others. For unless he develops the habit of taking into account the claims of all the requirements of a product, treating each as for the moment all-important, he may never be quite sure whether he has struck the right pattern of compromises—those which, technically are soundest and fairest.

Both the apprentice and the master will find it useful, moreover, to analyze their instruments in this way, to see why they *necessarily* are what they are. The apprentice will rid himself of the tendency to blame them for his mistakes. He will also see that if they were designed to meet his claims, they cannot do so perfectly unless he meets their claims. To control them, he must, in a sense, be controlled by them: he must meet their needs, if they are to meet his. And the master will benefit by making full analyses of the requirements of his instruments, since, although he never blames these for his failures, he is always trying to improve them —even when this may mean only slight adjustments to new materials and conditions. Both men, therefore, can benefit here: the one by learning how best to *con*form to the nature of his instruments, the other by learning how to *re*form them as well.

Does it handle well?

So far, we have only touched on the requirements of operation briefly; now we shall take them up in greater detail.

After a designer has hit upon the pattern, then, which insures efficiency of function, he may need to modify it more or less radically to insure ease of operation. So it is that the pattern for the bowl of a spoon, for example, even when it satisfies the requirements of the functions to be performed—the dipping, carrying, sipping, digging, measuring—may still need to be modified noticeably for the sake of the handling. The bowl may need, that is, to be shortened, flattened or rounded (or all three) so as to accord with, have the right proportions and heft for, a handle that can be manipulated naturally and gracefully by an adult. And so for every similar product: its design will depend not a little on the demands of efficient and pleasant handling—on its meeting the requirements of what is called in sport good form.

More specifically, a pattern will be determined in part by *all* the factors of the event of operation: the immediate purposes, the nature of the material acted on, the characteristics of the user. Depending on whether an instrument is to make a change that is slight or great, delicate or crude, sudden or gradual, the maker of it will be called upon to increase or decrease its weight or length, assure unusual balance or heft, shape it for quick or deliberate, steady or shifting grasp, and so on. Again, the pattern of an instrument will depend very much on the condition of what it is designed to work on: whether this is relatively uncontrolled (like a tennis ball) or controlled (like a woodblock); whether it be thick or light, homogeneous or heterogeneous; whether its variations in fiber require subtle variations in stroke or pressure.

Moreover, a designer should have full awareness of the requirements of skillful performance, both generally and particularly. He should certainly know what he is demanding of an operator. He should be aware of how old habits interfere with new, so as to take account of so-called "natural tendencies" which are often acquired or merely habitual tendencies. Certainly, he should be thoroughly familiar with the basic anatomical and organic determinants of graceful movement—especially with man's being so constituted as to have any one part of him, when set in motion or even fixed in position, affect every other part of him either directly or indirectly. (The position of a typist's feet, for instance, can have a surprisingly good or bad effect on her typing.) Moreover, a human being is so built as ordinarily to find it easiest to make large, sweeping, circular, full-bodied and rhythmical movements so that the effective part of a stroke often seems only a tangential by-product of the stance, the preparatory movement and the follow-through. Again, every user of an instrument wants to feel it as one with him, as an extension of himself: the wearer of a glove feels, not merely the glove, but the surface it touches; the oarsman, not merely the oar, but the "catch" of it in the water; the cyclist, not merely the balance of the bike, but the traction and tilt of the road. The designer must accordingly pattern his product with these various tendencies in mind, conforming it to both the limitations and the powers of the human being using it.

There may also arise the problem of adapting it to the medium in which it operates—air, oil, snow, water—so that often enough a racket, a shaft, a ski, an oar, must be shaped in accordance with what it is going *through,* as well as what it is finally working *on.*

Ideally, a designer thinks here of the needs of an individual expert. Since no two masters execute a stroke in exactly the same way, no two of them should have exactly the same instruments: each should have one that is tailored, as it were, to his own individuality. For this reason, the bats of famous ballplayers, the clubs of famous golfers, the scalpels of famous surgeons, are often made to personal specifications. To an expert, in fact, an instrument may hardly seem "his" until it has been adapted (and "broken in") to his physique, his temperament, his nervous disposition and his technical habits.

There are other reasons too why a designer should keep in mind the requirements of expert users. For one thing, unless he does so, he may never learn what can be legitimately expected of his product, and therefore what it could be made to achieve. It is only when he can be sure of what can and cannot be gotten out of it that he can design it to work as efficiently as it should in meeting requirements that are inevitable. Otherwise, he can never be sure when he is sacrificing the product to the needs of the inexpert; and unless he is on guard against the promptings of democratism, he may do this altogether too readily. The result may well be that both the potentialities of the user and of the instrument may never be fully realized.

Again, it is only when the designer knows what an instrument can legitimately be expected to do that he can be sure of the varieties of it that he should devise—as well as of the special qualities of each variety. Often enough, he will be called upon to work out at least two general types of instrument: those needed to gain only a crude effect with comparatively little skill; and those needed to gain a fine effect with unusual skill. The somewhat surprising consequence may well be that the instrument designed for the inexpert will prove complex and heavy, while that designed for the expert will prove simple and light—this latter usually being a member of a set, each member of which is called upon to perform a relatively small, but vital and delicate operation. The ordinary whittler, let us say, will be content with a pocketknife containing two or three blades; whereas the skilled carver will be content with nothing less than a family of knives and gouges. Generally, in short, the greater the skill, the simpler and more responsive the instruments. Clearly, then, it is only the designer with an exact appreciation of the normal grades of skill who can turn out instruments in the proper variety, the proper complexity and the proper heft and sturdiness.

All of which implies that to design a thing well, one should, ideally, be an expert user of it. The man who knows through personal experience the needs of both tyro and master—who has done some coaching, perhaps, of both—is the one best able to *feel,* as well as conceive what is most efficient because most manageable. So it is that Howard Hill, as a master archer, has learned to make bows and arrows, and that great skiers, like Alf Engen, Thor Groswald and Hannes Schneider, have been among the foremost designers of skis and skiing equipment. What is true of them, indeed, should be, as far as possible, true of all other designers—even if this requirement means that before a man works out the final blueprints for a garbage truck, he should ideally have worked, for at least four or five days of each of the four seasons, as a garbage collector.

All these considerations should help make clear how the pattern of an instrument—and it should not be forgotten that most things are made to be instruments of one sort or another—depends not a little on the conditions of its operation. Its length, for example, will depend very much on how near or how far from it (and from the material he is working on) the operator must stand to ply it tactfully and guide it accurately, since he must enjoy freedom of stance, stroke and follow-through. Similarly, the weight of shaft and head will depend largely on the strength of the impact and the pressure to be exerted; the shape, on the kind and form of the material on which it is to work, as well as on the medium through or against which it is to do so; the specifications of the grip (its shape, balance, diameter, smoothness, roughness), on the strength, size, flexibility, sweatiness, angle and manner of grasp of typical users. And the overall pattern will result from the maker's striking a proper compromise between these various claims—fairly, reciprocally, coalescently.

Is it well protected?

Like the requirement of ease of operation, that of protection can also prove demanding. It, too, may cause a maker to modify an otherwise satisfactory design radically. This requirement does not, to be sure, lay claim to as much consideration as other requirements; but it is never to be neglected. It naturally calls for our attention at this point since it is closely related to the requirement of ease of operation; for the operator, if he is to be at ease, must feel, not only that he is protected against the instrument, but also that it will be continuously available in a sound state through having been protected against both accidental abuse and environmental assault.

Since the need for protection (as against the need for conservation) means the need for being taken care of against external, rather than internal, enemies, the designer is here concerned with four types of safeguarding: that afforded by the thing itself; by a sheath or covering; by artificial environment; and by supervisers.

To modify his design in accordance with these possibilities, the designer must take into account many factors, such as: the number and kind of "enemies" his product will be threatened by in being made, stage by stage; in being set up; in being plied or used; in being taken down; in being stored away. What shocks will it have to bear, what temperatures (what expansion or contraction, as a whole and part by part); what sunlight (fading, melting); what magnetizing, corroding, staining, warping, adulterating, contaminating, "stenchifying," souring, rotting, under foreseeable conditions of making, using and abusing?

In attempting to answer general questions of this kind, a designer naturally encounters many special questions to which the answers are not always easy to find. Does the painting, repainting or later cleansing of the thing suggest simplifying the shape—so as to eliminate, for instance, niches, chasing, fritillaries and other such inaccessible dirt pockets? May not a covering be dispensed with, since it must be taken off and fixed back on easily and securely, and so demand the enlargement of the general structure or the addition of parts for screws or clamps? Must it not be designed to aid the knowing and to guide the ignorant user: indicating by its shape the kind of element it covers and (as with the rear covering of some cameras, for instance) blocking its being put back on in any but the right way? Does the cover make it unnecessarily difficult to get at the mechanism underneath it? If the protective agent is a tight-fitting one (a lamination, for instance, or a varnish on a painted canvas) the question may arise: will it have the same rate of expansion or contraction as what it covers? under all conditions? or what can be done to prevent undue conflict here? Again, to what extent must the product adapt itself to the conditions of being capped (like a fountainpen), cased (like cigarettes), bottled so as to be free of sunlight (like some pills) or given, as it were, a cold pack (like water-cooled engines)? How can it be protected against itself, through being so designed as to govern or shut itself off or resist mishandling? And if a supervisor proves inevitably necessary, how much can the thing be simplified in reliance on his attentive and expert care, with the elimination of special fenders or cumbersome foolproofing?

In dealing with this requirement of protection, as in dealing with other basic requirements, the designer will do well to concentrate on it first as if it were independent of them and, for the time being, all-important. Then he is likely to be just to its claims as he goes on to see how they are covariantly determined by the other claims—of functioning, operation and conservation.

Naturally, he must not favor the claims of protection unduly and fall into the fallacy of what might be called antimacassarism, and this is sometimes manifested in the design of bicycles, for instance, or automobiles. A bicycle should not have a single element of safeguard that is not necessary for the protection of it and its rider against rust, dust or slush. And much the same can be said of automobiles, as the popularity of compacts and small European cars suggests.

One is reminded here of the story about Thoreau and the chickens of Miss Emerson, daughter of Ralph Waldo. To assure her that their feet would not get too cold in winter, Thoreau made bootees for them. With these on, they could not scratch for their food and they died. However, apocryphal, it is a good parable of the dangers of technical momism.

Is it easy to maintain?

The need for conservation means, of course, the need for preserving a thing against internal exhaustion, deficiencies or self-impairment. It raises much the same kind of problems as does the need for protection—the preserving of a thing against external enemies. For the parts of a thing may be regarded as separable, whole units, each in need of protection individually—especially against the surrounding or neighboring parts: each, that is, may need to resist being pushed or pulled, rubbed, strained, shaken, jolted, scorched, worn or corroded.

The designer must therefore be alert to such dangers and plan how best to forestall or cope with them throughout the working life of his product. He must make sure that it is not only durable and well-integrated, but also easy to "shake down," break in, govern, adjust, lubricate, nourish, restore, repair or remake.

To insure durability, he is likely, of course, to think first of density, hardness, solidity; therefore of heaviness and largeness. But he will not cherish these latter qualities simply for themselves. What he mainly aims at is making each part duly resistant and stable. And this may well mean making it supple and resilient —able to yield as required without breaking. To be strong, a thing need not be in any sense gross; on the contrary, it is likely to be refined, but all of a piece, homogeneous, with its sturdiness resulting from its structural pattern as much as from its stuff. As is proved by the suspension bridge, the Gothic cathedral, the buildings of Fuller and Nervi, to say nothing of that astonishingly durable, yet mainly liquid, structure, the human body, the strength of a thing may have little to do with its mere thickness. Nor, for that matter, does strength imply mere largeness, especially if a thing is to be of any height: the higher and bigger the wall, the greater the need for buttressing. A suspension bridge, with its relative thinness of material, can be quite as strong as a pyramid.

Not that the designer calculates parsimoniously. On the contrary, he keeps in mind the requirements of a margin of safety and he takes carefully into account both the general, "lifetime" wear and tear or shrinkage and the special jogging that a product is to receive while being broken in or tuned up. He asks himself first such questions as: How small or thin can this thing be made without loss of efficiency? How supple, pliable and resistant can it be made through the use of tensible strength and interlocking stress patterns? It is only when he has answered questions like these that he will concern himself with massiveness.

The requirement that a product be well-integrated is much the same as that which we have just been considering; what is true of constituents or elements individually is also true of combinations of them. These larger units should also be light, flexible, coalescent, homogeneous. Materially, they should be attuned to one another; formally, they should interact reciprocally, like the sections of a finger. The designer must therefore consider how few parts this or that sectional unit must have, how small they should be, how complementary or compensatory—all without jeopardizing the sturdiness of the unit as a whole or its resiliency.

The conservation that is assured through the harmonious cooperation of parts is not always something that a designer may expect to attain at once. More often than not it has to be achieved. The designer must frequently plan to have a thing run *down* into smooth action, so that it may thereafter be kept *up* easily—prevented, if you will, from running down too far. He may, therefore, at the outset, overmake it: make it tougher and stiffer at the moment when it is assembled than the casual observer might think necessary. Only much using and testing, often enough, may enable a maker to determine, therefore, just how sturdy each part or section must be made. If he is to design well, he must always keep in mind the possibility that almost everything (from penpoint on up) may need to be carefully broken in.

Further, there is tonal or vibratory unity to be taken into account here; obviously, no instrument should shake or jog itself apart. On the contrary, it should be provided when necessary with shock absorbers and so constructed as to make easy the adjusting of one part to another. The designer is under the obligation to devise suitable ways for "cushioning the shock" with everything from buffers to escapements and systems of recoil and feedback. At the same time he must be heedful of what might be called the claims of proportionate harmony, making certain that each part be given the size, tightness and flexibility essential to cooperation, especially when they will wear down at different rates. For these, as well as many other reasons, he will once again be induced to keep his product simple, homogeneous and light in all its principal elements, if only to offset the deteriorative complexity it acquires through its secondary elements. These latter too have their rights; and the good designer learns to treat these as justly as he would, let us say, the elements of a whip—through perhaps

the norm here should be not the whip but a more organic one—
the snake.

Even in things perfectly designed, however, there is often some
unavoidable friction; and for that reason the designer may need to
think also of the requirements of lubrication. A thing may need to
be chemically treated either internally or externally; fed as leather
is fed; imbued protectively, as wood is by creosote; ventilated;
housed with oil or grease, which itself must be drawn off and
replaced or purified. All of which requirements enforce the claims
of simplicity, because each such minor need compromises the
design of the major elements or of the thing as a whole.

Finally, in addition to the requirements of preventive, there are
those of redemptive conservation. These are reducible to three
kinds: reconditioning, restoring and remaking.

The designer has obviously to keep in mind the need which a
user may have to get at the inner parts of a product, so as to free
them of rust, dirt, grime or rubble; to drain off used up oil; to re-
inforce, loosen or tighten, reconnect, reorient, and so on. A user
will therefore welcome coverings which, while they protect, also
indicate, by their transparency or configuration, what kind of
parts lie beneath them.

Like other requirements, ease of restoration also implies that
the general design of the product be as simple as possible, with
the fewest number of elements to restore. And, obviously, these
should themselves be as simple as possible. Ideally, moreover,
they should be capable of being readily modified to suit the product, not as it was when it was first made, but as it is at the
moment of being restored: they may need to be ground down or
even slightly remade themselves at this moment, in tactful adjustment to the general wear and tear, shrinkage or expansion of
other parts about them.

Certainly, the requirement of restoration is not to be regarded
lightly. It raises such questions as: Will it really cost more to
repair this product than to make a new one? Should we ignore
this possibility simply for the sake of profit-making? More specifically, will the requirements of repair, as they affect the choice of
material and form, jeopardize too much the requirements of func-

tion? Can the thing be best used only once and then thrown away? How skillful in keeping it in condition can one expect the user to be? At what point does it become false economy to try to repair it? Are any units of it worth trying to save?

Naturally, in answering the claims of conservation, the designer has to make sure that he is not scanting those of operation and protection, as well as ignoring the limitations of making. Against the questions raised by the requirements of integration, durability, ease of adjustment, of governance, of lubrication, of reconditioning and the rest, he must set such questions as: How costly, in terms of material, time, effort, skill and money, will this thing be if made easy to conserve? How light must it be to be operated gracefully and effectively? How small can it be, as a whole and in each of its systems of parts, if it is to have the desired heft, pressure, flexibility? Is it essential that the operator have the sense of projection through this thing to the material on which it operates. Must it therefore have the "ring" of homogeneity, all its parts blending in a chordlike unity—or can this quality be sacrificed somewhat to sturdiness? In short, the designer must balance carefully the answers he gives to the demands of conservation with those he gives to the demands of operation, so as to steer between unwieldliness on the one hand and fragility on the other.

The main admonition he has to keep in mind is that which has come down to us in countless proverbs: An ounce of prevention is worth a pound of cure. A stitch in time saves nine. For lack of a nail, the horse was lost. . . . Ideally, of course, a thing should be so cautiously and circumspectly made, so well and carefully wrought in the first place that it can be kept in condition with little care—and so that whatever care it does need can be given it readily. It is vitally necessary to heed these requirements since a weak or disjointed element strains or disrupts all the other elements, often starting a kind of chain reaction of disintegration, a progressive deterioration. When one part has worked loose, it may not only fail to contribute its share of work, but also prevent other parts from contributing their share—obstructing, jolting or sundering them. The defective cog in the mechanism can be far worse than the rotten apple in the barrel.

'Must I be a functionalist?'

We have explored thus far the implications of what might be called designing with a purpose. We have noted particularly how this requires conceiving of a purpose as dynamic, rather than static; as possibly multifold; as playing a concrete, rather than a general, role; as satisfying needs; and as also determined or limited by the needs of the thing made.

If it be asked, however, whether the theory presented here is functionalism, the answer will have to be, "yes and no." For the present theory, while incorporating (the author hopes) what is good in functionalism, differs from it radically in several ways.

Certainly, as functionalism is ordinarily set forth, it seems to be hardly more than a set of half-truths, or of whole truths wrongly emphasized. To many it suggests that purpose is all-important; that it is very strictly determined by a combination of complex economic and simple aesthetic needs which can be met by simplicity of design, neatness and brightness. It suggests also that designs are also strictly governed by requirements of convenience as this is understood by sophisticates leading suburban lives; that designs are normally limited by the kinds of materials and elements that can be turned out by mass-production methods; that, within these limitations, the buyer is not only king, he is absolute monarch.

Let us therefore take a close look at these notions.

Purpose is, of course, a primary determinant—but not one with which a designer should be obsessed. Even among the dynamic factors alone, there are three other kinds that determine the pattern of a thing intimately. They are, as we have seen, those of operating, protecting and conserving. Purpose in the usual sense, therefore, is only first among equals; it is as limited by other factors—or almost as limited by them—as they are by it.

Again, purpose is one thing and what is commonly *called* function is something else; the two are not interchangeable. When a thing is spoken of as functional, what most often is meant is that it is adequate for answering mainly three sets of needs—those of the body, the senses and the imagination; not of the will, the intellect and the conscience. The result is that too often the functionalist, either as maker or user of things, is in danger of overlooking the demands of humaneness, custom and religion, blithely sacrificing their claims to the economic and aesthetic requirements laid down by the sophisticated. Frequently, a so-called functional house, for instance "works" better for those who have little use for a really functional home: it serves better as a setting for those who wish to hold cocktail parties than for those who wish to pray, meditate, study, work, dine, raise a family, nurse the sick, rest, hold meetings, die in it. It is better suited, in other words, to those who wish to live decoratively than to those who wish to live, if not too tidily, at least somewhat heroically. And a similar criticism often holds for other kinds of things called functional.

Again, the functionalist's tendency to concentrate on all forms of convenience may prove no less unfortunate. Obviously, to be well-designed, a thing must be convenient—but not primarily for those who want a slothful and specious way of life. A "machine for living" is all to the good provided that it fosters the client's living profoundly as well as graciously.

Certainly, an intense preoccupation with the satisfying of *all* possible wants can prove highly undesirable. In a civilization in which people have learned to hunger for a wide range of conveniences, almost everyone comes to prefer the shoddy answering of many wants to the genuine answering of basic needs. And to satisfy such a preference would hardly seem to be truly functional.

In short, what may be, and often is, called "modern functional design" often consists in a jugglery (somewhat analogous to the Renaissance jugglery of Greco-Roman elements) of mass-produced elements which are the products of commercialism, all in satisfaction of a high level of mass gluttony. Elements easily produced and inexpensive are thrown into a shipshape pattern which satisfies the aesthetic sensibilities of the semisophisticate, enabling him to feel quietly superior to the Mid-Victorians. True functionalism is, as we have seen, something else again.

CHAPTER 14

ON THE RELATIONS
OF CLIENT AND MAKER

As experience shows, many a product turns out to be something that is not quite what the client expected. When this happens, the client is liable to blame the maker, and the maker the client, for not respecting his rights. It is therefore important for us to consider what these sets of rights are: what the maker may properly expect of the client; and what the client may properly expect of the maker.

In all fairness, the maker has a right to expect that:

—The client will concern himself principally with *specifying* his *needs*. He has little or no right to specify the exact pattern or nature of the thing which is to meet these needs—although, of course, he may venture reasonable suggestions. He can be expected, for instance, to describe fully what he needs in a home—to what uses he intends to put it, and what way of life he hopes it will foster—but he has no right to begin by demanding something "Dutch Colonial" or "like the latest ranch house."

—The client will specify his needs *exactly* and *fully*. In building a house, for instance, he may not simply require, vaguely, that there be a large dining room; he must enable his architect to visualize clearly the particular kinds of dining that are to go on there, and determine the relationship of these to the rest of the client's activities and his way of life.

—The needs which the client states must be both *possible* and *legitimate* for the maker to meet. A client cannot ask him to produce something to accomplish absurd, contradictory or miraculous effects. Nor can the client ask to be pandered to: he has no right to demand that a maker satisfy needs that are in fact mere, idle wants. A customer is no more a king over a cabinetmaker, for instance, than a patient is king over a doctor. An architect cannot be asked to plan a room that will serve equally well for a dining room, a study, a drawing room and a bedroom. Nor should he be called on to design a grandiose structure, mostly facade, simply because his clients wish to appear at least as wealthy and fashionable as their neighbors.

—The conditions of time and money will be stated exactly by the client. He must also make clear his willingness to accept such modifications of the plans as contingencies of execution may require; if, as the designing proceeds, he finds he is expecting too much too soon, he should welcome this information and accept the changes that it calls for willingly.

—The client is not to judge the work of a maker by any other criterion primarily than its capability to answer the needs which both of them agreed should be answered. Naturally, he may ask other expert makers about the goodness (though not necessarily about the kind) of its material and workmanship; but he has no right to judge it by its degree of conformity to past or conventional patterns or to the client's purely personal likes or prejudices, especially before he has lived with the product and tested it. He has no right to object, for example, if his architect turns out something stylistically unexpected—something which, strictly, is neither Romanesque nor Gothic, neither Beaux Arts nor Bauhaus —provided it answers his needs as these could not be answered otherwise. If a building or, for that matter, any other work of skill, is soundly conceived, if it fits the requirements of an acceptable way of life for the client, if it is pleasingly organic, sturdy, duly symbolic and humanly livable, as well as thoroughly functional, then it is what it should be, whether it looks like anything previously admired or not.

The client, on the other hand, has a right to expect that:

—The maker will confer with him and advise him, while yet leaving to him the final statement of needs. Naturally, the maker may help a client arrive at a clear, exact and thorough grasp of these needs; but it is not for him, *on his own,* to say which needs are to be answered and which not—or even which are most important. Obviously, a maker cannot be expected to pander or go against his artistic conscience; but neither must he try to do his client's thinking for him. An architect has no right, for instance, to tell a client that he should not have a toy theater built into his house if the client is interested in the theater. All he can do is make the client see how distorting or wasteful such a room may be if it is not really going to be used, and help him decide if he really will use it; how often and for what kinds of performances.

—The maker is to use ingenuity in giving *fresh, uniquely* appropriate answers to the client's needs, having familiarized himself with these thoroughly and sympathetically. As no one client is exactly like any other, so, ideally, no product should be exactly like any other: unique needs call for unique answers, and the maker can be required to arrive at these answers through careful study and ingenious *inventing.*

—The maker will be required to hold himself to the use of the best material, the best instruments and the best methods available for doing the work satisfactorily and justly (that is, with primary justice to his client and ultimate justice to himself and his co-workers), profit being for him more of a necessary evil than a main objective.

—The maker can be expected, at least as a master, to know his craft exceptionally well; that is, to know how to strike wise compromises between what the client should have ideally and what the available time and money will permit him to have really.

—The maker is, of course, not to promise the impossible; nor is he to pander or turn out routine products that are shoddy—things that look right, but do not do what they properly should do.

Naturally, there will be all kinds of give and take between maker and client, and these rules are not given here as constraining or binding. They are merely basic for the *modus vivendi* of the two men.

What happens when even one or two of them are ignored is well brought out by the following passage from a novel by James A. Michener:

At the seventh washed-out bridge we had to ford a river much deeper than we had anticipated and got stuck in the middle with our bottoms wet and our engine useless, waiting till a truck came along to haul us out. We had nothing to do but study the bridge overhead, and it was perhaps the loveliest of all; its arch was graceful, its turrets solid, its brickwork neat, and its impression substantial.

"Beautiful bridge," I admitted grudgingly. "Who built it?"

"A German. One of the worst tragedies that ever hit our nation."

. . . "What happened with these bridges, Nur?"

He replied in careful Pashto. "A disaster. We were taking our first step out of the Dark Ages and the Germans said, 'It's stupid to have your two major cities unconnected by a road.' They arranged a big loan and gave us experts who surveyed the road and showed how it could be built. When the king saw the survey, very neatly drawn with little pictures, he approved and said, 'We're a modern country now. We must have a modern road.' Then he asked who would build the bridges, and the Germans lent us a learned professor-architect that had built many bridges, and the work started."

Nur pointed up at the bridge. "He was a brilliant man who demanded the best. Look at that brickwork. You don't find much of that in Afghanistan. It was his idea to mark each bridge with distinctive turrets and ornamentation, for he told us, 'A bridge is more than a bridge. It's a symbol connecting past and present.' He said that towers and intricate brickwork were part of the Afghan soul. In a famous speech he gave in Kabul he said that he had taken the idea of towers from the family forts that mark Afghanistan."

"I don't see the relationship," I remarked, but Nur pointed down the river toward a private fort and then I knew what the professor-architect had been after.

"He built some twenty bridges," Nur explained as we sat in the cold river— and I mean in the river, for the jeep kept settling—"and all the time he was working, a handful of Afghans like Shah Khan and my father kept warning him, 'Doctor, that bridge is fine for a well-controlled European river, but has anyone told you about our Afghan rivers in the spring?' He replied angrily that he had built bridges over some of the finest rivers in Europe . . . much greater rivers, he assured us, than these trivial desert streams."

Nur looked sadly at the bridge and said in English, "You understand, of course, that this all happened before I was born." Then he explained in Pashto, "But I remember my father telling us later, "We went to the government and warned them, 'Those German bridges will not stand up against our rivers in the spring.' " They were told, 'You think you are smart enough to tell a German how to do his job? A man who has built bridges all over Europe?' My father replied that he had never seen a European river and it looked to him as if the German had never seen an Afghan river, and there the matter was left."

The jeep settled deeper and Nur said in English, "Shah Khan is a learned man and a brave one. In those days he was without the dignity of his present position, but he refused to drop the matter. He told the Germans—and here Nur Muhammad reverted to Pashto—'These bridges are far more important to us than they are to you. They're our first contact with the western world. If they succeed, we who want to modernize this nation will succeed. If they fail, dreadful consequences may follow. Now please, Professor-Architect, listen when I tell you that sometimes in the spring what you call our trivial desert streams roar out of the mountains two miles wide. They move boulders as big as houses. They destroy everything not perched on a hill. And the next day they're little streams again. Professor, build us big broad bridges and leave off the pretty towers.'

"The German professor was furious that Shah Khan would dare speak to him directly. He insisted that a meeting of the government be convened, at which he made an impassioned speech. 'I want to tell you that I have sunk my pillars to bedrock. I have built as no bridges in Afghanistan have ever been built before. When the floods that Shah Khan speaks of meet my bridges, not one bridge will fall down.' I must say that Shah Khan was a fighter. He replied, 'Professor-Architect, you're entirely right. The bridges will not fall down. Of that I am convinced. But the rivers of Afghanistan, like the people of Afghanistan, never attack the enemy head-on. Your stout bridges are like the British army. Their soldiers were ten times better than ours . . . better fed . . . better armed. But we didn't march up to the British in double file so they could shoot us down. In a thousand tricky ways we surrounded them. They protested, "This is no decent way to fight,' and we destroyed them. Our rivers will destroy your bridges, Professor-Architect, because they're European bridges and they're not prepared to fight Afghan rivers. What we want, Professor-Architect, are tricky Afghan bridges.'

"The German replied, 'A bridge is a bridge,' and Shah Khan shouted, 'Not in Afghanistan.' The quarrel was taken to the king himself, and he ordered Khan to shut up. The German ambassador explained everything by pointing out that Shah Khan had been educated in France and was thus emotionally unstable.

"So the bridges were built, and the next year there were no spring floods. For eighteen months we enjoyed a wonderful road between Kabul and Kandahar, and Afghanistan was spurting to catch up with the world. In that second winter there was a great snowfall in the mountains followed by an unusually warm spring, which sent towering floods down the gullies, moving boulders as big as houses. When these floods struck the bridges, the German was proved right. His stone pillars stood fast, as he had predicted. The bridges were as strong as he said. But they were so narrow in span that our rivers simply went around them. All the approaches were gouged out and the bridges stood isolated."

"Why not rebuild the approaches?" I asked.

"We did," Nur replied. "Another flood took them out. So we rebuilt again. Another flood. My father calculated that to keep the bridges operating would require a hundred thousand men working around the year. So after the third flood the government said, 'Let them go. Who needs bridges?' And the dream road that was to have bound our nation together remained an aching monument to the folly of man."

"What happened to the professor?" I asked.

"After the first flood he travelled from Kabul to Kandahar, refusing to believe what he saw. 'I've built a hundred bridges over some of the greatest rivers in Europe,' he shouted. He stood in the middle of one little stream and wailed, 'How could this little puddle wash out a bridge?' He refused, even then, to see the boulders which that little puddle had moved down from the mountain."

"Did he leave the country?"

"No, he went back to Kabul and boasted to everyone who would listen that not a single one of his pillars had been destroyed. He made himself what the English call 'quite a bore.' He insisted upon explaining about bridges. The German embassy finally called him in, and what they said we never found out, but that night he went to his room and blew his brains out."

Nur shook his head sadly, still waiting for a truck to appear. "You can't imagine the tragedy those bridges became. Whenever the government wanted to do some new thing the mullahs and the mountain chiefs would laugh: 'Remember the German bridges!' You're an American and you may not like Germans since you fought them twice, but in Afghanistan they were wonderful people. Most of what we have that's good came from the Germans, but after the bridges even they were held in suspicion. Their effectiveness was chopped in half. Those damned bridges!"*

---

*Caravans, by James A. Michener (Random House, N.Y. 1963).

CHAPTER 15

ALL PRODUCTS SHOULD BE COSMETICALLY SOUND

Everything made for man is, as we have seen, meant to fit into a human act. But a human act is a formal one: it has a certain pattern which has been rationally determined and spiritually felt as right; otherwise, it will be, as we say, indecorous or inhumane. Properly executed, it has a kind of splendor of proportion and fittingness (decency) as has whatever plays a part in it. Especially does all this hold good of anything that figures in social activity.

In other words, everything made should be cosmetically sound. Not that it should be bedaubed or bedizened to make it "look pretty." On the contrary, a true cosmetic never calls attention to itself nor tries to deceive, its sole purpose being to enable something to function more humanly than it might otherwise. A house, a garment, a hair do, a chair—all should enable the persons who use them to live not only efficiently, but also in accord with their best selves, with their nature as human beings. As the derivation of the word *cosmetic* implies, it is meant to enhance the splendid orderliness of the action performed; it has nothing to do primarily with allurement or false glamor.

It does not, therefore, in any way cover up, substitute for or distract from the essential beauty of that which it, as it were, equips.

Its first requirement, in fact, is the one suggested by the famous remark of Beau Brummel: "The best dressed man is the least conspicuous." For this remark does not mean that when we have met the best dressed man in a group, we walk away with no memory of him; it means that we remember him as a person, not as a clothes horse: his style has been expressive of his personality, not of his tailor's virtuosity.

The first set of requirements which a designer has to meet are, clearly, those that we have been considering up to now. Part of the function of everything is to play a role; in the sense of making the right kind of appearance in the actions in which it figures, it must be given the pattern, the proportions, the coloring, necessary for fulfilling this requirement as well. The designer has therefore to be mindful of making his product both pleasantly appropriate and inconspicuous.

For a concrete example, let us consider the designing of a hair-do.

In this process, a coiffeur will first aim at achieving a certain negative inconspicuousness; he will try to make sure that the client's head will not strike the observer as abnormal in its proportions, or as in conflict with her environment. As the jargon has it, he will try to normalize and socialize the coiffure.

For, in profile, the human head normally divides into three sections, bounded by lines almost equidistant from one another: one extending from the top of the head to the eyebrows; another, from the eyebrows to just below the nose; and the third, from just below the nose to the bottom of the chin. If, because of size or shape, any of these sections, any feature of them, or anything worn on them (eyeglasses, earrings) calls undue attention to itself, then, of course, the coiffeur masses and accentuates the hair in such a way as to deemphasize it and assure an impression of normal proportions. Sweeping the hair too high off the forehead, in obedience to the dictates of passing fashion, may simply dwarf a nose already too small (especially if it is competing with glasses), just as lowering the hairline too much may exaggerate the heaviness of a big chin and jeopardize what could be the delicate effect of small, high, shell-like ears. To avoid such mistakes is not to be dishonest; it is only to be fair to the good qualities of the client and charitable to those who have to look at her, especially her husband and her family. It is, in fact, to keep her pleasantly undistracting.

A hairdresser can also assure a fitting inconspicuousness by making the hairdo accord with the main environments in which it is to be worn. Obviously, a stenographer should not dress like an actress; in any ordinary business office she will merely look silly. Her hairdresser should therefore see to it that her coiffure "rhymes" properly with the kind of clothing she normally wears at work and at home. Ideally, of course, he should make it adaptable to occasions of different degrees of formality, enabling the client to go from office to theater and back again without too much adjustment.

While avoiding conspicuousness, however, the hairdresser assures positive enhancement; this, by exercising care in choosing the pattern of lines and light modulations that will emphasize the characteristics of the client's personality which might otherwise go unappreciated; it is legitimate for him to try, though not deceptively, to bring out her essential strong points. The eye of the observer is to be conducted, insensibly, toward the naturally good features and kept from dwelling on the less pleasant, without, however, any misleading emphasis. If the client's natural expression is quite serious, and yet she is endowed with a lively sense of humor, the hairdo can properly be given a subtle gaiety of line to suggest this fact. To put this in precise and accurate terms: the physiognomy can be given a coiffure that assures a truly expressive countenance: even at rest, it will then still be eloquent of the client's essential personality. There should be no attempt, of course, to make the design tell a lie: it should only enhance the truth of what is really there. The person with a witty hairdo but with no great wit is worse off than one with a commonplace hairdo and great wit: the one will seem absurdly dry; the other, drily amusing.

Nor does bringing out the strong points mean emphasizing those which make a person romantically attractive; it simply means accentuating the features and the expression that tell what a person essentially is. In the long run, the second has much the same force as the first is meant to have, anyway, since it is with her reality that the right man for a woman will fall in love, just as it is with mere appearance that the wrong man will become infatuated. And there is no good reason why a woman should want to make herself romantically attractive to every male who happens to pass her on the sidewalk. There is nothing more pathetic, in fact, than the woman whose only concept of "making herself beautiful" is that of making herself as "attractive," not to say seductive, as a Parisian *cocotte* or a Hollywood courtesan—especially when this means vainly trying to appear several years younger and more "sophisticated" than she will ever be. And no true coiffeur would lend himself to this sort of enhancement.

For, however subconsciously, he would be aware of four basic aesthetic requirements: those of appropriateness, unity, variety and vividness. A good hairdo will be *appropriate* in all the senses we have been considering; it will have the *unity* of balance and symmetry, as well as of blend with the whole countenance and the ensemble; it will have the *variety* of line, color, chiaroscuro, indicative emphases; and it will have the vividness of color, sheen, fluidity, liveliness, fluffiness, thickness and aura.

Naturally, the possibilities will depend on the health of the hair, its variable thinness, stiffness, refractoriness—in short, on the condition of the material on which the coiffeur has to work. They will also depend on the potentialities of the instruments that must be used, as well as on the coiffeur's imaginativeness and dexterity. But they must be at least hoped for at the outset and settled for afterward.

And what has been said here of hairdos applies, *mutatis mutandis,* to all other products that cannot but be frequently observed.

It may be asked whether, in modifying his design to make the product look humanly acceptable, the designer will not inevitable be sacrificing one set of requirements (the objective) to another (the subjective). So put, however, this question proves misleading. First of all, it gives the impression that the meeting of objective requirements does not also entail the sacrificing of one set of them to another; and this kind of sacrificing is, as we have seen, inevitable. Then, too, because the kind of compromise that is usually struck between the claims of functionally determined inner structure and those of appearance is usually commercialistic and meretricious, the assumption may be that any favoring of the claims of appearance unavoidably entails a betrayal of those of inner structure. The chicanery of disguising a jerry-built shack with a glamorous facade should not blind us, however, to the possibility that the requirements of beauty of appearance more often than not correspond quite closely with those of beauty of construction—far less of a compromise being usually required than might be expected.

One of the time-honored ways of assuring beauty of appearance, for instance, is that of dividing spaces, not into exactly equal units, but into units the smaller of which is to the larger as the larger is to the whole: the rule of the golden section. These are proportions in which the mind and the eye naturally take delight. That there is no reason for holding them to be purely subjective in any derogatory sense, however, that they are not merely what the knowing powers demand, is shown by the way in which they recur, over and over again, throughout the human body and variously, in terms of the Fibonacci thereom, through the structures of different species of trees. And even when the basic structure of an object inevitably requires that it fall into two exactly equal divisions, the designer can correct the resulting unpleasantness by his choice of colors in the paint he uses for protection —applying, let us say, a relatively bright color for the base and a pale color for the top, thereby achieving something the visual *effect* of a golden section.

It must be remembered here, of course, that what the designer does in making such modifications is not plaster on some beauty, sugar-coating the pill of ugliness with, so to speak, a palatable prettiness. He merely tries to bring out its intrinsic beauty and to *complete* the product by making it humanly acceptable. A thing made for human beings is obviously not fully itself until normal human beings find it suited to their human nature. If it is so bare as to satisfy only those who have no sensitivity to human style, or if it satisfies only those who have a taste for the ornate, it is simply, in the full sense of the term, unsightly.

The proper form

If we are to deal successfully with the factor of form—if we are to meet its claims justly in making something—most of us, it would seem, need first to rid ourselves of the habit of focusing on it both too narrowly and too statically. We must learn to think of it, in fact, somewhat more subtly than we do ordinarily. And to this end we may well begin by jogging ourselves with a few basic questions about it such as those that are raised in the following socratically arranged cases:

—A kindergarten teacher hands a child an orange and asks what the form of it is. When the child says, "round," the teacher accepts this answer as for the moment satisfactory. But she realizes that, at some time or other, she will have to show how inadequate it is. Why will she have to do so—is it simply because an orange is never exactly round?

—A geometry teacher, using a large compass with white chalk, draws a circle on the blackboard, and then, without changing the compass in any way otherwise, he substitutes a piece of red chalk for the white and draws another circle. Would he be right if he then said that, despite their difference in color, these two figures were obviously the same in form? Or would his remark be, ultimately at least, just as inadequate as was the answer of the child in the first case?

—Another geometry teacher, a rheumatic one this time, draws a three-sided figure, the lines of which are all slightly wavy, and asks what the form of this is, expecting to be told that it is isosceles. Instead, a facetious student answers that it is three wavy lines that join. The teacher then replies indignantly: "Now, don't try to be funny! You know as well as I do that the lines on the board are not what I am referring to: they are only the form of the *picture* of what we are studying." And to bring home his point, he draws another isosceles triangle, using a ruler, which is larger than the first and suggests that he can use either of these for dealing with the form of an isosceles triangle—for demonstrating its nature. "Therefore," he concludes, "it is obvious that we cannot be studying the forms that we have here on the board in chalk; we are studying the form which they both merely represent." Is he right? Can we speak of the form of a triangle that is not the same thing as the form of the image of a triangle?

—A Western scientist, in trying to describe geometry to a primitive tribal king, says that it has to do with the forms of things: the round (the circle); the four-pointed (the square); etc. The king, following his natural interest, asks which of these is the strongest. He is told that, for most structural purposes, the triangle is. Then he asks, knowing that the scientist is from a democracy: "And do you think, then, that a democracy is the most triangular form of government?" If the scientist were to answer that form did not strictly apply to a government, but only to physical things, would he be right? Can we say, then, that there really is such a thing as a form of government—even if we can say that there is such a thing as a form of a triangle distinct from the form of its physical picture?

—A theatergoer, on his way home from a musical comedy, finds himself whistling the hit tune without a false note. Can we say that he has captured the form of it exactly?

Whatever else such examples and questions should do, they should stimulate us to see, once and for all, how unfortunate it is to narrow the term *form* down to either shape or figure. They should help us, positively, to discern how inclusive this term is, aiding us to see that the best way of conceiving of it is as referring to everything that is other than its purpose, material or instrumental source. Whether a thing be physical or not, its form includes its whole system of qualities, the whole complex of properties peculiar to it. In this broad philosophic sense, which is the one least crippling for the maker, the form of an orange, for instance, consists in its sour-sweetness, its color, its size, its structural pattern, etc., as well as its shape; just as the form of the red circle on the blackboard differs from that of the white by its color —though the form of the geometric circle to which they both refer is the same: that of a pure circle in pure space. Moreover, a given type of government can have quite as complex a system of properties—every bit as much form—as, let us say, a battleship. And we can hardly say that the man whistling the hit tune has captured the form of it since notes made by pursed lips can hardly have the same system of qualities (volume, timbre, etc.) as those made by a singer accompanied by an orchestra. Tempo, pitch, melody line—the figure of the tune—he can reproduce more or less accurately; but he can no more reproduce its full form than he can whistle a sextette.

Viewed as a maker should accustom himself to viewing it, form is comprehensive in another way as well. It is never merely a generic form he is concerned with, nor merely a specific, nor merely an individual one: it is all three. A good landscape garden, for instance, cannot ever be simply a garden in general; or even simply a special kind of garden (Japanese, French formal, English romantic); it has also to be an individual garden, unique in its makeup and effect. And so for everything else that has been designed thoroughly.

There are obviously several reasons why a maker has to think in terms of concrete individual, as well as generic and specific, form. He is called upon to do so, first of all, by the requirement that his product serve the needs of an individual client. Even when these needs turn out to be negligible (no one ordinarily needs sheets of paper to be made for him alone, for instance) it is still good practice to visualize these first and then ignore them when they are seen to be of no great importance. Then again, the final form of a complex or delicately wrought product cannot ordinarily help being particular, in the sense of being uniquely different, since its material, its designer, its instruments, as well as its user, are not the exact same as any other; and the designer might as well take this fact into account deliberately.

The maker should also think of form as dynamic and genetic. He must see his blueprint as diagramming a direction of embodiment or growth—as disposing his product to take, stage by stage, its final form. He may here, in fact, take to heart the lesson of the acorn or the egg. For what is the basic form of an oak but that system of qualities locked up as a living principle in the acorn; the living pattern which branches up, down, out, taking on gradual full embodiment through, as it were, dominantly absorbing earth, air, moisture, warmth and light as these are made available to it? And what is the basic form of a rooster but that tiny bit of living "programming" which, feeding on what it finds in the shell, differentiates itself methodically, stage by stage, into the whole creature?

The ancients thought of the physical world primarily in terms of growth, as the derivation of our words "physics" and "nature" both indicate: the one being derived from *phuo,* to bring forth, to produce, to make grow; the other form *natura,* the condition of being born for certain activities. These men thought of things as basically lifelike; and it is this attitude which is most fruitful for the maker. For it accustoms him to thinking of his blueprint as only an indication or suggestion of the ultimate form of his product—to think of his design or pattern of specifications as primarily a virtual, unfolding one, like the life-principle of the oak implicit in the acorn. He will thereby learn to visualize it as determined by the stages through which it has to pass in becoming embodied; by the reciprocally determined potentialities of the materials and instruments he will have to use; by the needs of seasoning and, above all, for revising: by the requirements, in short, of a quasi-organic growth. Certainly, with such a view of it, he is not likely to make the mistake of conceiving of a form as something cut out, once and for all, like a die and then automatically "imposed" on "raw" material.

In other words, he is not likely to fall into the error of taking his blueprint or his mock-up too seriously. He will see that at best these can only be indicative. They are simply what is first *suggested* by the requirements of function that we have been studying, and then limited, as well as realized, by the capabilities of the material, the maker and the instrument. They constitute a set of guidelines which, however stimulating they may be, are to be followed no more closely, let us say, than the guidelines of lettering. They are certainly not to be copied mechanically or followed slavishly. The moment a blueprint, an outline or a model proves constraining, it should be thrown away or radically modified. It is not for the final product to look like the model; it is for the model, even at the cost of distortion, to look like the final product. A stone statue so carved that it looks like something that was first done in clay is a failure; just as a coin (like almost any of ours) is a failure when it looks like a silver imitation of a plaster of paris model. In short, every blueprint or model should be looked upon as a kind of experimental hope, never as a determinative crystallization.

It may be objected that we have been regarding form altogether too dynamically. Yet this is hardly possible; for even the deadest of material is acting with astonishing power merely in holding itself together and continuing to be itself. The power by which its atomic forces maintain their pattern and synthesis is so great that when this coalescence is loosened, the energy that is released can devastate a continent. From one point of view, the borders of a thing are only the lines by which its energy defines or bounds itself. And the maker who does not feel this will never think of his material or his form respectfully enough to get the most out of them.

The type of mind which thinks that a form is something that can be readily, almost mechanically, abstracted from one matter and imposed on another can wreak havoc—has wrought it more than once—in technology and the fine arts. For this type of mind proceeds "scientifically" to imitate either nature or other men slavishly, treating the forms of things created or of things made as if they were absolutes. To cite a classic example: wishing to fly, this sort of person studies a variety of birds, defines their "forms," and then tries to duplicate these in wood or canvas. Naturally, as long as he does this, he never gets off the ground. It is only when he begins to study things that can be made to fly— like kites—that do not happen to be very birdlike in figure, that he begins to turn out machines that will fly—machines which ultimately come to resemble giant birds so closely that it would seem that they had been designed as imitations of them in the first place.

As the examples presented at the beginning of this chapter suggest, it is also important for us to see how the concept of form applies, not only to physical objects, but also to institutions and events or performances.

The basic form of an institution, for instance, is its system of responsibilities, its final full form being the complex of all the qualities manifested by the whole organization in maintaining due relationships between all its parts and in fulfilling its overall aims. Since it is a huge instrumentality made up of coalescent small instrumentalities, it gets its form from them primarily as meeting one or other of the requirements of the general process they all subserve. A factory, for example, being constituted to carry on a process of making a given thing, is determined, first, by the stages of this process and then by the stages of insuring the elements it requires—whether these elements be materials, let us say, or trucks needed for carrying these materials.

To put this a bit more concretely, the determining of a factory as such (not as a fullfledged business) is the system of responsibilities (indicated by a flow-of-authority chart) implied, ordinarily, by such necessities as those of collecting, purifying, seasoning, molding, combining, compounding, shaping, adjusting, breaking in, testing, housing, shipping: responsibilities for assuring logistically the money, the materials, the instruments, the designs, the research department, the working conditions, the men, the instruction and the leadership required for producing a given thing well and economically—and for continuing to do so. The form of a factory is determined mainly, therefore, by the form of the stages of a large event, each of which is made up of many small events.

What, then, do we mean by the form of an event and by the stages in a large event, or process?

The first part of this question can be answered easily by elimination: if the material in an event is what is being acted on, (dough) and the instrument or agency is that which is acting (the stove), then the form of the event is what takes place between them (cooking). In a process, it is the kind or pattern of action that takes place in a given stage.

But what do we mean by a stage and how does it differ from a mere state? The answer is that it is a sequence of actions determined by a recognizable or definable *goal*. A stage begins when a new intention is adopted by the maker; it ends when this intention is either achieved or decisively balked. A minor stage in a golf game, for instance, begins with the setting up of the tee and goes on through the estimate of the distance and the hazards, the preparatory stance and the gripping, the waggling, the adjustment and the final stance, the stroking of the ball and the follow-through. For all these clearly comprise a sequence of actions determined by a single intention. Even the follow-through does, for unless this too was intended from the outset, the stroke will be defective.

The form of a stage, then, is like the form of a thing in one important respect: it is a coalescence* of actions as a thing is a coalescence of energy-constituents.

It is in view of all this that the sound designer thinks of his blueprint or model as something which enables him to guide what he is fashioning through the various stages, and their constituent actions required for the final emergence of a product with right specifications.

Unless he does think of form in this dynamic or organic way as something beyond mere diagramming, he is likely to prefer forms of things that are ultimately "dead": stiff, angular, mechanically regular, spare, bleak, dull. Nor will he be able to relieve their ugliness by trying to cast them into mathematically pleasant proportions and ornament them with chrome.

---

*This word does not mean crystallization: it means having parts that are helpful to one another.

The correct materials

The most important single necessity in dealing with the material of a product is that we respect it and treat it diplomatically. The reason why we must make a special effort to do so is that we are surrounded by a materialism which encourages an almost complete disrespect for matter as we find it. We still hear people speaking of *dead* matter, of *raw* material, of *imposing* a form on it, and of substituting one form of matter for another at will—as if matter had no rights of its own or as if, in fact, it did not matter. And yet this attitude is directly opposed to that of the skilled maker. For he knows from experience that even the simplest form of matter is never strictly "raw" in any usual sense of the term; it has always, as our very language indicates, a "will" to do this or not to do that. Nor can it ever be substituted for indifferently with any degree of success since it has its own subpersonality and its rights do matter a great deal.

Matter is essentially subtle because, as Aristotle pointed out, it is essentially unknowable. Even today, when we have equated it with a system of electrical charges, we can hardly say that we know its essence since, after all, what is electricity? Again, if matter is energy, and energy is matter, why have we two different words for them—unless they are two different forms of something which is essentially indefinable?

If we worked down in a kind of reverse evolutionary process from man to animals to vegetables to minerals, if we worked down from the most complex form of matter to the simplest, there would still seem to be little likelihood that we should ever reach at last a matter without any form whatsoever—especially one which, by lifting itself by its own bootstraps, could take on more and more complex forms. And if we say that the first matter was always "there," and was always filled with all the potentialities that have since been realized, we have certainly not made it seem less subtle or more raw.

The truth is, of course, that we never know matter directly

apart from some form: we know only this or that unit of a certain form of matter, which expresses its nature in this or that set of operations. We know it primarily, that is, as possessed of certain properties capable of certain combinations and compounds, able to receive or give, resist or cooperate, in its own way. As material for a product we know it in much the same way as a coach knows his "material." And if we are as wise as a good coach, we learn to respect the individuality of its units, so as to bring these along as he brings his men along in transforming them into a team. Just as he organizes them, trains them and encourages them to cooperate, to coalesce, so, analogically, must we do with the various units of our material—only then can we transform them into what their potentialities fully permit.

Now, because material can best be known, from a maker's point of view, as it is related to the agent that works on it, we can clarify our notions of both these factors correlatively by reflecting on the following socratically arranged instances and the questions they raise.

—You are watching a game of billiards, and you notice that when the cue ball hits the object ball, the cue ball slows down— sometimes even stops. Does this mean that the cue ball which stops has transferred its motion more successfully to the object ball than does that same ball when it does not stop?

—A friend asks for a light for his cigarette. You strike a match and hold it to the end of his cigarette so that his begins to burn. Has the flame been transferred from the match to the cigarette? Is the flame of the match diminished by the amount of flame taken over by the cigarette?

—You leave the room and go into the library, where you pick up a copy of *Don Quixote*. After reading a chapter of it you feel refreshed. Does this mean that the book, or Cervantes, has lost the energy which you have thus gained?

—Next you go to the refrigerator for a late snack. As you open the door your hand feels a positive chill. But if physics is right, cold is nothing but the absence of heat. How can the absence of an energy transfer itself, seemingly in waves, to the senses: how can a negative state or quality make the senses respond to it positively?

—Then, in slicing bread for a sandwich, you cut your finger slightly. Is the pain that you feel transferred somehow from the edge of the knife through a pain nerve to the mind?

—If a teacher does not transfer his knowledge, what does he do?

These various examples serve to bring home two extremely important truths about the way in which the material receives a new form from an agent. They show that it does so by having its own powers activated—*not* by accepting the transfer of a quality or condition. They also show how erroneously we are likely to think of a material unless we see it as having its own nature, powers and disposition, which are set in motion by the energy of the agent. As the scholastic principle says, "Whatever is received is received in the manner of the receiver." The cue ball, for example, does not transfer its motion to the object ball; it releases the power of the object ball to move in a certain way—whether the cue ball follows after or stops dead still. The match does not lose any flame to the cigarette: the energy of its flame causes the cigarette to explode, as it were, into its own flame. Cervantes does not, of course, lose energy; but the instrumentality he left behind, *Don Quixote,* when applied by its user, the reader, to his mind, sets that mind into its own actions of remembering, imagining, correlating, interpreting and appreciating. The knife evokes the chemical effect that awakens the nerve (or the mind through the stimulated nerve) to an awareness of the harmfulness of the cutting. And the teacher certainly does not transfer information to the student, pouring it, as it were, from a truck into a tank; he merely presents specimens, data or symbols in such a way to prompt the student to acquire a new insight from them, a new principle to be contemplated or acted upon. "Books," as the architect Gropius has said, "are for making clear what has already been experienced."

The attitude toward material, then, which is adopted by the wise maker is that of eliciting changes from it in accordance with its nature—that of political persuasion, of diplomacy. He regards the whole universe of creatures as in a sense a democratic commonwealth; each is to be respected as having its own nature and rights; none is to be coerced. And so for materials: each of these he looks upon as a kind of subperson, with rights that must be respected; and he regards all of them as cooperating to constitute the product as a kind of organization. His materials, in short, are to be set in motion in accordance with their own natures to form something which will act in accordance with its nature.

To put this in chemical or biological terms, he tries to turn out something that resembles more nearly a compound or an organism than a mixture. The skilled maker knows that it is only in mathematics that the whole equals the sum of its parts, and that he is concerned with producing something which may be as different from its constituents as water is from either hydrogen or oxygen, or as Abraham Lincoln was from the handful of chemicals of which he was composed.

He certainly comes to feel that the normal attitude for him in dealing with material is never to think of it as raw in any usual sense. He treats it as a *personne manquée,* an "almost person," rather than as a kind of putty plus. The term "raw," then, he always sees as purely relative: a material is raw only in respect to its refinement for incorporation into a given product; and what will be raw for one product may well be refined for another.

In the light of all this, and of what has been said in previous chapters, we can make out clearly what is meant by a maker's "knowing his material." Obviously, it does not mean simply knowing its chemical composition, though there is certainly nothing wrong with his knowing that. Nor does it simply mean knowing where it can be found or bought at a given price, though this information too is likely to be very valuable. Primarily, it means knowing what qualities his material has in the form it takes at the final stage of manufacture; then, what qualities it has in the earliest state of it; and, finally, how the spread between these two is systematically lessened, stage by stage, throughout the process. Moreover, it means that, through long familiarity, a maker knows how to adjust to the inevitable uniqueness, the peculiar excellence or flaws, of each new batch of materials, and how to take advantage of or compensate legitimately for these. It means, ultimately, that he has acquired a "feel," as we say, for his material that enables him to obey it considerately and persuade it diplomatically to take the right form for his product.

It means, too, that he never adopts a kind of "race prejudice" attitude toward it, as if any one kind of material should be regarded as the norm for all other kinds of it, or as if one kind could really substitute for or adequately imitate another. He does not condemn a material like plastic, for instance, simply because it is not wood or marble. He treats it respectfully, using it for what it, and nothing else, can do and allowing it its own self-expression—without trying to make it do what only wood and marble can properly do or look as only wood and marble can really look. Nothing would amuse him more than such a remark as, "Isn't that a wonderful plastic soda fountain: it looks just like marble." For he would wonder, why not have a wonderful plastic soda fountain that would look just like a wonderful plastic soda fountain; and if that is not possible, why not have a good wooden one which would look just like a good wooden one? Having an honest love for material, in other words, he loves it for what it is, not for what it is not or for what it can be coerced into resembling.

The effect of this way of thinking, were it to become universal, would be almost incalculable. There would be hardly a single item in many of our churches, for instance, that would pass muster, from the phony stained glass and the half-wax candles to the shoddy vestments and the imitation organs. The whole art of eye-catching deception, as practiced by everyone from our packaging agencies to our contractors for nonranch ranch houses; all the tinny automobiles made to look like solid ones; all the motorboats made to look like automobiles; all the trains made to look like airplanes—but why go on? One need only walk down any big city street and estimate how much of what meets the eye is materially, as well as formally, honest to see the point. For it is hard to deny that we are overwhelmed with the pinchbeck and the shoddy; so much so that we seem to have learned to take it for granted, and even to prefer it.

CHAPTER 16

THE AGENTS OF ARTISTIC METHOD

THE HAND

We come next to the hand. By this, however, is meant, not simply the hand alone, but it, the arm and the whole body viewed as the wielder of the instrument. The reason why it is necessary to extend the coverage of the term in this way is that the hand cannot properly be thought of in an act of skill as disconnected from the rest of the organism to which it belongs—as operating independently of it.

For we are so constituted as to act as a unit. And we are meant to do so in easy, circular movements, rhythmically, being guided kinesthetically—that is, by patterns of impulse suggested by mentally conceived purposes. Certainly, we are not meant for short, spasmodic, unrhythmical, externally guided, unintellectual action. Effective actions, in other words, are gracefully organized wholes. A good stroke, whether in sport or work, is such that its three main stages are unitary: they affect one another integrally. The follow-through determines the stance just as the stance determines the follow-through and as both of them determine and are determined by the central, the applicative, part. It is fatal not to think of them as constituting a single more or less circular movement which does its work almost tangentially, almost incidentally.

220

This condition requires that, in executing a stroke, we stand at a reasonable distance from the material we are operating on: far enough away from it (usually somewhat farther than most beginners think right) to allow for the free play of hands and body; yet near enough to work on it surely. Moreover, we must often get used to a stance that at first seems strange and uncomfortable. And we must learn not to hurry through one or other stage of the stroke.

We often, in fact, find a new stroke difficult because it seems, as we say, "unnatural." We subconsciously resist mastering it because we fail to realize that we must learn to obey an instrument as much as command it—indeed, that we cannot command it until we have analyzed the inevitable requirements of the stroke and come to obey them logically, rather than neurally. There are few technically skillful movements that are completely natural to us as human beings, and almost none, even walking and talking, in which we reach perfection automatically. Although, therefore, we should always, after we have clarified our intentions, heed the promptings of instinct—especially those of natural talent—we must always, even with that talent, learn to habituate ourselves to postures that at first sight seem strangely cramped. We usually pay for excellence by the pain of making second nature a "good form" that originally strikes us as constraining.

In making such an effort, we should realize, above all, how rhythmically we are meant to move. We should take as our guides here the ancient Athenians, who practiced nothing, not even oratory, without a musical accompaniment to go by; for every good worker or athlete learns, whether consciously or subconsciously, to set up for himself a felt inner pattern, a kind of subtle dance to an unsounded music. He learns to experience each stroke as a system of tensions and releases that are harmoniously rhythmic.

There are three things that may prevent most of us from doing likewise: our subjection to the wrong image of a stroke; to tension; and to timidity.

We frequently set up and obey the wrong kind of image because we have come to identify, mistakenly, all imagery with visual imagery, so that we fail to see that we are guided by the un-visualizable imagery of the kinesthetic and static senses (the sense of movement and balance) quite as surely as by any other. (If it were not how could we—or a blind person—guide the vocal organs to speak and sing?) And as a result of trying to follow the wrong kind of visual image, we set up within ourselves a conflict between it and the motor imagery that may almost paralyze us, or at least constrain us gravely.

The solution to this sort of conflict, however, is not necessarily to discard all visual images and to rely wholly on kinesthetic. Sometimes, we can profitably have recourse to visual images which, because they are pleasingly fantastic and stimulating, can act safely as dynamic guidelines, as we see from precepts like these: "To make a good forehand drive, try to throw your racket into the net—but just don't let it go;" or: "For a thin note, blow as if your breath were not to touch the sides of the horn; for a full, fat note, try to make your breath scrape the sides of it." As yoga has shown, fantastic imagery of this kind can often help to assure a control not otherwise attainable.

Tension is another great enemy of skillful action since it disrupts the rhythm which this normally requires. Partly, this disruption results from our failure to distinguish carefully between the speedy action of light pressure, the speedy action of heavy pressure, the slow action of light pressure and the slow action of heavy pressure; and then to master the patterns of tension and relaxation required for gliding quickly and smoothly from any one of these to any other. And we frequently fail to master these patterns because of the tension of uncertainty about them; we do not understand and "feel in our bones" how they are *necessitated,* how they are inevitably required by the action as a whole and in all its stages: by the nature of the material and the instrument on the one hand, and our structure and tendencies on the other. We are unduly tensed through not seeing *why* it is that what we are doing must be the kind of thing that it is and no other: we do not, in short, rely confidently enough on our sense of its inner logic.

As a result, we fall prey to a timidity that prevents our achieving anything like the perfection normally open to us. For it causes us to be easily hypnotizable into unthinking and inept action. As we all know, when we are fearful and nervous, we often find ourselves doing things we have little or no conscious intention of doing. We find ourselves yawning, for instance, simply when someone else has done so—even when we are trying hard to resist the impulse out of politeness. The reason for this kind of lapse, the psychologists tell us, is that when we are weary and fearful we tend to lose control over our faculties and subconsciously take the very suggestion that our apprehension is warning us not to take. The classic example is that of the person who, in learning to ride a bicycle, becomes so fearful of a telephone pole, warning himself to do all he can to avoid it, that he rides straight for it, even though there is plenty of space all around. He does so because it is the fearful suggestion that registers in his mind and acts as a kind of hypnotic one which he obeys in spite of himself. Timidity, then, may disrupt skillful action by causing us to substitute for a confidently held, accurately directive image one that is hypnotically inadequate or seductive.

To summarize: in the use of the hand, understood in the broadest sense, the important thing for us is to have a clear intent based on a sound analysis of the requirements of an effective stroke freely and gracefully executed; an image that guides us into the proper kinesthetic pattern of balance, rhythm and controlled, relaxed firmness; into a musically harmonious unity; into the peace of mind that comes from an awareness of the rightness of our technique; and into the confidence based on the experience of the "feel" of a successful stroke that we have often achieved. These are the requirements of mastery.

THE HEAD

We consider next the intellectually founded habits which are to be exercised subconsciously yet prudently in the performance of a skillful action: those which assure a procedure at once orderly and inventive.

Roughly, an action of this kind consists of the following stages: the careful determining of its purposes; the sketching of a possible design; the choice and collecting of materials; the choice and application of instruments; the rechecking of all the factors at every major stage, with the consequent readjustment of them to unforeseen difficulties or unsuspected possibilities. Commonly these large stages break down into similar substages to be scheduled more or less interdependently and concurrently, as experience dictates.

In going through all of them, the maker will guide himself by what are known in traditional philosophy as the eight integral "parts" of prudence. He will acquire, first of all, a knowledge of the whole situation and of the needs of the client—a "knowledge of the facts of the case." Next, he will try to acquire an insight into the central, or crucial, problem it raises. Then, of course, he will work out reasonable inferences about the probable claims of the material, formal and instrumental factors. He will next try to exercise foresight in visualizing probable requirements and estimating possible contingencies. Nor will he neglect any guidance he can acquire from masters who have dealt with a similar task in the past. He will not follow these slavishly, however, but try to deal with his problem freshly, with the special ingenuity its uniqueness inevitably calls for. He will be circumspect, taking into account all determinants, and making frequent reestimates and revisions. And he will proceed with the cautious leisureliness which waits on and fosters inspiration and inventiveness.

Efficient scheduling and management (what the military call logistics) require that these parts of prudence be exercised, not merely one by one, or one after another, but discursively—back and forth, from one to another, as simultaneously as possible. The collecting and laying out of instruments, for example, may need to be done concurrently with the collecting and preparing of the materials; as was said earlier, the maker is an impresario as well as an inventor.

To understand how this prudentially controlled art is to be cultivated and exercised, we must first identify and observe the mental power of which it is the virtue. This is called, in scholastic psychology, the cogitative sense, and, in modern psychology, intelligence or the creative imagination. It is a power at once sensory and intellectual: it enables us to see a thing as a concrete instance of a general nature—this particular animal before me (concrete instance) as a police dog (general nature). It therefore enables us to play an intellectual hunch—to follow aptly a general principle—in dealing with a particular thing, so that we can deftly control or avoid it if it threatens or make use of it if it favors us. It is the power, in short, that prompts us to do the intellectually right thing "instinctively."

Now, it is this power that the maker relies upon most. It is this above all that he needs to have trained in order that its hunches will be sound both intellectually and imaginatively; so that what he makes will be rightly determined by both universal principles and particular purposes, materials, instruments.

How, then, is this power to be trained best?

As being intellectual, it should be made cognizant of the general nature of every act of making—hence this book; for we are dealing here, of course, with the principles governing any and every act of making. And a knowledge of these makes it possible for the creative imagination to focus on its work readily and surely, in the assurance that everything that is being done is *necessitated* by the nature of things, not merely prompted by mere instinct, whim or convention. Knowledge of this kind makes possible, moreover, the adjusting, rectification or perfecting of a method. Knowing what the general requirements of building any house are, an architect can the better focus on the particular requirements of a given particular house, and so play the best hunches about its materials, design and mode of construction. One of the first necessities here, then, is that of realizing that we are concerned with an imaginativeness that is guided and aided intellectually.

All this seems, however, to raise an insoluble dilemma. A maker must devise things either consciously or unconsciously. But no one would contend that when he sits down to work out a design, he must advert consciously to all the intellectually determined principles that govern his technique. But neither can one contend that all he needs to do is let himself go and obey unconsciously the promptings of instinct, or even of great natural talent. Where, then, are we? If he is to work neither consciously nor unconsciously, how in the world is he to work?

An example from athletics may prove helpful here. It is obvious that a player who sets out to tackle another on a football field cannot, at the moment of doing so, say to himself: "Remember all the things the coach told you in that last practice session. Be sure to bend forward at just the right angle, etc." Obviously, if he did, he would never get near his opponent. Nor would he do so any more effectively if he relied on his natural talent alone. He would succeed only when he tackled in the proper way without having to think about the principles he was obeying.

In other words, the answer to the seeming dilemma here lies in there being a state of mind between full consciousness and unconsciousness; namely, subconsciousness. It is a state, as we all know from experience, in which through habit we can concentrate on one thing while only partly concentrating on—only giving "half our mind to"—another. When we are walking down the street conversing with a friend, we are subconscious of our technique of walking—until, by chance, we hit a projection in the sidewalk and start to stumble. When that occurs, the habits of walking that we have developed from early childhood help us, automatically, to regain our balance while still continuing to converse. Moreover, this is not a merely mechanical (completely unconscious) reflex action of adjustment. If we find that it is the result of our awkward way of walking that we stumble often, we can deliberately master a new technique, develop a new set of habits that will enable us to walk gracefully. We can, that is, through intellectual analysis and the practice of the methods it suggests, improve our *art* of walking.

So, too, for every other habit of making or performing things well: we can consciously practice our technique in accordance with intellectually determined principles until we obey these habitually and subconsciously. And as the simpler habits required for a performance become second nature, we can bank on these to free us for the mastery of the higher or more complex. Shakespeare, for instance, could rely on his habits of obedience to grammatical, rhetorical and poetic principles as he devoted his attention primarily to dramaturgy: never being, while he was composing, either analytically conscious or merely unconscious of any of them, but always capable of correcting himself when he had accidentally failed to obey one of them.

Here, then, is one of the keys to training for an art. It must be *practiced* in accordance with clearly understood intellectual analyses and formulations of its exigencies and principles. It must be *exercised* without special attention to these, though without disregard of them since obedience to them has become second nature. To enable himself to devote almost all his attention to solving the problems that arise from moment to moment, the maker or performer should have acquired an armory of habits which he can perfect at will by special exercises, rely on subconsciously, and call upon readily as his higher technique requires.

It is possible, of course, to become too intellectually calculating here. Technique follows intention; and once intention is clarified, the creative imagination can often be relied on as trustworthy to an astonishing extent—much more so than is suggested by the kind of academic, pseudoscientific analysis that is often made by those who have had little or no experience in making. What we must do is train and then trust our powers of invention: never becoming too self-conscious about them, yet always enlightening them with the clear vision that results from careful study. In short, we should never practice too subconsciously, nor perform too consciously: the first fails to generate an intellectual habit; the second frustrates the imaginative use of it.

Moreover, in guiding himself in his inventing, the maker, especially the apprentice, must distinguish carefully between the true and the false concepts of both imitation and originality.

Concerning the first, he needs to keep in mind particularly the admonition: *never copy products,* whether of men or of nature, and never imitate anyone slavishly. As was pointed out earlier, so long as inventors tried to make heavier-than-air craft that looked and worked like birds, they never got off the ground. And when we try to turn out a Gothic building by imitating Rheims or Notre Dame, we produce what the architect Barry Byrne calls a corpse. The last thing that a Gothic architect would do, were he building today, would be imitate the cathedrals of his own time. Following the principles that he would have followed then, but correlating them with those that had been discovered since— especially those of engineering—he would use modern materials and techniques to produce a structure that would satisfy the requirements of worship as we know them today. As a consequence, his building would be Gothic in the sense in which a modern airplane is Gothic—and, in fact, a modern airplane will stand next to a great Gothic cathedral in quite pleasant concord with it. A sound medieval master-builder could be said to imitate others insofar as he followed the principles they had found valid, but not insofar as he merely imitated exactly either their products or their methods.

Yet, is there no way in which we can learn from the masters by imitating them? Did not Benjamin Franklin, for instance, learn how to write, as he tells us, by imitating Addison? Yes, of course; but not by trying to become another Addison. He did not set before himself this or that passage of his master and then try to write one that looked like it—a practice which results only in a near parody. Rather, he would first summarize the thoughts of a passage and then jumble these up. Next, when he had forgotten the original, he would arrange these thoughts again in what he considered their best order and phrase them as well as he could in his own style. After this, he would compare his writing with the original to see wherein and why it fell short. By a like method, Victorien Sardou, though he had nothing much to say, became a skillful dramatist even as a young man. He would read the last two acts of a successful play, then write his own first act for these, and finally compare, analytically his first act with the original, which, of course, he had not seen up until then. Later, he would leave out two acts (sometimes the first two, sometimes the last) until, ultimately, he was able to take any section of a story line, or any good plot germ, and develop it by himself. Insofar as he faced himself with the same conditions, imaginatively visualized, of audience, staging and acting as confronted the original author and then solved the problems they raised in his own way, this method was certainly valid; for it taught him to produce, not something reminiscent, but something advisedly original.

And so for all other imitating, the imitating of nature included: the model must be regarded as an *exemplification* of principles and as a *standard* of achievement, but never as something which is to be duplicated either in pattern or in mechanism. When the learner sees that imitating means acquiring the habit of following inventively and, as it were, adoptively the principles of sound workmanship as well as his own imagination and technique permit, then he can imitate profitably, but not otherwise.

If we are not to be wrongly conventional through slavish imitation of masters of the past, neither are we to try to be original in equally slavish rejection of them. If there is anything that has warped the development of architecture and the fine arts, it is the "politicalization" of thought with which they have been afflicted; each new school trying to solve problems, not in accordance with the potentialities open to them, but in reaction to the previous school. This tendency has regularly resulted in the temporary prizing of a certain kind of limited and standardized "originality," against the pretensions of which it is normal for any succeeding young group to rebel with an equally limited and standardized originality.

Such partisanship is all the more ridiculous for being tragically unnecessary: originality is the one quality which will take care of itself if the maker merely concentrates on doing each particular job as thoroughly as possible. After all, no two users or clients— even when they are twins—are ever exactly alike; no two conditions of use; no two batches of material; no two minds of makers; no two blueprints, therefore; and no two sets of instruments or techniques. How, then, can any product fail to be original if the maker simply obeys, as searchingly as he knows how, with the means that he alone has available and the technique that he alone possesses, the requirements of all these kinds of uniqueness? And how can he ever be really as original as he should be when he tries to meet them in an ideologically doctrinaire way?

Another necessity for developing sound technique is that we do so, not through memorization, but through familiarization. This point has to be made here because so much of our education today has overlooked it—even though we are not always inclined to do so outside our schools. Certainly, none of us would ordinarily set out to master a game, let us say, in the way favored by elementary schools and textbooks; that is, by memorizing one rule or item of information at a time until we had "covered" the subject and were able to pass a written examination on it. If we set out to master the game of bridge, for instance, we should certainly not spend the first week in cutting and shuffling, the next in counting points, the next in bidding only club hands, and so on, taking quizzes on each of these subjects and playing a half game at midyear and a whole game for the final examination. Or, again, if we set out to master cooking, we should certainly not begin by classifying and defining and memorizing all its elements and processes, from the smallest on up: classifying all the kinds of basic foods, all the kinds of spices, all the kinds of utensils; then going on to practice, one by one, independently, the various kinds of subprocesses—cutting, mixing, "aging," boiling, roasting, broiling, etc.—all in some purely alphabetical or chemically logical order, until finally we might feel ready to confect, following a very exact traditional recipe, first a simple dish, then a more complex one and, at last (oh, glorious day!) a whole meal. Such a method would seem, of course, monstrously unnatural, and therefore self-defeating. Yet many of our courses in English Composition do much the same thing, beginning with words and working up through sentences and paragraphs to whole themes—as do, analogically, many of our other courses in the liberal arts. For, all too often, we have been taken in by the so-called scientific approach to an art, the approach that sanctions logical order as more important than either psychological or technical and makes it easier for a student a) to memorize b) doctrines c) about the general nature of a process than a) to develop habits b) of acting in accordance with these doctrines in c) performing more and more difficult feats of skill.

True training in an art means that we acquaint ourselves with it as a whole both quickly and naturally, and that we acquire the technique and the science governing it as we go along, learning to know it as we know our own families (hence the phrase, "familiarizing ourselves with it"). We come to know it through experience and cogitation, as well as through formal study; we become, as it were, more naturalized in it, more acclimatized to it, more and more personally acquainted with its general nature and all its elements.

This requirement does not mean that we should in any way misprize the scientific knowledge required for an art or that we should fail to order this knowledge, at some time, systematically. It simply means that the memorizing of the scientific doctrines of a liberal art is not the mastering of that art—the acquiring of its special form of skill. This is a truth long since recognized by our graduate schools, which afford, as well as they can, a case-method apprenticeship in their arts; but it is a truth, alas, that most of our liberal arts colleges and many of our technical schools have still to learn.

In the light of all these considerations, then, it would seem that the best method for the acquiring of skill is that of an apprenticeship. For this method, when made sufficiently philosophic and liberal, rather than merely routine and imitative, fosters the most natural and fruitful kind of familiarization. To have been a liberally trained apprentice, then an experienced journeyman and finally a master means to have acquired authority, in the strict sense, naturally and easily: through familiarization, through supervised practice and study, through the inspiring challenge of real and increasingly responsible work, through the experiential guidance of common interest and companionship. It is no wonder that this is a system still followed in the medical and military professions, where success is a matter of life and death.

APPENDICES

INTERMEDIATE TECHNOLOGY

by E. F. Schumacher*

Pope Paul's encyclical *Populorum Progressio* speaks of "the judgment of God and the wrath of the poor" which will be provoked by the rich unless they make much greater efforts to help the poor: "The very life of poor nations, civil peace in developing countries and world peace itself are at stake."

The current efforts—indeed, the efforts of the last twenty years—are not enough to stem the tide of world poverty. In many places, the poor are getting poorer, while the rich are getting richer. Societies lose their inner cohesion and become "dual economies," with a few "modern" sectors in the cities on the one side and a vast hinterland of misery in the rural areas on the other. Aid fails to reach those who need it most, because they are separated from the aid-givers by three great gulfs—the gulf between rich and poor; the gulf between educated and uneducated; and the gulf between city and countryside (of which that between industry and agriculture is but a part).**

The central problem of development aid is how to bridge these three gulfs. A great effort of imagination, study and compassion is needed to do so. The methods that suit relatively affluent and educated city people are unlikely to suit poor, semi-illiterate peasants. Wealth generated by the wealthy in the cities does not percolate to the poor in the rural areas. As the "duality" of the economy becomes more extreme, the rural areas fall into ever deeper decay, and three giant evils threaten the life of all society: mass migration into cities, mass unemployment and the specter of famine.

---

*Reprinted from *Good Work,* Autumn, 1967.

**In this regard, see Victor Papanek's extremely important book *Design for the Real World.*

It is too often taken for granted that the methods and technologies which have proved their worth for the rich will also be advantageous for the poor, and that the poor should be able to adapt themselves to these methods without delay. But poor peasants cannot suddenly acquire the outlook and habits of sophisticated city people. If the people cannot adapt themselves to the methods, then the methods must be adapted to the people. This is the whole crux of the matter.

The great peasant populations of the developing countries generally fail to benefit from the rich man's development efforts, because modern technology favours industrial developments in and around the big cities, and small-scale industrial production in the rural areas tends to die away, so that nothing remains there but the most abject poverty, to which unemployment adds another dimension of misery.

The rural areas—on whose health the health of the cities ultimately depends—need technical assistance of a kind appropriate to their actual conditions. They need a technology that is more powerful and efficient than their own, yet at the same time very much simpler, sturdier and cheaper than ours: an *intermediate technology*. They need technical assistance in a form they can assimilate and make their own. They need the chance of "taking the next step." In short, they need help to help themselves.

As Mr. Atma Ram, the Director-General of the Indian Council of Scientific and Industrial Research, put it: "The transition of traditional economy to industrial economy can be achieved better and possibly quicker through an evolutionary rather than a revolutionary process," and "evolution" *means that intermediate levels of development are attained by means of intermediate levels of technology.*

The life, work, and happiness of all societies depend on certain "psychological structures" which are infinitely precious, yet highly vulnerable. Social cohesion, cooperation, and above all mutual respect, self-respect, courage in the face of adversity, and the ability to bear hardship—all this and much else disintegrates and disappears when these "psychological structures" are gravely damaged. A man is destroyed by unemployment or the conviction of uselessness. If the rate of change is such that nothing is left for the fathers to teach their sons, or for the sons to accept from their fathers, then even family life collapses. No amount of economic growth can compensate for such losses, though this may be an idle reflection, since economic growth itself is normally inhibited by them.

Everything points, therefore, to the need for organic, evolutionary processes of development, and hence to the need for *intermediate technologies* to help the poor to help themselves.

It is to meet these needs that the Intermediate Technology Development Group has been set up in London. It is a private, non-profit-making organization, formed in 1966 by some thirty specialists in development problems.

As a small firm endeavouring to pioneer industrial enterprise in an underdeveloped country . . . . we have on numerous occasions found that modern plant and machinery offered to us by U.K., U.S., and European suppliers

. . . . are far too highly automated, apart from being very costly; that the minimum output is far in excess of our entire market requirements . . . .

This is a typical letter, one of many received by the Group from all over the world. Everyone who has actually worked in the field is familiar with this problem—the problem of inappropriate equipment, of inappropriate technology.

Poor people, it has been said, are poor because of their poverty. This is more than a trivial tautology. It points to the basic truths that they cannot do the things they could do if they were already rich, and that they cannot become rich by the means which the rich use to maintain or increase their wealth. Their problem is how to take the first step out of poverty; and the first step for an unemployed man is to get some productive work, and for the man doing things inefficiently with inadequate tools, to get improved tools and equipment. Whether unemployed or under-employed, the man is too poor to afford the tools and equipment which the rich man would choose. Either he gets something cheap and relatively simple, or he gets nothing at all and "development" bypasses him altogether. These are the stark alternatives; and it is no use saying that only the best is good enough and that intermediate technology is a second best.

Approaching the same problem from a different angle, one can say this: the people currently unemployed in the developing countries and the annual increment of the population need *new* workplaces, while many of those currently in work need *improved* workplaces. If each workplace costs, on average, $300 of capital investment, there can be twenty times as many new workplaces as when each costs $6,000. Even if it could be demonstrated (as it cannot) that in a *poverty-stricken* community one man at a $6,000 workplace can produce more than twenty men, each at a $300 workplace, this would mean nothing at all. For we are dealing with real situations and real people, not with economic models, and the nineteen people left out could not, as it were, hold their breath for a generation or two until some of the surpluses of the favored one had percolated down to them.

From another angle again, it is clear that economic development is an illusion unless there is a genuine development of people. It is only when a significant proportion of the population has acquired certain aptitudes and disciplines that a broadly based economic development can gather momentum. But how can these aptitudes and disciplines be spread unless by setting large numbers of people to work? And how could a sufficient number of workplaces be set up unless each of them is relatively cheap, avoiding ultra-modern, sophisticated, highly automated, expensive, labour-saving capital equipment? We must learn to distinguish between the *tool element* of a machine and the *labour-saving accretions*. Intermediate technology equipment provides first-class jigs and tools, but does not incorporate elaborate devices for the sole purpose of saving labour. This should be obvious enough: no one has ever acquired education, skill, and discipline by his labour being "saved."

The Intermediate Technology approach to aid and development presents a new and interesting challenge to engineers. Production problems have to be solved, not simply by the further evolution of existing methods or designs, but by going back to first principles and finding a solution that fits into the narrow boundaries set by poverty. When working for the rich, the designer can specify exactly the material that is best for the job; for the rich have money, and money buys anything anywhere. But when working for the poor his design must be such that it can utilize the materials which the poor can get hold of, whether these are the best or not; for the poor have little or no money and face the alternative of either using what they have or going without. And just as the design has to be tailor-made—or "generalized"—to fit the available materials, so it has to fit the available or obtainable skills, the given size of markets, and all the other relevant conditions.

All this may sound pretty difficult, but it is also fairly simple—firstly because poor people have simple requirements, and secondly because practically all the necessary solutions already exist somewhere in the world.

The first task the Intermediate Technology Development Group has set itself is therefore to assemble the maximum of information about *low-cost techniques* in a wide variety of fields, from agricultural production and the utilization of waste products to small-scale manufacturing and building work of all kinds. *Low-cost techniques* means techniques that require only a modest capital outlay; that employ tools and equipment which are cheap but at the same time efficient and troublefree; and that are adaptable to local conditions of raw material supply and small-scale marketing.

In short, these are techniques appropriate to the actual conditions in which poor people all over the world subsist, and simple enough to be mastered by people lacking higher training and education. The knowledge of these techniques needs to be systematically assembled, catalogued, tested, and then disseminated in a suitable form. There can be no doubt that it exists, but existence and availability are not the same.

Countless research institutions and other organizations all over the world possess relevant know-how in their special fields; but who knows of the know-how? Countless practical people have found their own original solutions to their own problems of economic survival; but who knows of these solutions? Poverty is silent, unable to communicate. Many industrial firms still manufacture equipment which was in universal use some hundred years ago but is now only in occasional demand—the very equipment which would ideally suit the purposes of the poor, but of whose existence they do not know.

Here, then, a very big job needs to be done, a job of organization and communication. The Group has set out to do it. For a start, it has undertaken a detailed survey of British industry, to assemble a directory or buyers' guide of suitable equipment of an Intermediate Technology character currently available in Britain. The *Buyers' Guide on "Tools for Progress,"* to be published shortly, attempts the widest possible coverage of every production process capable of raising incomes in rural areas—"All the Tools the Village Needs" and "Education for Self-Help."

The first edition of the Guide deals only with equipment obtainable in Britain, but it is hoped to internationalize the subsequent editions. There is also a section indicating the interest taken by British firms in overseas manufacture, by making available designs of products, by entering into licensing agreements and also into joint manufacture, and by releasing personnel to help local enterprises. This section, too, should be internationalized as soon as possible.

Intermediate Technology equipment is typically of a kind that itself can be produced simply, cheaply, and (where markets are small) on a small scale. It does not make the developing country unduly dependent on imports. In this connection it is worth listening again to Mr. Atma Ram, who can speak with unusual authority as one of the highest-placed scientists of India and also as the Director of the Central Glass and Ceramics Institute at Calcutta. With regard to the selection of technology, he complains that "during the last decade, although the glass industry has expanded very substantially, it has become more critically foreign-exchange-dependent, has not created significant employment potential and has tended to cripple local initiative. The reason is obvious," he continues, "and that is, lack of proper attention to selecting technology suitable to Indian conditions."

Gandhi once said that "it was not mass production but production by the masses that would do the trick." This is of the utmost importance. Economic development aid makes sense only if it leads to self-sustaining growth; but this will never come about if the development leaves out the masses, because it is based mainly on imported equipment, to be operated by small numbers of foreign, or foreign-trained, technicians. Unless the circle is closed (so that the internal demand for capital equipment, no less than that for consumers' goods, can *very largely* be met from indigenous production) the *leak* on the foreign exchange front becomes so great that drastic restrictions have to be imposed—with disastrous effects on any budding development. By and large, it is only for equipment at the Intermediate Technology level that indigenous production on a substantial scale can be quickly developed.

The Intermediate Technology Development Group's central task, therefore, is the systematic assembly and cataloging of data on low-cost techniques suitable for developing countries, particularly in the rural areas; and, together with the assembly of appropriate techniques, the provision of a buyers' guide and service to enable the needy to find the relevant equipment. These tasks can be satisfactorily accomplished only if there is a "feedback" system of information. The Group's London centre is already in the possession of extensive information on intermediate technologies and knows the libraries and research departments of national and international agencies where further information can be obtained. But this is not enough. *Intermediate Technology Information Centres* are needed in the developing countries themselves, both for the gathering in of further information and also for the dissemination of knowledge already assembled. The Group is currently in negotiations with interested parties in half a dozen developing countries for the establishment of such Centres. None of these should be large and costly. Their task is not to duplicate work already being done, but to know of it and make it available to those who can benefit from it.

A world-wide system of Information Centres, coordinated by the Group in London, but *based entirely on local initiative and finance* will ensure that the experiences of fighting and conquering poverty in rural areas become fruitful beyond the narrow geographical boundaries within which poverty tends to confine them.

Careful attention has to be given—and is being given—to the manner in which the precise knowledge of low-cost techniques is to be made available to those who need it most—that is, mainly to semi-illiterate peasants. The Intermediate Technology Information Centres must be well equipped with communications experts, capable of translating the information into simple terms for local use; of producing manuals showing every necessary step of the production process; and of introducing the elementary accounting systems that are a pre-condition of all commercially viable activities.

The question has been raised of whether all this work could not be much better done by an international agency of the United Nations. There is no doubt that the U.N. agencies, each in their special field, are doing invaluable work for the developing countries. They have been quick to recognize the contribution which Intermediate Technology can make to development and have established useful working contacts with the Group in London. But it is a mistake to think that a problem, merely because it is international and world-wide, must therefore be dealt with at the international level of organization. World poverty will not yield to any standardized application of textbook rules, but only to painstaking, detailed, self-sacrificing work on the basis of personal involvement. There is no shortage of either expertise or goodwill in the industrialized countries, but the mobilization of these forces still requires private initiative and this is more easily evoked by private, voluntary organizations than by world-wide bureaucracies. "As history abundantly proves," to quote from the famous encyclical, *Quadragesimo Anno,* "it is true that on account of changed conditions many things which were done by small associations in former times cannot be done now save by large associations. Still, that most weighty principle, which cannot be set aside or changed, remains fixed and unshaken in social philosophy . . . it is an injustice and at the same time a grave evil and disturbance of right order to assign to a greater and higher association what lesser and subordinate organizations can do. For every social activity ought of its very nature to furnish to the members of the body social and never destroy and absorb them" (paragraph 79).

The Group, therefore, welcomes the most intimate collaboration with governmental and supranational agencies of all kinds, but does not believe that the important task of "helping the poor to help themselves" can simply be left to any of these agencies.

The decentralized, personalized approach, while desirable on the donor side is in fact crucially essential on the recipient side. No doubt, there are a variety of "macro-economic" functions which no one can fulfill but the national government and which may even call for an overall "development plan." But no development has ever resulted from central planning; it has always and invariably depended on the initiative, daring, and entrepreneurial imagination of single individuals or small groups of men. As *Populorum Progressio* insists: "Basic education is the primary object of any plan of development" (paragraph 35); that is to say, not a great dam here or a magnificent steelworks there, but the unfoldment of latent aptitudes and abilities in human beings. This is an intensely personal task which can only be accomplished within small social units supported by local initiative and in the pursuit of locally meaningful aims. Basic education means teaching people to live in their community within their given environment. It cannot, therefore, be standardized. It must include practical and effective knowledge of low-cost techniques relevant to the actual problems of living in rural areas. In truth, "basic education" and "intermediate technology" are two related aspects of one and the same task—the task of rescuing the world's poverty-stricken peasantry from a misery which is not merely a human scandal but is now a threat to all civilized life.

A good example of Intermediate Technology leading to basic education is provided by the rainwater catchment tanks developed by a member of the Group, with the financial support of the Food and Agriculture Organization of the United Nations. These simple underground tanks of various sizes are suitable for individual families, farms, and villages, and embody all the principles of Intermediate Technology:

—their production is labour-intensive and cheap in capital;
—the materials are cheap and can be assembled in do-it-yourself kits;
—the necessary skills can be acquired by any able-bodied person without specialist training;
—simple booklets can describe, and give visual representation of, every step in their construction.

On the basis of an I.T.D.G. demonstration, the government of a developing country in Africa has agreed to incorporate the teaching of this low-cost technique—which can have the most profound effect on the entire life of the country—into the primary school curriculum; and the first instruction course for school teachers is now under way.

A further example is provided by a variety of methods of low-cost building construction. It is hard to think of any development that does not depend on and give rise to, a substantial amount of building. The Group has paid considerable attention to this subject and has found—hardly surprisingly—that a fair number of genuine low-cost techniques are being applied in various parts of the world, but that most of the people taking decisions on building projects in developing countries are unaware of their existence.

One of the Group's members in Africa reports as follows: "The District Councils have prepared a five-year plan for building primary school classrooms, which aims at a maximum of 40 pupils for each room. In the N. district, 400 classrooms will be needed . . . By the end of the five years, this number will be quite inadequate, because of the rapid increase in the number of pupils. It has now been agreed that the best way to go about this scheme will be to import only the steel sections and the roof sheeting, and to set up a local industry to manufacture the frames from standard imposted steel sections. Such an activity, starting on a small scale, might form the starting point for a larger and more diversified industry in due course . . . The steel frame and iron roof will provide a sound basis for a permanent structure, while the walls will be filled in with whatever material can be obtained locally. Burnt bricks, stone, concrete blocks, soil cement, mud bricks, even hessian or grass matting will give varying degrees of permanence and resistance to weather, at varying cost. Because of this use of local materials for the walls, the classrooms will have a certain amount of variety although based on the same framework. What is more, *the local people will be able to look upon them as their own.*"

No originality is being claimed for this approach, but the example none the less points to the urgent need that low-cost building methods should be systematically assembled and made available to those who need them. Availability means that they are presented in brochures which can be assimilated by semi-illiterate peasants and can be used as teaching material in primary schools.

Why is it so difficult for the rich to help the poor? We have already spoken of the three gulfs that separate the helpers from those they wish to help. It must become the primary concern of all education among the privileged groups in the developing countries to bridge these gulfs. The all-pervading disease of the modern world consists in a total unbalance between city culture and rural culture. The former has become over-extended and the latter has atrophied. The city has become the universal magnet, while rural life has lost its savor. Yet it remains an unalterable truth that, just as a sound mind depends on a sound body, so the health of the cities depends on the health of rural life. The cities, with all their wealth, are merely *secondary* producers, while *primary* production, the pre-condition of all economic life, takes place in the countryside. A lack of balance has developed which threatens all countries throughout the world, the rich no less than the poor. To restore a proper balance between city and rural life is perhaps the greatest task in front of modern man. It is not simply a matter of raising agricultural yields so as to avoid world hunger. There is no answer to the evils of mass unemployment and mass migration into cities, unless the whole level of peasant life can be raised, and this requires the development of an agro-industrial structure in the rural areas, so that each community can offer a large variety of occupations for its members.

Intermediate Technology is not a master key to solve the problems of this difficult and tormented world, but it is at least relevant to *Populorum Progressio* and, thereby, perhaps, also to *Pacem in Terris.*

[The address of the Intermediate Technology Group is: 9 King Street, Covent Garden, London, W. C., England.]

CHALK MILL EOLITHS

The following is another good example of just how futile it may prove to apply scientific method to a work of art (an artifact) without sufficient regard for the factor of purpose.

(An eolith is an intentionally chipped or utilized stone, shaped or employed during the Tertiary Epoch. An artifact is an object produced by human art.)

That natural processes such as torrential action, pressure of overlying beds, change of temperature, and wave action might suffice to produce eoliths, was thought to have been demonstrated by the appearance of flints that had passed through a chalk-mill. The first observation of this kind was made by Laville, preparator at the *Ecole des Mines* (Paris), at a cement factory southeast of Mantes, near Paris.

In extracting chalk from the quarry, most of the flint nodules are cast aside; some, however, pass unnoticed by the workmen and are carried with the chalk to the factory. These, together with a certain amount of clay, are emptied into circular basins or diluters. In their passage through the basins, the flint nodules receive thousands of knocks, some mutual, some from the iron teeth. At the end of twenty-nine hours the machinery is stopped, and the nodules are removed, washed, and piled up to await their ultimate use as a by-product. It was in one of these piles that Laville's discovery was made. Later, he revisited the place in company with Boule, Cartailhac, and Obermaier.

According to Boule, the flints that had passed through the machine had all the characters of the ancient river gravels. Most of them had become rounded peb-

243

bles, but some were chipped in a manner to resemble true artifacts. He and his companions were able in a few minutes to make "a superb collection including the most characteristic forms of eoliths, hammerstones, scrapers, spokeshaves," etc.

Boule does not pretend that all eoliths have a natural origin more or less analogous to those made by machinery. He does claim "that it is often impossible to distinguish between intentional rudimentary chipping and that due to natural causes." In his opinion, the artificial dynamics of the cement factory are comparable in every respect with the dynamic action of a natural torrent.

After a careful comparison of machine-made eoliths from both Mantes and Sassnitz with eoliths from Belgium, Hahne's conclusions are as follows: (1) the chalk-mill flints are all scratched and otherwise marked by the iron teeth of the mill; (2) the sides of all the larger pieces are bedecked with scars from blows that were not properly placed to remove a flake; (3) almost every piece shows more or less of the original chalky crust of the nodule; (4) anything like a systematic chipping of an edge or margin is never found, except for a very short stretch, where one would expect it to be carried along the entire margin; this is quite different from the long retouched margins of most eoliths; (5) the same edge is often rechipped first on one side and then on the other, absolutely without meaning or purpose (the "reverse working" of true eoliths is quite another thing); (6) in the mill product, coarse chipping alternates with fine retouches along the margin, while on the eoliths there is a regular and orderly sequence of chipping; (7) the repeated rechipping of the same edge, while others are left untouched, does not occur in machine-made eoliths; (8) the chief difference is between the haphazard and meaningless, on the one hand, and the purposeful, on the other. The most prominent and easily breakable parts suffer most in passing through the mill. They are often retained intact, or only slightly altered to serve as a handhold on the eolith, and there is a logical relationship between the worked and the unworked portions.*

---

*George Grant MacCurdy, *Human Origins*, as quoted by Daniel Sommer Robinson, *Illustrations of the Methods of Reasoning*, D. Appleton Co., New York, 1927.